Dear World

Wisconsin Studies in Autobiography

WILLIAM L. ANDREWS
Series Editor

Dear World

Contemporary Uses of the Diary

Kylie Cardell

The University of Wisconsin Press

The University of Wisconsin Press
1930 Monroe Street, 3rd Floor
Madison, Wisconsin 53711–2059
uwpress.wisc.edu

3 Henrietta Street, Covent Garden
London WC2E 8LU, United Kingdom
eurospanbookstore.com

Printed in the United States of America

Library of Congress Cataloging-in-Publication Data

Cardell, Kylie, author.
Dear world: contemporary uses of the diary / Kylie Cardell.
    pages   cm. — (Wisconsin studies in autobiography)
        ISBN 978-0-299-30094-4 (pbk.: alk. paper)
        ISBN 978-0-299-30093-7 (e-book)
        1. Diaries—Authorship.   2. Autobiography.
    I. Title.   II. Series: Wisconsin studies in autobiography.
        PN4390.C27   2014
        808.06′692—dc23
        2014012691

For

Peter, Sylvia, *and* Avery

Contents

Acknowledgments

Some parts of this work have appeared elsewhere: *Biography* 29, no. 4 (2006), *a/b: Auto/Biography Studies* 27, no. 2 (2012), and *Continuum* (2014). Much of the work that now appears in this book had its first articulation at various International Auto/Biography Conferences (IABA) and I thank the generous and collegial scholarly community at these events for inspiration and impetus.

I have encountered exceptionally generous readers of this work. I am extremely grateful to Michelle Dicinoski for her intelligent and precise comments on the manuscript. Kate Douglas is another valued reader who has supported this project steadfastly in so many ways. My deepest thanks go to both. The reviewers for the University of Wisconsin Press offered insightful advice at crucial stages of the revisions. My thanks also go to Raphael Kadushin at UW Press and series editor William Andrews for encouraging and supporting this book from the outset. Gillian Whitlock and Jude Seaboyer were my doctoral supervisors when this work began and remain crucial intellectual and professional role models. Gillian's ongoing work in the field of life writing, particularly in relation to the cultural politics of autobiography, is an important interlocutor for me in my work and in this book. Thank you to friends and colleagues near and too far: Kalinda Ashton, Angi Buettner, Danielle Clode, Kate Douglas, Gay Lynch, Michelle Dicinoski, Julie Rak, David Sornig, Deb Thomas, and the many others who have read parts of this work, encouraged its progress, or generously supported my work (and me) over the years. I am fortunate to have at my home university the creative thinkers of the Flinders Life Narrative Research group. Thank you to my codirector Kate Douglas, to Tully Barnett, Pamela Graham, Sandra Lindemann, Emma Maguire, and Threasa Meads among others for discussion, support, and writing "lock-ins" at just the right time.

To my parents, Jim and Mazz Cardell, who let me take mountains of books to remote destinations, to my sisters, Melanie Duncalfe and Lauren Cardell, and to Norm and Danielle Bain and my wonderful extended family, thank you for your love, care, and outstanding good humor. Peter has been with me the entire journey. Sylvia and Avery were born during the writing. I dedicate this book to my family—to the passion, joy, and wonder I find in every day with them—and in memory of Betty and Bill Cardell, and Harold McClelland.

Dear World

Introduction

So perhaps the humble, guilty diary still has its uses.

Thomas Mallon, *A Book of One's Own*

*W*hat is a diary now? Who uses it? What kinds of diaries are published? Where does diary fit in the much-remarked-on memoir "boom" in contemporary life narrative? The diary is a highly recognizable form of life writing, and it is also a diverse and shifting genre that has been interpreted in contemporary media and by contemporary users in a variety of ways. The diary now is a performative space, a print genre, a digital platform, a behavior regime, a smartphone app.[1] It is the subject of ongoing controversy—the repository of persistent beliefs, myths, desires—and it is a clear and distinctive rhetorical style deployed by television producers, by bloggers, by journalists or self-help gurus as a directive and inducement, what Sidonie Smith and Julia Watson might name "coaxing" (*Reading*, 66) in the elicitation of particular kinds of self-display and certain ways of self-knowing, and as the visible reminder of certain doggedly persisting ideas of the true and authentic self. In all kinds of ways, contemporary diaries make visible the intimate and the personal, they blur and destabilize conventional boundaries between public and private, and they foreground processes of formation and reformation of subjectivity in self-representation.

This study explores the diary as a mass-market and published commodity, as a popular and highly divergent digital mode, and as a representation of self still widely associated with particular expectations, assumptions, and desires. The particular shape of the contemporary diary is underwritten by centuries of practice from which the diary emerges as a flexible and hybrid genre and as an autobiographical mode that, as I argue here, requires its own particular critical

3

and theoretical apparatus. Early life narrative scholars, however, identifying an overlooked "canon" of diary writing, constructed the genre a priori: as not only historically marginal but aesthetically too. Valued as a sociohistorical document to be mined for detail or as a cultural artifact, the diary has only recently been considered an autobiographical genre in any "proper" sense. Indeed, while memoir has recently become the domain of "the young," as Leigh Gilmore puts it in *The Limits of Autobiography* (a radical shift from the autobiography of "great men" that constitutes the genre historically), diaries are already historically and traditionally by "other" kinds of subjects, in unpublished forms and on topics conventionally regarded as peripheral to matters of public importance or historical significance. The diary is both critically and popularly established as a marginal mode, a ragged edge to erstwhile "public" discourse. In this book, however, I examine contexts in which the diary has become a central cultural form, and I respond to some of the dominant cultural motifs that shape and surround the genre as a popular contemporary life narrative practice. What does it mean to think about diary in the age of mass "reality" media franchises like *Big Brother*, where individuals are surveyed so relentlessly at one turn and in the other encouraged everywhere to confess? Is a Facebook update a kind of diary?[2] Can serial autobiographical posts on Twitter come to constitute a diary narrative of some kind?[3] What myths about diary are powerful now, and why? In a time of unprecedented access to the private lives of public individuals, how do we understand the enduring relationship of diary forms to scandal and secrets?[4] What do long-held assumptions about diary as "artless" or natural signal for a genre now so widely published? Even shallow data on diary publishing reveals that diary is an increasingly popular contemporary genre.[5] Complicating any survey of this field is the diversity of texts that fall under or are described as diary—the category ranges from calendar forms through to examples that are closer to memoir than diary in any conventional formal sense.

As a life narrative form, the diary is highly recognizable; yet it is also a genre, and it is discursively constituted. Diary signals a status as intimate, personal writing, and it may or may not also take a conventional formal shape as, for example, dated entries.[6] That "diary" is used to market or identify works that don't necessarily respond to ostensible formal conventions, or that take new forms in, for example, reality television or online, indicates a demand for autobiographical works that connect to the discursive traditions of diary writing and reading. Long associated with private lives, secret knowledge, and the threat (or promise) of self-exposure, the contemporary diary is a highly popular form, a matrix through which key social discourses are played out and made visible.

Like other autobiographical modes, the diary is an icon of confessional culture, the embodiment of a widespread fascination for the lives of others and a signifier of powerful desires for contact with a literary "real." The "humble, guilty diary" that Thomas Mallon (*Book*) remarks on, however, is both proximate and unique to the genres of life narrative that have proliferated or evolved in the last decades of the twentieth and the early parts of the twenty-first century. For example, a persistent belief (or is it a hope?) in the diary as a primarily *private* form of writing means that even when published, it is reflexively associated with intimate disclosure and private life. "It is hard to think of a more private place outside the skull—at least in the West—than the toilet," remarks Fiona Capp, musing on the posthumous eBay listing of novelist J. D. Salinger's toilet, emphasized in the sales blurb as "uncleaned and in its original condition" ("Salinger's," 13). The case is "bizarre," yet instructive, an indicator of the extreme limits to which confessional culture has reached and a signal of the extent to which the private lives of public figures are desired and fetishized: "The ad for Salinger's loo would have us believe that to possess this unlikely throne is to have access to his seat of inspiration. The toilet, it is implied, is the place where the writer metaphorically as well as literally spills his guts. (Hence the symbolic importance of it being uncleaned)" (14). Less viscerally associated with private ablution, the diary is a literary genre in which an association with rawness and intimate self-display, to the literal as well as figurative "trace" of the author, has equally functioned to attract or repulse readers and critics.

Scandalous, sordid, unmediated, associated with "unprofessional" writers, or with adolescent girls,[7] the diary is a genre desired as much for its promise of rawness and unself-consciousness as it has also been derided for excess interiority, solipsism, or an unrelentingly emotional register. This is particularly so in popular representations, where both the diary format and its particular rhetorical effects have become synonymous for what have been seen as the worst excesses of the contemporary autobiographical turn: confession, narcissism, and unmediated exposure of self.[8] Consider *Big Brother*. Developed from a Dutch format and shown in more than forty-seven countries (including the online world of *Second Life*[9]), the "reality" game show documents the lives of a set of housemates for television and online audiences. Through a premise of surveillance, the show relies on secrets, gossip, and candid confession in establishing a context where housemates are voted out for not appearing "real" enough or for not convincingly displaying their "true self" and behavior within the artificial parameters of the contest.[10]

Employing discourses of confession, voyeurism, and analysis, one of the most recognizable "spaces" of the *Big Brother* house also manifests the fascination with private and public selves that the show promotes: the diary room. Here the all-seeing narrator of the show, "Big Brother," engages directly with contestants in the *Big Brother* house, and they in turn reveal secrets, or receive information selectively shared with fellow housemates (information, nonetheless, relayed to the viewing audience). Observing that the *Big Brother* diary room functions as an embodied space for private and confessional behavior is to notice, to paraphrase Carolyn R. Miller and Dawn Shepherd, that genre shapes action ("Blogging"). It also shapes reception: audiences for *Big Brother* expect (and usually receive) certain kinds of representation and disclosure when subjects are in the diary room.[11]

Big Brother is frequently hailed as the most significant antecedent in a raft of reality television programming that employs, in various guises, confessional to-camera sequences that allow the subject an opportunity to offer an "authentic" or "truthful" interpretation of their behavior within the staged context of the show. As such, these sequences mesh with assumptions about public and private selves that are also played out in literary forms like diary. Genre is important here. The explicit designation of the *Big Brother* diary room as a space where contestants are encouraged to "let the mask slip" shows that conventional understandings of the diary as an intimate, secret, and confessional genre have become fixed in popular culture.[12] Imagining an alternative, awkward designation of this space as a "memoir room," or an "autobiography room," implies that it is not just a context of self-talk that makes this space intimate and confessional. Instead, it is through the generic designation and association to "diary" that the effects of "liveness" and therapeutic surveillance crucial to the show's rationale and success are invoked.[13] Here, as elsewhere, the diary is conceptualized as a private and personal genre and as a mode with particular implications for the formation of individual identity and in the representation of personal experience.

Big Brother and its reality television successors employ diary as both a discursive mode and a generic format. As television media, they also draw on the specific technology that enables and produces "live" or "unmediated" content in this context, and they respond to specific audience expectations in doing so. The case studies of diary texts and practices that are the focus of this study, however, are literary texts largely produced within the last ten to twenty years, and they represent both the continuation and evolution of diary traditions in the past. They are also, despite their contemporaneity, recognizably conventional as "texts"—even the blogs that I consider in this study usually have a print published edition. Given the proliferation of technology and forms for self-representation now available, why this focus on conventional modes, on the diary as "book"? My focus in this study is not on form as such but on "published," whether in print or online; this book considers diary texts that have found an audience and that circulate widely in the public sphere. Moreover, while a focus on published work is usually invisible in most literary studies, where the condition of publication is reflexively assumed, diary studies differs in that a substantial focus of scholarship has been directed to unpublished writings. Indeed, a great many diary scholars are also diary editors, and the difficult work of shaping and producing a published text from a diary artifact has its own vibrant category of scholarship.[14] The published diary, then, is a relatively recent phenomenon, a product of determined scholarship, shifting social and cultural mores, and a well-remarked memoir "boom" that has seen the emergence of mass markets and publishing apparatus aimed at the elicitation and publication of autobiographical representations of all kinds.[15]

In choosing to focus on published diaries this study responds not only to the growing visibility of diary publications in marketplaces and bookstores but also to a shifting context in which diary publications are also more likely to be the product of their living author. That is, the contemporary diary, like other genres of life narrative, is produced and published as an autobiographical object—a self-representative mode in which generic choices (or transgressions) must be read into the characterization of self and experience that also makes up the text. In what way is diary understood to both shape and represent the self differently (for the reader as much as the writer) compared to other narrative modes? What is the rhetorical position of the contemporary diarist? Who uses diary now, for what ends? The diary is a generic and rhetorical choice (one that reveals a social and cultural context as much as an authorial intent) that must be explored as such.

Just what diary does in a contemporary context brimming with ever more diverse opportunities and modes for acts of self-representation is one of the key interests of this study. Ultimately, I am interested in diary as a cultural practice, one that both reveals and negotiates with concerns of intense desire in contemporary life: authenticity, subjectivity, and truth. Diary is a genre that appears at once inordinately simple—a personal expression—and infinitely complex: it is a text created by the self, but that may also create it.[16] It is a representation that reflects not just the individual, but also discourse, culture, society, and power. It functions as evidence of the world and in reference to it, but it is also a construction of that world and a representation of it. This is not particular to diary—such problems are foundational in autobiography studies—but in this book I look carefully at how diary forms become significant in certain discursive constructions of self and subjectivity, and I explore how diary is particularly imbricated in ideas of authenticity that energize and complicate acts of self-representation now.

In the chapter that follows, "A Public Private Self: Diary Now," I establish a foundation for the exploration of the contemporary diary in this book. Here I consider some of the major aspects of diary criticism, and in particular I explore changing concepts of diary as it has moved from an assumed condition of largely private and marginal practice to a highly visible and central genre of popular culture. My aim in this chapter is to establish a critical perspective on assumptions and expectations about the diary genre that characterize it as a life narrative text and this critical survey underpins the various case studies that follow.

Chapter 2, "How to Be the Authentic You: Therapy, Self-Help, and the 'How-to' Diary," explores a particularly prominent commodification of the diary genre. In this chapter, I explore how what I am calling the "how-to" diary—guided journal programs or workbook style manuals—makes visible discourses of authenticity and assumptions of therapy that coalesce in form. How-to diary manuals by self-help authors like Sarah Ban Breathnach, Julia Cameron, Stephanie Dowrick, and Michelle Weldon reveal the significance of diary as a genre connected to authentic self-representation and they advocate a form and a regime of the diary that reproduces this ideal. The how-to journal mobilizes discourses of redemption through self-representation that also characterize autobiography and memoir more broadly, but in this chapter I look at how and why the diary has acquired traction as a unique and specific methodology. That is, I explore how particular uses and forms of diary have become privileged as tools for self-knowledge and for the representation of authentic knowing and I argue that this has significance for considering diary writing in other locations and contexts of contemporary culture.

Chapter 3, "The Ethics of Being There and Seeing: Thomas Goltz, Paul McGeough, and the Journalist's Diary of War," examines the production of contemporary war journalism and explores how diary narrative accrues particular rhetorical effects in this context. The war correspondents Thomas Goltz and Paul McGeough use diary strategically to represent their respective experiences reporting from the sites of modern conflict in Chechnya and Iraq. These diaries map a site of practice and an ongoing tension between diary and journalism—as "daily" forms—that is further played out in writing about war. The use of diary narrative by journalists in zones of recent conflict is also connected to new technology; the Internet, with its capacity for live streaming or real-time discourse, both responds to and fosters a desire for immediate, grounded, and urgent narrative forms that are producing new variants of diary.

Chapter 4 also explores diaries of war, but in this chapter I move to a different context for bringing into view stereotypical disjunctions between public and private perspectives. "The Intimate Appeal of Getting Closer: The Diary as Evidence and Testimony in Nuha al-Radi, Riverbend, and Suad Amiry" discusses the diary publications of three Arab women. These recent publications offer a further context in which to explore the effect of diary in representing a highly valued perspective "on the ground." That is, these diarists are women with urgent stories to tell and who desire to reach audiences beyond the local, who want to intervene in cultural and gender stereotypes of Arab lives, and who seek to testify to the traumatic everyday of life during conflict. This chapter explores the way in which diary narrative enables, but may also constrain, certain exchanges or crossings of such narrative into the West. These diaries enter Western markets as highly desirable commodities, and they draw our attention to critical issues of gender, genre, and place that remain resonant in contemporary uses of the diary.

In chapter 5, "Sex, Confession, and Blogging: The Online Diaries of Belle de Jour and Abby Lee," I look at a recent yet nonetheless now well-established venue for personal writing that draws distinctively on diary discourse in both its production and reception. The blog is a mode of writing that many critics have observed retains structural and thematic links to diary writing. However, while a great many bloggers reject the designation of their practice as linked to diary writing, historically or in the present, others have actively asserted their role as online diarists, naming their blogs as "diaries" and producing personally in-flected representations that directly engage with assumptions and expectations of the diary genre. This chapter focuses on a category of bloggers where blog as diary has particular force. The online sex diaries of British bloggers Abby Lee and Belle de Jour perform the taut relationship between personal narrative and confession in contemporary culture that has frequently been encoded into perceptions and representations of diary narrative in particular. This chapter focuses on the sex blog as a form of online writing that draws on stereotypical assumptions about diary writing as more authentic, more intimate, and more "real" than other kinds of autobiographical representation. In a coda to this chapter, I frame a consideration for the blog as "digital manuscript" in order to further interrogate the assumptions of authenticity and privacy that attend to personal writing like diary and even in very new contexts.

In chapter 6, "Graphic Lives: Visual Narration and the Diaries of Phoebe Gloeckner, Bobby Baker, and *The 1000 Journals Project*," I again look at a rela-tively "new" form for diary writing: this chapter is a consideration of graphic diaries as modes that offer innovative ways of thinking about diary texts and that further counter enduring stereotypes of the genre as private or naïve.

Graphic diaries foreground the increasingly significant phenomenon of a visual-verbal grammar for self-representation and the formal capacity and flexibility of diary is responsive to this context. Bobby Baker's *Diary Drawings: Mental Illness and Me* (2010), a visual document of Baker's struggle with a period of mental illness, and the *1000 Journals Project* (2007), by San Francisco artist Someguy, an art project to randomly distribute (and retrieve) 1,000 blank journals among strangers worldwide, as well as Phoebe Gloeckner's graphic autobiography *Diary of a Teenage Girl* (2002), are some recent examples of the continuing interest in the diary as a personal mode of self-exploration or identity creation that are also part of a contemporary turn toward graphic and visual styles in autobiography more broadly. Graphic diaries turn attention to the diary as assemblage and to the possibilities of fluid and multiple self-mediation and self-representation that are literally made visible in this context.

The conclusion to this study returns to some key findings in order to reflect on why readers and authors use the diary genre and what they expect when they encounter it. In doing so, I consider what diary now has to tell us about the significance of privacy and interiority in autobiographical writing and what this might signal about contemporary concerns for authenticity and confession that so vigorously circulate around and through the contemporary diary as a discursive mode.

1

A Public Private Self

Diary Now

> The aesthetic of the "unfinished," which is that of the notebook, of the
> diary, of fragments (not the novel, which is supposed to be cultivated,
> worked over, finished).
>
> Kate Zambreno, Heroines

*A*n attention to diary forms in contemporary culture is in dynamic tension to
a historical moment in which autobiographical modes of all kinds have gained
attention and visibility; the diary is part of a broader and much remarked upon
"boom" in memoir and self-representational forms. The ascendancy of memoir
is linked to the advent of postmodern consciousness, a loosening of reference
and veridicality, an instatement of fluidity, fragmentation, and metaphor and
even in genres of "nonfiction." Moreover, as Leigh Gilmore has noted, a turn
to memoir as a prominent genre in contemporary life marks a cultural-historical
shift: "Previously associated with elder statesmen reporting on the way their
public lives parallel historical events, memoir is now dominated by the young,
or at least the youngish in memoir's terms, whose private lives are emblematic
of a cultural moment" (*Limits*, 1). G. Thomas Couser notes this shift has also
been defined in value terms: memoir is "minor," "subliterary," and "shallow,"
while autobiography is "literary," "deep," and "canonical" (*Memoir*, 18). Etymology further clarifies the distinction: "The term derives from the French word
for memory. . . . [C]alling a narrative about yourself memoir usually signals
that it is based primarily on memory, a notoriously unreliable and highly selective faculty. In turn, this creates the impression that the narrative may be im-
pressionistic and subjective rather than authoritatively fact based" (19).

Ordinary lives, private lives, fluid, fragmented, and flawed, highly subjective
representation—this is also the domain of the diary. Rachael Langford and

Russell West, for example, describe diary as an "uncertain genre uneasily balanced between literary and historical writing, between the spontaneity of reportage and the reflectiveness of the crafted text, between selfhood and events, between subjectivity and objectivity, between the public and the private . . . a misfit form" ("Introduction," 8). The appeal of diary as an "in-between" genre is cited by practioners; Virginia Woolf's famous description of diary as a mode that does "not count" as writing—natural, impulsive, and naïve, "like scratching or having a bath"—foregrounds the quality of capaciousness and freedom perceived as unique to this genre (*Diary*, 2:179). Kate Zambreno's meditative reflection in the epigraph to this chapter further extends this ideal. However, and with Woolf in mind, Rachel Cottam notes that "not counting as writing" may also be why "most of the work on genre theory omits to consider diary, or, at best, dismisses it in a single sentence" ("Diaries," 267). Conventionally, the diary has been devalued as an autobiographical (literary) mode even though it has also been prized as a unique self-representative text. That is, lacking qualities of teleology, linearity, or stability, diary is positioned as a marginal form of life writing, one that opposes or undermines a classic construction of autobiography as a literary genre. Indeed, while the diary conforms to a Greek etymology of the term "autobiography" as self-life-writing,[1] autobiography has also been defined as a specific style of narrative linked to the emergence of Enlightenment subjectivity. Though the word is "a post-Enlightenment coinage," it invokes "a particular genealogy, resonant ideology and discursive imperative" that is connected to the Enlightenment ideal of a self-knowing subject at the center of a universalizing life story (Smith and Watson, "Introduction," xvii). The autobiographical narrative produced by such a subject has, in the past, been favored as the definitive mode and constructed as an ideal form. "One creates," says James Olney, "from moment to moment and continuously the reality to which one gives a metaphoric name and shape, and that shape is one's own shape. This is *my* universe" (*Metaphors*, 34). In this traditional sense, autobiography is retrospective, linear, and unified—a composition of disparate parts into a metaphor for the whole self.

Though contemporary life writing resoundingly demonstrates that autobiographical narrative is far from the singular and teleological mode imagined by early critics, this dominant view of autobiography has meant that diary narrative, characterized by qualities of informality, discontinuity, and fragmentation, could not count as an autobiographical form in any "proper" sense, and this has consequences for how the diary has been both used and understood in literary contexts. Philippe Lejeune, in his famous definition of autobiography as "retrospective prose narrative written by a real person concerning his own existence, where the focus is his individual life, in particular the story of his personality," considers diary and journal to be subcategories, closely related to but not fulfilling the requirements of autobiography (*On Autobiography*, 4). For Lejeune, diaries are temporal documents, written from the perspective of immersion; the end of the story is not clear to the author, and meaning is gathered through accretion rather than retrospective construction. In short, he considers autobiography as a self-consciously literary text and the organic and "structureless" form of the diary as one that fails the aesthetic criteria. Here Lejeune joins early critics like Olney or Georges Gusdorf in viewing this characteristic of diary as a negative quality, though in recent years he has retraced this dichotomy, arguing instead that immediacy and immersion is the particular (and redeeming) character of diary narrative: "The diary's value lies in its being a trace of a moment" (*On Diary*, 182). Nonetheless, Lejeune has also remained attached to an ideal form of the diary as a "private" mode, and so one in which naturalness and lack of artistic intent become definitive qualities: he opens a paradox that surrounds diary as a "pure" form, one in which alterations "kill" (182). The diary is here idealized for its *form*, to which the author must submit. Technology thus has a primary effect. Lejeune exhorts that "with computers, corrections can be made on the fly: I only close my entry once it sounds *right*" (182). It is a capacity Lejeune remains wary of because he prizes the diary as a private, unself-conscious representation of self and the computer alters this prospect radically. Indeed, a temptation to tamper with or alter the diaristic "moment" is for Lejeune also representative of a cultural shift: "A diary is a place where you're not afraid to make spelling mistakes or be stupid. Of course, ever since we've developed the vile habit of publishing diaries, many people put on a suit and tie to write about their private lives" (175). For Lejeune, the diary is quintessentially a private (and *unpublished*) text and is attenuated or diminished as a public, published mode. As more and more authors choose diary as a literary form, such ideals come under pressure. The contemporary diary, especially as a widely published genre, nonetheless negotiates with desires for purity and naturalness that are tied to expectations of the diary as a record of the moment, and to the text produced as ideally uncensored and "uncorrected."

Understanding diary as an artistic and literary mode must invite consideration of the form as a rhetorical and strategic device. While, for a number of years now, critics have valuably turned attention to recovering and reading unpublished diaries (most notably, as projects of reclaiming women's life writings), the contemporary diary is a mode that no longer precludes or makes publication exceptional. Indeed, Lejeune's diarist who is "intimidated" by the prospect of baring their thoughts and who would prefer to "hunker down and barricade" themselves in the diary—his "you and I" who "wear our old bedroom slippers and don't give a hoot" (*On Diary*, 175)—is not the subject of this book. The diaries that constitute the texts for this study are published, sometimes in more than one medium (as in the case of blogs), and they are by subjects for whom the diary constitutes a specific rhetorical mode. Nonetheless, perceived distinctions between diary and autobiography, between natural representation and artistic construction, between public and private writing, continue to inform both how these subjects use diary and how these diaries are circulated and read. That is, the kind of distinctions critics have made between diary and an autobiography "proper" represents a discursive split. Where autobiography is perceived as the more literary or "high" form of self-representation, diary has been considered a more natural, less mediated form. It is a perceived "naturalness," in the form, as Woolf and Lejeune each indicate, that has then allowed for constructions of diary writing as outside of or antithetical to "proper" writing. Yet, though this is often framed as a kind of detriment, a perception of naturalness in diary forms is also valued as authentic. Paul Fussell, for example, argues that "the memoir is a kind of fiction" because it employs artificial structures and recognizably literary character-narrators. For Fussell, "the further personal written materials move from the form of the daily diary, the closer they approach to the figurative and the fictional" (*Great*, 310).[2] Diary is valued as a document written in medias res.

This perception of diary, which is also a perception about personal discourse in general, remains very powerful. Indeed, in his discussion of Holocaust diaries and memoirs, James E. Young explains: "because the diarists wrote from within the whirlwind, the degree of authority in their accounts is perceived by readers to be stronger than that of texts shaped through hindsight" ("Interpreting," 414). Young spells out further how this perception operates: "On the same phenomenological basis as print journalism, in which the perceived temporal proximity of a text to events reinforces the sense of its facticity, diaries can be far more convincing of their factual veracity than more retrospective accounts. Like photographs, which represent themselves as metonymical remnants of their objects, the diary accrues the weight and authority of reality itself" (414). Even in "literary" incarnations the diary is stereotypically perceived of as an "unskilled" writing form and as a nonliterary and spontaneous mode.[3] In this, it has links to other aesthetic modes where spontaneity and the "natural" have been highly valued (and contested). For example, in *Regarding the Pain of Others* (2003), Susan Sontag observes that photography is one of the only art forms in which "professional training and years of experience do not confer an insuperable advantage over the untrained and inexperienced" (24–25). The amateur photo-graph competes with professional images because "so permissive are the stan-dards for a memorable, eloquent picture" (24). Is diary a genre of literature that does in fact approach what Sontag finds in the amateur photograph? This is mostly about aesthetic effect: Sontag observes that grainy "home video" footage now makes regular appearances on news bulletins, even when more professional footage may be available. These "amateur" images have a particular authority that is in turn an aesthetic: they carry "the weight of witnessing without the taint of artistry, which is equated with insincerity or mere contrivance. Pictures of hellish events seem more authentic when they don't have the look that comes from being 'properly' lighted and composed" (23).

Like the photograph, the diary is privileged as both an "objective record and personal testimony, both a faithful copy or transcription of an actual mo-ment of reality and an interpretation of that reality" (Sontag, *Regarding*, 23) and even as the final product, the production of a representation, calls all these things into question. Though Sontag argues that "there is no comparable level playing field in literature, where virtually nothing owes to chance or luck and where the refinement of language usually incurs no penalty" (25), the diary is a mode in which "natural" and "amateur" are aesthetic qualities that confer sig-nificant value. As in amateur photographs, the context of the representative act is more important than the quality of composition.[4] This is the case with the Holocaust diaries that Young considers, and Andrea Peterson indicates a similar interpretation in her entry "War Diaries" for *The Encyclopedia of Life Writing* (2001): "It would seem likely that war diaries might eschew both literary cre-ativity and style simply because they are often written hastily by exhausted, traumatized and terrified people" (926). For both of these critics the urgency to record is seen to impair, or preclude, aesthetic intent. This "loss," however, is in correlation to an increase in authenticity.

A tension between aesthetics and authenticity that characterizes the con-temporary diary mode, especially in particular contexts, is explored throughout this book: the journalists' diaries of war that are the focus of chapter 3, for ex-ample, throw into relief larger questions about the use of personal narrative in the telling of public history. Here, popular assumptions about what a diary should be (naïve and nonliterary), and what a diary should do (confess private experience), are in tension with the journalistic role and identity. Indeed, the association of diary forms with ordinary writing and everyday experience and the value accorded to the natural and unmediated as an aspect of representation is part of a widespread stereotype of the genre as artless, and it is also part of an apparent confirmation for a condition as "private." Diary scholar Lawrence Rosenwald has indicated the authority of this perception, and its troublesome effect.

In his introduction to *Emerson and the Art of the Diary* (1988), Rosenwald catalogues what he takes as certain "errors" proceeding "from our deep beliefs regarding diaries" (4). "Beliefs" is a key term here, indicating his sense that diary forms are mostly understood through conclusions and assumptions "acted on rather than thought about" (4). The diary, argues Rosenwald, is a genre that has been only "shallowly examined," and he hopes then to assess and perhaps "modify" certain persistent beliefs: Rosenwald is "Against the Myth of Privacy," for example, and "Against the Myth of Veridicality; Against the Myth of Art-lessness" (4). Some of these "myths" can be "refuted through an appeal to fact," though "the myth of the veridical diary cannot be; it is founded irremovably because it is founded upon a void, founded not on error of fact but on truths we hold to be self-evident" (14). The myth of privacy, however, cannot be thus defended, because it ignores the common practice of diary texts shared among readers: "New England Transcendentalists," he notes, "passed their diaries around as scholars pass around drafts of essays," and while New England Puritans "seemed not to have passed them around to their contemporaries," he argues that they were nonetheless alert to future readers; they were used to reading the diaries and journals passed down by their ancestors (10).

In the contemporary context, diaries are increasingly common as published texts, circulating as commodities—marketed, distributed, and serving various ends. This is one clear way in which contemporary uses of the diary need to be reconsidered against assumptions of the genre as a private mode, or indeed, as part of a reconsideration of what "private" can indicate apart from "unpublished." Discussing the myth of "artlessness" in the diary, for example, Rosenwald makes a distinction not "between degrees of finish" but "between inexorably opposed and sundered antitheses: between 'art' and 'nature,' that is, between a well-wrought urn and some mode of spontaneous utterance wholly unshaped by convention" (*Emerson*, 21). Artlessness is in itself an aesthetic value and one with distinct rhetorical effects; it engages desires for transparency and "naturalness" in representation and contributes to the value of this condition as authentic. The perceived "privacy" of the diary is thus less about its status as withheld—as unpublished, kept under a pillow, or otherwise resistant to outside readers—than its relation to uncensored and unmediated self-narration. Perceptions about diary as a text written with a greater sense of "privacy" (no matter the actual status of the document as a circulated or published text) confer

utilization of "practical techniques . . . to reshape the soul in the service of an art of living" to the Stoic, Epicurean, Socratic, and Platonic traditions: "one who would lead a philosophical life must practice self-examination, cultivate attention to the present moment, devote oneself to duties, cultivate indifference to indifferent things, keep certain things 'before one's eyes'" (242). Discourses of the Christian confession emerged from this tradition, as did the sense of "cultivation of an attention to oneself in order to achieve a transfiguration of the soul" (243). A historical link between this kind of religious discourse and the practice of diary writing is traced by Felicity A. Nussbaum, who notes that following the expansion of literacy in the seventeenth and eighteenth centuries, Quaker, Methodist, and Baptist sects commonly promoted diary writing as a disciplinary device for fostering proper spiritual and moral conduct ("Eighteenth-Century," 153). These writings were considered as largely private and individual, and were not generally published (though Nussbaum notes Quaker journals are an exception). However, though working on the self was thus largely a private task, it was one implicated in the social fabric and public life of the whole community—a discipline for producing moral individuals and upright citizens.

Contemporary ideas of self that accompany a confessional turn are also the result of particular institutional forms and organizational contexts, and one of the most powerful of these, according to Furedi, is therapy: "Contemporary society transmits the belief that problems of the emotion ought not to be faced by people on their own" (*Therapy*, 9). Peter Brooks is similarly concerned: "In a contemporary culture that celebrates the therapeutic value of getting it all out in public, confession has become nearly banal, the everyday business of talk shows, as if the ordinary person could claim his individual identity only in the act of confessing. We appear today to live in a generalized demand for transparency that entails a kind of tyranny of the requirement to confess" (*Troubling*, 4). The therapeutic imperative, which figures as redemptive, is also essentially a confessional one, manifested in an emphasis on "feeling in public" and in the widespread idealization of and conviction of the existence of a "true self" (Furedi, *Therapy*, 37). Thus, what may appear as an emphasis on individualism and a value for "spontaneous and natural emotions" is in fact a distortion of the "classical search for authenticity" in which social action is given over to personal contemplation. Importantly, therapy culture produces not "emotional literacy" but "emotional conformity" (39). Robert Van Krieken, who nonetheless situates Furedi as the latest in a long tradition of "cultural pessimists," notes that a perspective of culture in decline is centered on a particular perception of contemporary life: "The shifting boundary between public and private life, an inclination towards self-expression and self-gratification combined with a

declining interest in public life and communal social relations; an expansion of
the influence if not the power of a corps of psychologically trained experts who
define our system of meaning, replacing Christianity, family ties and institutional commitment with a secular, individualist, humanist, therapeutic concep-
tion" ("Decline," 54). The sense of a breakdown between public and private life
and self is of particular relevance in considering the contemporary diary. Again,
in her studies of eighteenth-century diaries, Nussbaum notes the effect of the
genre as a private space: "Though even secret writing cannot escape its inter-
sections with social relations, private writing in eighteenth-century England
was often an attempt to find words without masters, to speak 'outside' familiar
discourses" ("Eighteenth-Century," 156). For Furedi, the distinction between
spheres necessary for this sense of privacy—and so, the possibility of subversion
it encourages—is eroded in contemporary culture. Similarly, "in contemporary societies," notes Viviane Serafty, "the desire for transparency permeates
political and social discourse as part of a vast ideological formation, so that the
public and private sphere may seem to meld and merge" (*Mirror*, 83). The confessional television of Oprah Winfrey, Ricki Lake, or the *Big Brother* franchise,
as well as "the new genre of self-revelatory biography," are thus to be viewed in
terms of "new cultural norms about notions of intimacy and private space" that
validate the confessional imperative and encourage public disclosure as a project of self-knowledge and empowerment (Furedi, *Therapy*, 40).

Nick Mansfield argues that a "focus on the self as the centre of both lived
experience and of discernible meaning has become one of the—if not *the*—
defining issues of modern and postmodern cultures" (*Subjectivity*, 1), and in this
study, I argue that diary is *the* genre linked intimately to the representation and
construction of self and that it crystallizes a certain set of these ideas of self:
confession/privacy, surveillance/public presence. This activity has distinct historical and cultural links to other forms of diary writing and to how the form
has evolved or persisted into the contemporary moment. That is, an expectation
that surveillance will lead us closer to "reality" in representation, that the
confessional voice is authentic, and that our "true self" is achieved through
inwardness is key here, and these are ideals linked closely with diary practice,
both historically and in the present.

Radical Personal: Diary and Gender

In considering the diary explicitly as a contemporary genre, this book nonetheless returns to the varied and hybrid forms of diary practice. "At one moment

or another," says Rosenwald, "the diary may take on the supplementary functions of introspection or itinerary or confession; none of these functions is intrin-
sic to it" (*Emerson*, 6). K. Eckhard Kuhn-Osius explains, "it is very difficult to
say anything about diaries which is true for all of them" ("Making," 166). Diaries
take many shapes and forms. However, there are recognizable and standard
kinds of blank personal diary, and the form is a familiar mass-market commodity,
in its many gift iterations characteristically bearing gilt-edges and decorative or
hard covers. Personal diaries also (though this is less frequent now) often bear a
lock and key; Thomas Mallon notes they are more likely to be sold with a girl's
picture on the front.[6] The popular marketing of diary as a "book" carries with it
expectations of a document kept from first page to last—sequential and linear.
Yet a diary may be composed retrospectively, gathered through accretion and
selection, rather than as a text kept contiguously; this is the case with the Australian writer Miles Franklin's diary and countless others like it.[7] It may be
personal or practical, comprising intimate reflection or mundane daily detail; it
may be political or testimonial. A diary may be a photomontage, a file on a
computer, an online site, or a video stream. "It may be a book of court gossip,
or remarkable providence, or gleanings from other books, or notes on the
weather," remarks Rosenwald, nonetheless arguing that no matter the diversity of content it should be "a book of the self" and it "must be a book of time"
(*Emerson*, 6).

In his study of twentieth-century diary fiction, Andrew Hassam has argued
that it is less useful to see diary as a homogenous practice, a distinctive form,
than as a set of shifting and historical assumptions that attach to the word
"diary" (*Writing*, 18). Such a view accounts for multiple forms of diary, and a
diversity of effects. Which is not to say that categorization is irrelevant here.
Even without considering the multiple subvariants of diary that exist, a key
difference is often discerned between diary and journal, terms that are, just as
often, considered interchangeable; Mallon says they are "hopelessly muddled"
(*Book*, 1). *The Encyclopedia of Life Writing* lists "Diaries and Journals" together,
though diary is the term used throughout the entry. Nor does Lejeune make a
distinction between diary and journal, using the terms equally without signaling
any perceived accommodation of disparity between them. In his 1974 study
(one of the earliest critical works in the field) Robert A. Fothergill tells us he has
introduced the term "journal" into *Private Chronicles: A Study of English Diaries*
"for no other reason than to vary the monotonous repetition of the word
"diary" in almost every sentence" (14). Sidonie Smith and Julia Watson, however, note that "some critics distinguish diary from journal by characterizing
the journal as a chronicle of public record that is less intimate than the diary"

(*Reading*, 272). Nussbaum uses "diary to mean the daily recording of thoughts, feelings, and activities of the writer, entered frequently and regularly" and considers "journal" interchangeable in this context, though she also notes "diaries are often considered to be the less elaborate form" ("Toward," 130). There are gendered connotations here also. In her study of the journal as a pedagogical tool, Cinthia Gannett notes a "tense relation" between the terms: in North American educational parlance "journal" is the preferred term because diary "though denotatively similar . . . has come to be associated with connotations such as overly personal, confessional, trivial"—diary narrative is perceived as too "feminine" to be considered as a serious educational tool (*Gender*, 21). Mapping some of the fraught ideological ground of the American school system, Gannett notes that as writing that signals its intention to foreground the personal and intimate, calling personal narrative diary or journal does little to assuage those who cite a fear of indoctrination, invasion of privacy, and moral depravity as the accompanying dangers of personal disclosure (21). The tension between terms here reveals just some of the anxieties that attend personal writing in public settings.

In this book, I consider diary and journal as linked and closely related forms of serial personal writing. However, like Gannett, I also pay attention to where these terms are used preferentially and ideologically. Similarly, issues of gender remain fundamental in conceptualizing the diary genre. Sidonie Smith asks, in her revisionist theory of women's autobiography, "where in the maze of proliferating definitions and theories, in the articulation of teleologies and epistemologies, in the tension between poetics and historiography, in the placement and displacement of the 'self' is there any consideration of woman's *bios*, woman's *auto*, woman's *graphia* or woman's hermeneutics?" (*Poetics*, 7). As a form that has existed where other autobiographical modes might have been repressed or obscured, the diary is considered by feminist critics as a particularly important site for the expression of female subjectivity. That is, because it was so often practiced by women in particular—and mostly in lieu of other, more prestigious forms of life writing such as autobiography—diary has been considered a location where processes of resistance or compliance to cultural proscriptions of feminine identity can be seen. Katie Holmes remarks in her study of Australian women's diaries: "As I became more absorbed in the diaries I discovered that women did not simply write a record of their days. They could use the diary as a place of resistance to dominant prescriptions on women's lives, or, alternatively, as a place of rapprochement or accommodation, where conflicting and contradictory demands on women could be integrated. The very process of writing in this form gave women the space in which to define their own lives and to shape their identities" (*Spaces*, x). Holmes's linking of form to function here is a significant characteristic of feminist engagement with women's diary writing. In feminist critical interpretations, diary has received attention as an autobiographical genre with symbolic and manifest links to the cultural and ideological position of women and as a genre that both represents female experience and is feminine in form. In this vein, Suzanne Juhasz identifies "dailiness as a structuring principle for women's lives" ("Towards," 222) and diary as "the classic verbal articulation of dailiness" (224), while Estelle C. Jelinek, in "Women's Autobiography and the Male Tradition," sees diary writing as a popular mode among women because it is "analogous to the fragmented, interrupted, and formless nature of their lives" ("Introduction," 19).

Others, like Harriet Blodgett, have seen it as a circumstantial mode: "I do not make a case for the diary as an inherently female form, but rather as a characteristic one. I suggest that diary keeping has been practiced so extensively by women because it has been possible for them and gratifying to them" (*Centuries*, 5). Nussbaum suggests that diary is not only a popular mode among women, but that women may have invented it ("Toward," 134). These critics draw links between the cultural-historical circumstances of woman and to diary as a gendered and feminine form of writing. The essentialist and mimetic association of genre and subjectivity here is readily challenged by later feminist critics such as Sidonie Smith (*Poetics*), yet critics like Rebecca Hogan have still found it useful to see diary narrative, whether associated with women or not, as distinctly feminine: "Is the diary feminine? The obvious answer is no, since the names of many justly famous and less well-known male diarists will instantly spring to mind. On the other hand . . . we may describe a writing strategy as 'feminine' or 'masculine' regardless of the sex of its practitioner" ("Engendered," 95). In the introduction to her anthology of nineteenth-century women's diaries, Amy L. Wink also suggests that feminist readings of diaries might more usefully account for the stylistic choices women have used, rather than for determining their status as public or private utterances: "Women's diaries offer us a particularly powerful example of the manner in which women chose to structure their interpretations of their experiences" (*She*, xvii).

For feminists, diaries are sites for perceiving disruption and contestation, and also for observing the process of reconciliation in the formulation of individual identity. That is, the form is seen as able to reveal processes of the self as a social construction. Nussbaum argues: "In diary and journal, linguistic constructs of the self (or more accurately, the significations of the subject) are produced through social, historical, and cultural factors; and the self both positions itself in the discourses available to it, and it is produced by them . . . the discourse of diary is particularly open to a series of coterminous and contradictory subject positions" ("Toward," 129). Feminist interpretations of diary have been crucial in interrogating both the gendered assumptions that adhere to forms of personal writing like diary, and the expectations of subjectivity and selfhood these genres are often tied to. Diaries often reflect the dailiness, and so the ordinariness, of an individual experience, and this feature of diary narrative has made it an attractive genre for those interested in "other" kinds of representation—domestic, familial, and mundane. Moreover, diary is seen as a generic practice that undermines the assumptions of the autobiographical subject as a unified and coherent "I." That is, diaries are assumed to have a privileged relation to naturalistic representation, are often considered to be primarily private writing, and as narratives free from perceptions (and so distortions) of audience and public scrutiny. The assumed privacy of the genre is also linked to expectations of secret or subversive content: "The diary signifies a consciousness that requires psychic privacy in a particular way. Though the diary is not always strictly secret, it usually *affects* secrecy" (Nussbaum, "Toward," 135). The discursive location of diary texts as scandalous, forbidden, or dangerous, however, also carries the implication of narrative that is marginal or irrelevant to public discourse—inappropriate, disruptive, or not fit for public disclosure. In both cases, the appeal of the diary is linked to transgression. An association with secrecy, domesticity, and privacy has other consequences for the diary, particularly as a representation of self. Conceptualized as an artifact, diaries are assumed to be as idiosyncratic as the diarist, subject to transformation, mutation, and evolution in the process of the diarist's life. The form is privileged as a mode for individual self-expression, and this is connected to perceptions of diary writing as liberating and to assumptions of self-knowledge as enlightening and transforming, a construction that has special implications for the self-help diaries I examine in the next chapter.

The attention to a disruption of "norms" of autobiographical discourse that has characterized feminist critical engagement with diary writing is linked to the emergence of alternative voices and experiences in self-representation more broadly. Here, an ideological split between private and public forms of writing and experience that is otherwise understood as "natural" is contested. Positioning diary as a marginal form identifies a fertile location for intellectual and cultural interrogation:

> The diary thus emerges as a crystallization of overlapping practices which situate
> it not on the margins of various domains of social practice, but, in so far as it
> stands at the intersection of those cultural cross-roads, place it in the midst of

cultural practices, and make it a significant indicator of the contemporary cultural climate. Margins, after all, are places where distinct domains meet, where crossings from here to there, from sameness to otherness, are constantly being negotiated, and where mutually interdependent definitions of selfhood and alterity are necessarily reformulated again and again. (Langford and West, "Introduction," 7)

However, the dominant sense of diary writing as a marginal and resistant mode obscures another important aspect of the genre: the diary as a form of surveillance and constraint. The genre is often seen as subversive, yet it has also been used as a discipline to promote self-conformity—as much as it may also allow for self-exploration. Considering diary in this way draws attention to ideological boundaries between public and private discourse and to the differing values accorded to public and private experience at particular times. In the case studies selected for this book, for example, the role of confession in contemporary culture is critical—a discursive association of diary narrative with confession is clearly referenced in the reception and marketing of diary publications, to say nothing of shows like *Big Brother*. Contemporary uses of diary like those explored in this book are urgent sites of contest and reconciliation; they negotiate and make visible discourses of confession, audience, and privacy in the representation of personal experience and they force attention to how and why certain assumptions about privacy and interiority have so persistently emerged in characterizations of the diary as a life narrative form.

2

How to Be the Authentic You

Therapy, Self-Help, and the "How-to" Diary

> January: an exceptionally bad start.
>
> Bridget Jones, *Bridget Jones's Diary*

*I*n the early 1930s American expatriate diarist Anaïs Nin began analysis with the ex-Freudian psychotherapist Otto Rank. This transformative time in Nin's life, which eventually set her on the path to undertake her own training in psychotherapy, also saw Nin begin to think critically about her lifelong diary as an artistic and therapeutic practice. Under Rank's influence, Nin had lamented the diary as a practice that diverted her from proper artistic pursuit: "My poor diary, I am so angry with you! I hate you! The pleasure of confiding has made me artistically lazy. Such an easy joy, to write here—so easy. And today I saw how the diary does choke up my stories, how I tell you about things so nonchalantly, carelessly, and inartistically. Everybody has hated you" (*Incest*, 276). For Rank, the diary was an indulgence; it was a form that precluded artistic intent or purpose and that had kept Nin from her true calling, and from her art's true purpose as a public creation. However, Nin, though she lamented the diary's "diversion" of her artistic life, also believed it had kept her "alive as a human being" and eventually persuaded Rank that the diary was something that she could keep without descending into neurosis, indeed, that it ultimately functioned as a therapeutic mode, and a literary genre (277). In her essays on diary in *The Novel of the Future* (1968), Nin articulates her case directly, connecting diary and other subjective modes to articulation that moves beyond the "slicker, glossier, the more enameled surface": "the surface does not contain a key to authentic experience, the truth lies in what we *feel* and not in what we *see*" (*Novel*, 172).

A sense of the diary as a mode for self-work, and a shift to valuing its apparent "artlessness" as part of a creative therapeutic apparatus, one able to access the "subterranean" (Nin, *Novel*, 172) elements of human consciousness, was a feature of a new wave of diary writers in the late 1970s and early 1980s who advocated and published manuals for a proper creative and therapeutic use of the diary form. Nin is an important progenitor here; her preface for Tristine Rainer's 1978 publication, *The New Diary: How to Use a Journal for Self-Guidance and Expanded Creativity*, reflects on teaching a course with Rainer on diary writing, and she is an important influence for Christina Baldwin, whose spiritually focused journaling manual, *One to One: Self-Understanding Through Journal Writing*, was published in 1977. The psychologist Ira Progoff presents Nin in his *At a Journal Workshop* (1975) manuals as the key example of someone who used the journal for personal transformation rather than narcissistic contemplation, describing her *Diaries* as a "notable contemporary exception . . . where a person of great literary creativity used a journal also as a vehicle for her total life development" (25). The diary here features as a genre of personal narrative that can be "misused"; despite (or because of) its "artlessness" or "easy joy" for the writer, it is best incorporated into a program and conceived of as an instrument for therapy (Progoff, *At a Journal*).[1] This perception of the diary as a tool and a discipline draws from a historical role of the genre in religious communities, and it intersects with a contemporary shift to therapy in autobiographical discourse in contemporary culture.

As a trend that has continued in the first decades of the twenty-first century, telling personal stories has increasingly been considered in terms of therapy and healing. Indeed, as Leigh Gilmore observes in *The Limits of Autobiography*, the centrality of traumatic self-narration in contemporary autobiography is a thematic turn that has come to define the genre (2). More recently, Gilmore has drawn attention to the "neoconfessional" as a dominant contemporary mode of autobiographical representation (particularly for memoir) in which the representation of suffering is compulsively rendered into an optimistic, redemptive storyline ("American Neoconfessional," 658). The autobiography of trauma, loss, or suffering is intimately connected to a discourse of healing and overcoming, and in which the memoir as product becomes a manifestation as well as vehicle for this success—these narratives are generated by subjects for whom survival has become linked to the capacity for some kind of articulation about their experience (Gilmore, *Limits*, 7). The complicated playing out of trauma narratives in the public sphere has led to a recognition of the significance of ethics and rights in autobiographical discourse, as well as a more explicit understanding of autobiography's "weirder" positioning: "For many writers," argues

DeSalvo's *Writing as a Way of Healing: How Telling Our Stories Transforms Our Lives* (2000) does exactly this, connecting the therapeutic imperative to a self-improvement impulse and positioning autobiographical storytelling as a concrete methodology for bringing about "shifts in perspective" connected to general experiences of loss: "Now I felt connected to my feelings and to my life story. I was aware that I had honored my feelings of loss, but that I had transformed them into language so that I held these feelings differently" (8). In *The Power of Memoir: Writing to Heal* (2010), Linda Myers similarly encourages the writer to overcome "their shyness about putting everything in black and white. . . . It's enlightening to encounter the many layers of yourself and your memories" (3). Even manuals more directly concerned with mastering elements of writing craft (and with an emphasis on the prospect of publication that Lejeune says early manuals mostly foreclose on), such as Bill Roorbach's *Writing Life Stories* (1998), link skills in self-observation to personal growth: "Honestly examining whatever resistance you find in yourself and overcoming it (by just doing the exercises is the best way) is going to be a key step in your improvement as a writer" (6). The back cover description of *Writing Life Stories* further emphasizes the point: "Much more than a handbook for the rudiments of autobiography, this book will teach you to see your life more clearly."[2] Meshed deeply to hopes and aspirations of the power of autobiography, these manuals also speak to a contemporary obsession with authenticity: indeed, as Charles Guignon observes, "the ideal of authenticity is a project of becoming who you are" that instates a project of "self-transformation" in order to recover a lost "you" and reinstate it "to its proper place at the centre of your life" (*On Being*, 3). In this, autobiography is both a methodology and an aspiration: a way to "*be* that which you *already are*, the unique definitive traits already there within you" (4). This is an ideal that is also an industry: from the therapeutic genre of the television talk-show to the rise of makeover culture and in the emergence of self-styled "self-help gurus," the "basic assumption built into the ideal of authenticity is that, lying within each individual, there is a deep 'true self'—the 'Real Me'—in distinction from all that is not really me" (6). Moreover, excavating the "real me" is an arduous and stringent task: "It calls for constant self-surveillance aimed at finding out exactly what one wants and how one feels about things. There is a demand for total transparency of self to self " (9). In the texts I explore for this chapter, rigorous self-knowing is a central premise, and it is one that is extended through claims that are also attached to genre: Guignon "ironically" observes that "a number of large-scale programs have emerged to show people how to be themselves" (9). In this chapter, I explore how the diary is also a distinctive "program," and I consider what this indicates for how diary is conceptualized in this location and what it means for how it is used more broadly. That is, how-to diaries tap into a popular sense of diary as a unique genre more capable than other modes (for example the memoir) of representing an authentic self—while the memoir is commonly (if also contentiously) understood as a literary work that uses literary device to construct and control a representation of self, the diary is stereotypically conceptualized as a more natural mode, one that is literary less by design than accident, if it is literary at all.[3] A value for the authentic as the natural, the unmediated, and the unconstructed—as close as possible to the "real"—is also apparent here and this fits very powerfully with enduring perceptions of the diary as a less self-conscious, more "authentic" form of personal expression.

Puritans and Talk Shows

The contemporary diary as it is conceptualized by how-to authors not only indicates that concerns for authentic self-knowledge are prominent in contemporary culture but also offers a particular language for thinking about the self at the beginning of the twenty-first century. In contemporary cultures of the West, speaking for oneself, taking time for one's own story, is positioned as an elusive commodity; the modern individual is haunted by a sense of inauthenticity, of disconnection from the "self," and around this apparent void in self-meaning, an authenticity industry has emerged. Guignon notes that, through Oprah, over the Internet, in bookshops, and on television "the idea of achieving an authentic existence arises on a daily basis" (*On Being*, 1). In *The Authenticity Hoax: Why The "Real" Things We Seek Don't Make us Happy* (2010), Andrew Potter observes that "the demand for the honest, the natural, the real—that is, the authentic—has become one of the most powerful movements in contemporary life," a movement that is nonetheless haunted by the specter of its own impossibility (4). Increasingly suspicious of the mass, the multiple, and the generic, individuals seek out "authentic" ways of living and being: "A revolution is stirring, and it's crystallizing around a single word: *authenticity*" (Potter, *Authenticity*, 7).

In this context, it is perhaps unsurprising that an emphasis on quotidian progress toward self-realization might hold particular sway. That is, becoming authentic in a contemporary context takes on the form of sustained engagement by and with the individual in everyday life. In contemporary discourses of authenticity, "we learn that everyday life is spiritual, that there is spirituality in little things, that life is a spiritual quest and so on and on" (Guignon, *On Being*, xii). We learn that the self is a work of art and a product of invention and creation, but one achieved only through intensive labor and self-discipline. These ideas of the authentic self as available through a process of excavation and redemption, as a mundane but central project of the modern individual, underpin the position of diary as a unique disciplinary technology for self-analysis and authentic self-discovery. Moreover, it creates a context in which autobiography, authenticity, and self coalesce into a kind of contemporary spirituality and where diary is the iconic and definitive mode for this exploration of self. This is not only a modern phenomenon. The contemporary self-help diary emerges from a religious tradition in which self-surveillance figures as a crucial daily discipline, and this influences both how self-help authors promote the diary and how readers approach it as a methodology. Indeed, "taking care of the self" in and through writing, as Michel Foucault has noted, is an established Western tradition, already "deeply rooted when Augustine started his Confessions" (*Technologies*, 27). Yet the diary has a special relationship to this mode of writing (particularly as a method), and it is also a powerful *symbol*. As Roger Smith has observed in his analysis of seventeenth-century English diaries, the activity of diary writing has a metonymic significance:

> Boyle, who played a pivotal role in the legitimation of the new natural philosophy in England, referred to three "books," which carry authority—nature, scripture, and the conscience. The conscience, he believed, lies in each person and can be known by the use of right reasoning about moral things. From this perspective, the self is a book of truth comparable to the books of nature and of God's word. A sense of self reached its height in the diary, the book written by oneself for oneself as a means of self-reflection and self-control. ("Self-Reflection," 55)

The how-to diary intersects with and powerfully deploys the diary as object and symbol. That is, while many how-to diaries are conventional paperbacks dense with prose, a large subset of the genre take on the form of a gift book— they incorporate heavy bonded paper, or oversized "workbook" style pages with space for the reader to respond in text to exercises or questions; they can be hard covered, with ribbon bookmarks or other markers of luxury such as gilt-edged pages. Reviving the association of diary as keepsake and aesthetic object and offering the opportunity for a personal engagement allows an otherwise mass-market object to be "personalized" for the reader, by the reader. The how-to diary is a guided program that also promises to function as a personal record and embodiment of the unique self.

Constructions of the diary as a technology of the self represent a particular discursive ideal of the individual: the struggle of the self is assumed to be resolved—or at least, rendered visible—through writing. This is an essential appeal and founding rhetoric of the how-to journal genre, and it is amplified through a connection to self-help discourse that is also linked to a kind of secular spirituality. Indeed, as Micki McGee argues in her class-based analysis, *Self-Help, Inc.: Makeover Culture in American Life* (2005), "traditional religious and moral values are interwoven in the literature of self-improvement" (20). This has distinct effects: for McGee, it produces a kind of "moral values lite" (20), fostering the specific sense of an individual who now finds a "therapeutic imperative" attached to finding "self-fulfillment" (25). For Guignon, it also reveals the autobiographical conversion or "calling" experience as a dominant trope of self-help: he notices that self-help authors in particular have tended to draw on early Christian doctrine myth in framing or legitimating their work.[4]

As a journal workbook that draws explicitly on the programmatic "steps" of self-help methodology, Julia Cameron's bestselling *The Artist's Way* (1992) is one example of the how-to form that also clearly uses the classic religious narrative of epiphany and redemption. Cameron, though claiming to have carefully dissociated her use of "God" from its historical meaning (xi), narrates her life story with a plot that closely adheres to a conventional religious conversion narrative. In the introduction to her program, Cameron describes an epiphany—this moment of enlightenment is the catalyst for radical change: "One minute I was walking in the West Village on a cobblestone street with beautiful afternoon light. The next minute I suddenly knew that I should begin teaching people, groups of people, to unblock" (xiii). Cameron gets sober. She turns her "creativity over to the only god I could believe in, the god of creativity" and she learns "to get out of the way and let that creative force work through me" (xiv). Conquering the distractions of the material world (alcohol), surrendering to the forces of the divine (creativity), Cameron "unblocks" and finds a state of authenticity that she wants to share with others: "*The Artist's Way* is a spiritual journey, a pilgrimage home to the self" (203) and it is "a blueprint for do-it-yourself recovery" (xvi). As a practice of journaling, the program uses a ritual called "morning pages": "What are morning pages? Put simply, the morning pages are three pages of longhand writing, strictly stream-of-consciousness: 'Oh, god, another morning. I have NOTHING to say. I need to wash the curtains. Did I get my laundry yesterday? Blah, blah, blah . . .'" (10). Morning pages are designed to uncover the self through writing: "By spilling out of bed and straight onto the page every morning you learn to evade the censor because there is no wrong way to write the morning pages, the Censor's opinion doesn't count" (11).

In many ways, "morning pages" or other strategies such as "artist's dates" (a regularly scheduled block of "creative" time) are disciplinary practices that resemble the seventeenth-century journal of conscience. Practiced by "Puritans, and later by Quakers and other dissenting groups," the diary reflected a new sense of individuality and an orientation toward the personal (rather than the divine) as the basis for self-knowledge and moral behavior (Fothergill, *Private*, 17). Cautious of the seductions of self-scrutiny as self-indulgence, Puritan diarists composed their texts under strict moral terms: "What other business has man with his inner secret self, if not the business of improving it?" (17). This is a sentiment that Progoff, for example, recycles in his journal program.[5]

Contemporary methods of daily or routine writing practice such as Cameron's *The Artist's Way* also establish self-reflection as a serious discipline, one that demands to be guarded and defended: "in its most primary form, the artist date is an excursion, a play date that you preplan and defend against all interlopers" (18). However, as Catherine A. Brekus has argued, the contemporary spiritual journal offers a regime of self-reflection that also exists within a specific ideological framework: "Early American Protestants kept diaries in order to 'crucify' themselves and worship a transcendent God . . . today, Americans write spiritual journals for a very different set of reasons: to create an authentic sense of selfhood, to come to a deeper appreciation of their own worth, and to find God within them" ("Place," 2). While revitalizing the "intense self-loathing" and "self-denying piety" of Puritan diaries is not a turn she wants to make, Brekus finds contemporary journaling a decidedly bleak field: "In a consumer culture that treats the self as yet another object to be manipulated," journaling could "be understood as a protest against the dehumanizing forces of the modern world, especially the objectification and commodification of the self" (15). Yet contemporary journaling guides tend to "cultivate a kind of selfhood that is perfectly matched to the requirements of a capitalist economy. By insisting that self-love is an unqualified good, they contribute to a consumer ethic of self-gratification. The result is a vicious circle: these guides implicitly protest against the commodification of the self, but by urging people not to be guilty about self-indulgence, they unwittingly help fuel the engine of consumerism. 'I'm really glad you are taking time for yourself,' writes one woman on www.Oprah.com to another. 'You deserve to'" (16). Brekus finds this effect distinctive in how-to journals. Guignon identifies it as a central irony of self-help in general: "programs that are designed to help people get in touch with their true selves, supposedly motivated by emancipatory ideals, often have the effect of pressuring people into thinking in ways that confirm the ideology of the founders of the program" (9).

In a religious tradition, setting up a disciplinary framework for negotiating with the "self" produces the context for a strict examination of conscience (though it may also produce a kind of diary that is a narrow and exclusionary form).[6] Cameron's program of daily writing is also linked to the development of a particular ideal of self: "you are likely to find yourself avoiding your artist dates. Recognize this resistance as a fear of intimacy—*self*—intimacy. Often in troubled relationships, we settle into an avoidance pattern with our significant others" (*Artist's*, 20). Cameron's program, then, instates the self as a troubled other and posits writing as the means through which to both access (reveal) and incorporate (heal) this element of self. In doing so, *The Artist's Way* responds to a contemporary moment in which individuals seem to feel detached from an authentic sense of "self," yet this is not simply a matter of the individual. The rhetoric of self-help provides a set of dominant ideologies that have become influential in contemporary culture, and one of the most significant ways in which this has emerged is in an obsession with the self as a site of "improvement." Importantly, work on the self is a public preoccupation with a private focus: "the intimate sphere," argues McGee, "becomes a site of ongoing and tireless production, a design studio for reinventing one's most marketable self" (*Self-Help*, 22). The how-to journal is a mass-market response and a structured methodology in achieving this.

The Writing Cure for Weightlessness

"For nearly thirty years," reports Kathleen Adams in *Journal to the Self: 22 Paths for Personal Growth* (1990), "I have had the same therapist. This therapist is available to me 24 hours a day and hasn't gone on vacation in almost three decades. . . . I can tell this therapist absolutely anything. My therapist listens silently to my most sinister darkness, my most bizarre fantasy, my most cherished dream[, and] . . . best of all, this therapist keeps a detailed record of all our work together, so that I have on my bookshelf a chronology of my life. . . . [M]y therapist is my journal" (6). The spiritual underpinnings of the contemporary how-to journal are present in various ways. However, though the self-help diary is taken up as a spiritual genre, it is also more prominently a therapeutic one. Adams, for example, emphasizes a popular sense of diary narrative as nonliterary, amateur, and natural—a practice available to ordinary individuals for everyday transformation. But she also instates the practice of diary writing as a therapeutic engagement, and she positions the form as a unique method for this. Again, a sense of diary writing as a discipline of self-reflection that leads to self-control is key in this: "It's been proven," states the author of the *Body-Minder Workout and Exercise Journal: A Fitness Diary* (2003), "writing things down can help you be more focused and committed to your goals. . . . As you fill in

the pages of your BodyMinder, a personal memoir of an important achievement will be created—your true journey to physical fitness!" (Wilkins, *Body-
minder*, 1). Daily writing, as a way of recording, seeing, and mapping the "true"
progress of individual growth, is a powerful promise, one tied to a discursive history of the diary as a tool for self-surveillance. It is one Adams actively mobilizes,
for example, by constructing a distinct and teleological progress for the diarist:
"Your journal will serve as a scribe throughout the journey of your life, obligingly
recording your own uniquely forged path toward individuation, keeping an
accurate log of the uphill trudge, the view from the summit, the ambling strolls
through wildflower-strewn meadows, the terrifying descents into the abyss"
(*Journal*, 14).

Here, the journal, anthropomorphized into the figure of "scribe," records
an aspect of the self that is somehow outside of the self—a you "obligingly"
recording you. This idea of self and surveillance has special links to the development of diary as a genre. Stuart Sherman, tracing the development of a broad
range of technologies for the reckoning of the self in time that coincides with
changing ideas about temporality and time keeping in seventeenth- and
eighteenth-century England, finds the real success of canonical English diarist
Samuel Pepys as keeping to a "rigorously continuous, steadily serial narrative"
and so producing an account that could "foster the textual illusion of temporal
continuity" (*Telling*, 33–34). Pepys, according to Sherman, was the first to do so
in English, and his diary reflects the new capacity of clocks to track and report
newly small durations—minutes, seconds—in regular, perceptible succession.
Diary keeping as a technology for mapping the self, and especially for revealing
the otherwise invisible or unconscious aspects of one's character, is a powerful
concept in how-to diary discourse. The diary is desired (and privileged) for its
transparent representation of self. This effect, "as though diary and diarist were
one and the same" is an enduring hope of the genre (32). Lawrence Rosenwald
identifies it as one of a series of pervasive myths: "The first of these is a belief
about the self: that there exists in each of us a self independent of our consciousness of it. The second is a belief about perception: that the inward self is transparent to introspection. Setting out from these two positions, diarists may well
feel that if they can only resist the contemptible temptation to dissemble, then the
truth will come of itself, the fixed and immanent self will gradually be revealed
to candid introspection" (*Emerson*, 14). Though beliefs about diary that are
"mythic"—Rosenwald also argues they are simply "erroneous"—the "intoxi-
cating promise" of a more authentic or "truer" representation of self is exactly
what how-to authors claim. Indeed, the promise of these guides is that the
subject, inevitably figured as ignorant about the true nature of their life and

selfhood, can mobilize the formal capacity of diary for surveillance and retrieve an essence of self that has been lacking.

How-to guides to writing autobiographically connect to broader cultural aspirations for authentic living, and they both develop and respond to a sense of the modern individual as not only troubled but *traumatized* by a lack of authenticity. That is, the how-to diary is aligned very closely to certain clinical contexts, and where the diary format is interpreted as a therapeutic regimen. This is the basis for Progoff's influential *At a Journal Workshop* series as well as more recent work like James Pennebaker's *Writing to Heal: A Guided Journal for Recovering from Trauma and Emotional Upheaval* (2004). How-to diaries also draw on a specific tradition of diary keeping, for example, a gendered tradition of diaries by women and a status as private writing (even when in a communal or community context).[7] Indeed, as a regimen, and particularly when given therapeutic auspices, how-to diary authors conventionally insist on the diary as a private mode, and this is a defining characteristic also emphasized by influential progenitors such as Baldwin, Rainer, and Progoff. The emphasis here is not only on diary as private and intimate writing for the self and by the self but as a *form* that allows for unique and unmediated access to self. Rainer exemplifies this position when she states: "The diary is the only form of writing that encourages total freedom of expression. Because of its very private nature, it has remained immune to any formal rules of content, structure, or style. As a result the diary can come closest to reproducing how people really think and how consciousness evolves" (*New*, x). Instating the literate self and the writing subject as the authentic mode, how-to diaries move beyond the exemplary life of the memoir manual to provide a direct template for organizing and understanding autobiographical experience. Contemporary authors take up the ethos formulated in early works on the how-to diary, figuring journaling as an implicitly healing mode and arguing for privacy (unself-consciousness) as a key methodology in accessing an "authentic" inner self. In doing so, they support and promote a popular construction of diary as a unique genre more capable than other modes (for example memoir) of representing an authentic (because less literary, because more private) self.

The how-to diary taps into and reveals certain ideologies of selfhood that are prominent now. As Gilmore has argued, the contemporary memoir market is geared toward the production of "an increasingly generic and non-specific self," a shift away from the possibilities of systemic critique and social justice that defined the early emergence of the mode, as well as the possibilities engendered in the challenge to "dominant reading practices around truth-telling" ("American," 658). Thus, "the American neoconfessional primarily bears witness to personal pain," though "suffering, in this model, is ubiquitous, and insufficient to catalyze interest; what appeals is struggle and overcoming" (660). The appeal of "overcoming," as well as a ubiquity and flattening of "suffering," is an important context for the consideration of the how-to journal in this chapter. Indeed, for the broad range of how-to guides currently available, this is not simply a project of recording or documentation but resurrection: the how-to journal promises to rescue a self that has been lost and in doing so, to heal the wounded subject of contemporary life. This promise is unmistakable, for example, in Michelle Weldon's *Writing to Save Your Life: How to Honor Your Story through Journaling* (2001).

Just as her title promises, Weldon's journal program explicitly values articulations of experience as self-affirming and, literally, "life preserving." Drawing on popular psychology, she promotes life writing, and specifically the diary, as a comprehensive counseling tool in traumatic recovery and for building individual resilience. However, while many journal programs identify and address a specific clinical issue (such as Phil Rich and Stuart Copans's *Healing Journey* series, which publishes dedicated journal programs for conditions such as "addiction," "divorce," "grief," or, intriguingly, "retirement"), Weldon conceptualizes a broadly defined sense of the traumatized subject. That is, in *Writing to Save Your Life*, Weldon prioritizes journaling as self-witnessing—rather than as a specific guided recovery or therapeutic practice. Writing is a way of recognizing and treasuring experience in general, of valuing every day: "write to save your life," she encourages, "because your life is worth saving" (32). Notably, she distinguishes between talking and writing: "If you choose to respond orally, you are choosing not to give your words physical space. When you do commit your words to paper, they have a different, more concrete, less ephemeral power. They simply last longer" (4). For Weldon, forming experience into words on paper is a talismanic project, and *Writing to Save Your Life* figures daily writing as the crucial instrument in the achievement of a meaningful life and an authentic self.

Crucially, in the how-to journal, "becoming the person you are" is a project of writing about the self; telling life stories is a central trope of self-help literature. Eva Illouz, for example, argues that Oprah Winfrey, who "has reached a mass market through her ability to mobilize individuals and biographies" (301) on her talk show, uses pop psychology techniques to "rewrite autobiographical narratives through the discourse and techniques of therapy" (305). In this process, visible particularly on her talk shows, her own life narrative is foregrounded as exemplary and Winfrey, perhaps the single most influential proponent of contemporary self-improvement culture, is a dedicated journal-keeper: "I keep a gratitude journal, as Sarah Ban Breathnach suggests in *Simple Abundance*, listing at least five things that I'm grateful for" ("What," 298).[8] Sarah Ban Breathnach's best-selling *Simple Abundance: A Daybook for Comfort and Joy* (2001) embodies the authenticity ideal Winfrey advocates: *Simple Abundance* prioritizes dailiness and the mundane. Based on a calendar year, and with no page numbers, *Simple Abundance* is "organised as a walk through the year, beginning on New Year's Day" (x). Like Winfrey, Ban Breathnach uses her own story as the example and authority for her program. However, unlike Winfrey's well-publicized experiences of abuse and poverty, Ban Breathnach's discontent is generalized, linked to a vague sense of inauthentic living: "I was an angry, envious woman because of what seemed to be missing from my life, although I couldn't have told you what it was" (x). She has a contented relationship, a successful career, and a guilty "secret" longing: "how to reconcile my deepest spiritual, authentic, and creative longings with often-overwhelming and conflicting commitments—to my husband and daughter, invalid mother, work at home, work in the world, siblings, friends, and community" (ix).

Like Weldon, Ban Breathnach instates a noticeably vague sense of indefinable pain permeating the modern individual: Ban Breathnach is plagued by the sense that her life, though exceedingly good, is inauthentic. Suffering in her daily life from a sense of its "weightlessness,"[9] she addresses this condition as one that can be healed through daily writing. *Simple Abundance*, says Ban Breathnach, started out as a way of "creating a manageable lifestyle" but evolved into a mode for "living in a state of grace" (x). A calendar structure in *Simple Abundance* is an essential part of its therapeutic regime: written as a yearlong daybook, it promotes self-monitoring and instates the diurnal and chronological calendar as an organizing force. Here too is an ethos of the ordinary: salvation is available in simple steps. "If you consciously work to bring more gratitude, simplicity, order, harmony, beauty, and joy into your daily life," says Ban Breathnach, "your world will be transformed" (47). Figured as "simple," transformation Ban Breathnach–style requires a commitment to 365 days of self-improvement.

An emphasis on daily observation and on the diary as a distinct technology for self-knowledge characterizes the how-to journal. But while this process is framed as creative and self-directed (or "simple"), it instead involves a rigorous program of self-subordination. That is, a particular discursive self is already predicated in self-help journals and indeed, in self-help in general. As McGee notes: "the literature of self-help defines its readers as insufficient, as lacking some essential feature of adequacy" and "then offers itself as the solution" (*Self-Help*, 18).[10] The diary is figured in this as both a key methodology and a powerful symbol (and embodiment) of the time spent "becoming authentic." Moreover, the audience for the how-to diary is figured not only as essentially traumatized but also as overwhelming female. Ban Breathnach's "companion" text for male readers, *A Man's Journey to Simple Abundance*, offers a parallel and gendered version of the original text. For Will Tregonning, *A Man's Journey* is lacking in comparison; he prefers the original, ostensibly "female" version. However, following *Simple Abundance* requires more than submission to a gendered pronoun: "I had to compromise my position as a critical reader in order to accommodate its repeated interpellation of me . . . as a reader who came to this text with a sense of melancholia, with an insufficiency of meaning, seeking 'something more'" (Tregonning, "Authentic," 178). This criticism echoes Lejeune, whose response to what he observes in the early 1980s as an "American speciality" in practical autobiography guides expresses a similar discomfort:

> What I call *stabilization*, for lack of a better word, is the strategy of the personal journal found in the American guides. . . . Apparently it is a matter of helping people to "deconstruct" themselves, to free themselves through all sorts of exercises (fictitious dialogues, and so on). But this movement is contradicted by the perpetual fetishization of writing (appropriate to the genre of the journal) and the fixation of the self that it encourages, and especially the imposition of a moral balance and wisdom that perhaps has as its function to subjugate the individual by making him believe that he has become his own master. Such is the impression, a rather nauseating one. (Lejeune, *On Autobiography*, 225)

This effect of the how-to journal, the paradoxical offer to free the individual through strict adherence to an externally devised and guided program, makes visible inherent tensions in self-help and daily autobiographical writing. How-to journal texts diagnose the reader as suffering a lack of creative expression, a general malaise of inauthenticity, and they offer daily writing as the cure.

Bridget Jones and the Ideal Self

The prominence of diary as a commodity in contemporary culture and as a practice linked to a particular discursive construction of the self in therapy culture finds expression in various ways. From the mid-1990s, this shift was foregrounded in the proliferation of reality television and confessional talk shows, in the emergence of autobiography on the Internet, and in a boom in mass-market memoir publishing. In contemporary media and culture, a rhetoric of self-analysis as the proper task for the authentic individual has become a mainstream concept. In the novel *Bridget Jones's Diary* we see a fictional playing out of the tensions around diary and self-help, anxiously centered in therapeutic culture that I have been discussing so far. Here, the idea of using diary to take control of your life and to access an authentic self—a central promise of the how-to phenomenon—is what the novel both promotes and parodies.

At the beginning of the twenty-first century, the most famous diarist in Britain, when she wasn't masquerading as the international ambassador of "chick-lit," was the fictional character and eponymous "thirty-something" heroine of Helen Fielding's 1996 novel *Bridget Jones's Diary*.[11] Blamed for a dumbing-down of literary sensibilities, the promotion of an anodyne brand of "lipstick feminism," and the depoliticization of an entire generation of women,[12] Fielding announced in early 2013 that she was reprising the character for a new book (Flood, "Bridget"). Reaction to the news, as one commentator wryly noted, was "v. v. mixed" (Stevens, "Should"). Updating Bridget for the Internet age, Fielding has said in an interview that her character will focus more on Twitter followers than alcohol and cigarettes, but not much else will have changed: "She's still trying to give up [drinking and smoking], she's still on a diet. She's trying a bit harder, and is a bit more successful, but she's never really going to change" (Flood, "Bridget").

Bridget's failure to change, despite rigorous self-monitoring and documentation by way of her diary, is the narrative drive of Fielding's novels. A devotee of self-help literature, Bridget's New Year's resolutions, her lists and accountings of "units consumed," "fags smoked," or resolves broken appear as the manifestation of a broader cultural injunction to a certain kind of self; for the most part, feminist critics bemoaned Bridget's ostentatious pursuit of the perfect figure, partner, and lifestyle as symptomatic of a new generation of shallow, self-absorbed women and were disturbed by the level of kinship women felt for the character.[13] These concerns are intensified through form. As a daily diary, the sense of Bridget's life as shaped by obsessive and shallow concerns—she records with ritual regularity her fluctuating weight, "units" of alcohol consumed, cigarettes smoked, or lottery "instants" purchased—is exacerbated. *Bridget Jones's Diary* generates comic effect through its heroine's efforts at achieving a particular brand of unattainable self-perfection: "Being a woman is worse than being a farmer—there is so much harvesting and crop spraying to be done: legs to be waxed, underarms shaved, eyebrows plucked, feet pumiced, skin exfoliated and moisturized, spots cleansed, roots dyed, eyelashes tinted, nails filed, cellulite massaged, stomach muscles exercised. The whole performance is so highly tuned you need only neglect it for a few days and the whole thing goes to seed" (Fielding, *Bridget Jones's Diary*, 30). Bridget's exhaustive attempts to control her body's outward appearance are accompanied by equally extensive efforts at creating an ideal interior. Concerned not just with the perfect body, Bridget

reflects back another kind of cultural obsession, and a feature of self-help literature: the perfected character. She monitors calories, "3879 (repulsive)," but she
also counts "negative thoughts" per minute (approximately "942") as well as
"minutes spent counting negative thoughts 127 [minutes]" (30). Surveying and
detailing the transgressions of body and mind, as they meet or fail the ideals of
Cosmopolitan culture, Bridget draws on a panoply of self-help literature. From
fitness books to *The Road Less Traveled*, she implements a regime of improvement
and a diet of good intentions that is circumscribed by and created in popular
media. "Bridget's diary," says Kelly A. Marsh, "reveals the external pressure she
feels to be better than she is, pressure that exists without reference to her own
qualities and qualifications—improvement for its own sake" ("Contextualizing,"
57). The diary, rather than an empowering mode for addressing, determining,
and constructing a self, becomes emblematic of a narcissistic culture that has
trumped feminism by rerouting attention inward and down, toward the navel.
Here are revealed the pervasiveness of myths of both kinds—feminist and
self-help—in productions of the female self in contemporary culture.

Yet what does her use of diary tell us? Critics have paid more than the usual
attention to the genre of Fielding's novel. Indeed, if, as Imelda Whelehan has
put it, "Bridget Jones is a term which has entered our lexicon and itself conjures
up the image of a single woman of a certain age who obsesses about her body
and its shortcomings, whilst loudly bewailing the inadequacies of men with her
close friends" ("Sex," 30), then the fact that she has done so as a diarist seems
an equally important consideration. For readers and critics alike, Fielding's
"first person confessional idiom" and the organizational structure of the novel
as a diary is key to its appeal (Maddison and Storr, "Edge," 4). Nonetheless,
what some readers have found profoundly relational, a "that's me!" response
noted by Whelehan among others, has also been seen as problematic. Maddison
and Storr, for example, see this kind of response as a "slippage from self-
conscious suspension of disbelief to interpellated over-identification" (5). In
their article "The Edge of Reason: The Myth of Bridget Jones," they dismantle
the hyperbole around Fielding's creation and assert the fictionality of Bridget—
an insistence they claim as necessary in the face of the extraordinary claims
made for the character.[14]

Alison Case, in an early critical consideration of Fielding's text, also correlates the enormous popularity of *Bridget Jones's Diary* to the "authentic voice" of
the main character: "By far the most common response I got at the Narrative
conference to a short excerpt from the novel was from women who expressed
delight and a kind of rueful identification with Bridget's voice" ("Authenticity,"
176). By implication, outside of the "chick-lit" demographic, Case's academic

audience had "confessed that Bridget's voice 'hit home' for them" (176). For Case, however, the authenticity of Bridget's voice is not simply about its "verisimilitude to contemporary women's lives" but instead, "has as much to do with gendered literary convention" (176). It is as a diarist that Bridget, with her "telegraphic style," abbreviations, misspellings, and "rambling entries to suggest entries written while drunk" (177), draws the reader into a sense of naïve revelation with their narrator. It is as a diarist that Bridget Jones so effectively "speaks" to audiences, however "rueful" their identification.

Fielding has said that she deliberately chose the form of a diary because it allowed her to use the intimacy and directness of a conversation with a friend, and also as a voyeuristic device that readers enjoy. Indeed, responding directly to the question "why did you write *Bridget* as a diary?" Fielding replies:

> The best advice I ever had about writing was to do it as if you were writing for a friend. The diary form's very good for that, very direct and intimate. Because it's an imaginary character, you can hide behind a persona. It also allows you to write the sort of shameful thoughts that everyone has but no one wants to admit to, since you're not trying to make anyone like you. A diary is an outlet for your most private thoughts, a very personal way of writing. And that feeling of peeping behind a curtain at someone else's life is good for a reader. (Applewhite, "Penguin")

Fielding's use of the diary trades on the privileged relation between self and subject celebrated in therapy culture. Even the errors in the diary are crafted for achieving this effect; so too is its shamefulness. Nonetheless, critics like Case have viewed the choice with more suspicion. Bridget's diary and its obsessive concerns with things mundane and bodily, its fragmented narrative style and gentle but consistent self-delusions, appears less a vehicle for subversive revelation than an occasion of extended adolescent narcissism. However, beyond this, Case argues that Fielding's use of the diary also deprives Bridget of the control that, by keeping a diary, she ostensibly desires: "Diary almost by definition serves a purpose beyond the purely informational. It represents an effort to process experience, to order it, to make sense of it, and in that sense, to narrativize it" ("Authenticity," 177).

Bridget's failure to obtain control of her life, even as she writes about it, is the humorous ballast of the text. The comic trajectory of the plot is signaled from the opening pages—Bridget's New Year's Resolutions are a diaristic trope, and they are, as Leah Guenther notes, "annual goals notoriously idealistic and thus doomed from the start" ("Confessing," 85). In her reading of the novel, however, Case finds something more than the mere dignity of the narrator to be at stake: she interprets the diary form as a textual signifier for a lack of agency. She argues that Fielding's novel holds parallels to the seventeenth- and eighteenth-century novel. While "diary or epistolary narration" of this period may sometimes "underscore the authority of the narrator," Case says this is rare ("Authenticity," 177). Instead, the diary is more often called into play to represent a narrator who aspires to be transgressive—a "material plotter," but one who is continuously "thwarted by actual plot developments" (177). In Bridget's inability to control the trajectory of her life, Case proclaims a continuing tradition of ineffectual women diarists—she argues that it is precisely as a diarist that Bridget's quest for autonomy, agency, and authenticity is inevitably undermined.

Case's suspicion that the diary form operates, in literary terms at least, to undermine individual agency and authority in "plotting" a female life trajectory is useful to consider in relation to claims made for the self-help or how-to diary. After all, Case argues that Bridget's diary allows authenticity, but precisely at the cost of self-control and self-knowledge: "I am struck by the way the plot routinely attempts to punish Bridget for attempts to manage her own life while rewarding her for being out of control. . . . My suspicion is that women readers are willing to identify with her because of those trappings—her wit and (intermittent) self-knowledge—but that a large part of her appeal is the reassurance that our own failures of control are not only loveable, they may be the most loveable, feminine things about us" ("Authenticity," 178). In an argument that shares some perspectives with Case, Guenther notes that Bridget's main objective is "to perfect what she sees as her inherently flawed self" ("Confessing," 85). In this context, her diary is a form of self-help, albeit one that ultimately becomes a confession of failure. However, unlike Case, Guenther also sees Bridget's flawed diary-keeping as something more complex than only the record of a failure of self-discipline and control (the perpetuation of a lack of feminine narrative agency). For example, Bridget finds that her dedicated self-surveillance and efforts at self-improvement regimes may not necessarily produce the results she feels she has been promised. "Saturday 22 April," writes Bridget, is "an historic and joyous day. After eighteen years of trying to get down to 8st 7 I have finally achieved it. It is no trick of the scales, but confirmed by jeans. I am thin" (Fielding, *Bridget Jones's Diary*, 105). The expected benefits of this longed-for state, however, are not forthcoming. Donning a "tight little black dress to show off figure feeling v. full of myself," Bridget's friends remark that she looks tired and drawn—that she looked "better before" the weight loss: "Eighteen years—wasted. Eighteen years of calorie and fat-unit-based arithmetic. Eighteen years of buying long shirts and jumpers and leaving the room backwards in intimate situations to hide my bottom. . . . Eighteen years of struggle, sacrifice and endeavour—for what? Eighteen years and the result is 'tired and fat.' I feel like a scientist who discovers that his life's work has been a total mistake" (107). Within the comic frame of the novel Bridget's best resolutions (no matter how mundane) inevitably come undone; even her successes are hollow. Marsh notes, "the myth of self-perfection, the idea that the self can be completely remade, saturates Bridget's consciousness" ("Contextualizing," 59). Bridget's diary, ostensibly a technology through which she will achieve transformation, becomes instead a narration of subjection and conformity. Her daily labor, recording in minute detail consumption and activity, does not produce a new self, or a more authentic one, but only a "belaboured" one—rather than achieving self-sufficiency, the individual is forever at work, caught in a cycle of eternal vigilance and the need for constant reinvention. The diary, positioned by therapy culture as a technology for self-sufficiency and autonomy, is revealed as complicit to a conservative social rhetoric—inadequate, or simply misleading in its promise to produce a "unique" and authentic "you." Bridget's failure to use diary "correctly," and the labor diary demands of her, shows that autobiographical genres like diary are also tools for disciplining the individual to specific cultural ideals; the authentic self is a specific cultural and discursive position and the diary is a distinctive mode in connection to this.

Diary and the Regime of Self

The practice of the journal, as delineated in how-to literature, predicates an idea of self that locates authenticity as a primary objective of the modern individual. Granting individuals the power to authorize an authentic self depends on strict adherence to a regime of daily writing that is further focused on the mundane and the everyday. But what falls away in the relentless inward pursuit of the self? This is also a reminder that genre is ultimately conservative—the commitment to the power of the individual to produce change, for example, elides social causes of discontent or inequality in contemporary life, because the model of subjectivity available may be too narrow—the transformation promised is unobtainable because only certain kinds of identities are ever "authentic." Bridget Jones's "failure" to transform herself through her diary— her failure to achieve the standards of *Cosmopolitan* womanhood—parodies the imperatives for self-inspection, self-surveillance, and self-control that characterize the self-help industries.

What is enduring about diary as a mode for a certain kind of self-representation? What assumptions and expectations are still present in contemporary conceptions of diary writing like those in how-to guidebooks, and what assumptions and expectations are lost? Thomas Mallon, reading Oscar Wilde's satire of diary in *The Importance of Being Earnest*, finds the avid, and somewhat salacious, diary-keeper Gwendolen as representative of a historical shift: "Having been brought to life by dour Puritans of the seventeenth century as a place in which the faithful might expiate their sins, diary narrative had become, by the nineteenth century, more typically the place in which they could savor them" (*Book*, 208). The pleasurable narcissism implicit in Mallon's assessment is what how-to authors, with their emphasis on self-examination as a spiritual obligation to the self, attempt to displace. Daily self-writing becomes a practice of spiritual and therapeutic transformation, a way of accessing an authentic, secular spiritualism, of revealing the authentic self. Or rather, it is a turning inward to the self that they frame rhetorically in terms of work and improvement, as opposed to vanity and selfish self-absorption. Ultimately, and Mallon's quote also indicates this to some extent, how-to diaries represent a site of intense commodification that is tied to a cultural moment that values personal and individual experience as authentic.

The self-help "how-to" journal is a particularly potent use of diary now: a central claim of this genre in turn represents a tension of diary in general. Self-help diaries are paradoxical: they advocate inner resilience, creative free expression, and authentic self-knowledge as part of a program of self-improvement based on vigilant self-surveillance and externalization. Because "writing a journal involves externalising your thoughts, ideas and impressions," writes Dowrick in *Living Words*, "it lets you see in black and white, what your dreams and ideals are . . . putting them out there, onto the page of your journal, shifts the energy in a distinct and more helpful way" (3). In self-help discourse, the labor of self-study, the time required for monitoring and recording "thoughts, ideas, impressions," is framed not only as a therapeutic practice but also a spiritual journey. After all, "becoming authentic takes serious effort; it calls for spiritual exercise comparable to those to which religious initiates were formerly subjected" (Guignon, *On Being*, 5). Diary narrative—with its discursive connections to the daily and the mundane—appeals to individuals seeking spiritual transformation within a quotidian, secular frame, and how-to authors take up this rhetoric. Paradoxically, these authors emphasize assumptions about the naturalness of diary form—its lack of rules or prerequisites, a form available to the most inexperienced writer—even as they construct detailed guidelines for its proper practice. In *Living Words*, Dowrick emphasizes the agency of the reader: "No one knows you better than you know yourself" (3). Yet *Living Words* is a collection of highly detailed instructions and rules: "Your turn," encourages Dowrick: "Make a list (in this journal) of what will support you in your journal writing. Start with what you need to buy. New pens? Additional paper? What kinds? Where will you go to get them? When?" (14). The blank pages in the text encourage reader participation, fostering a sense of intimacy appropriate to stereotypes of the genre as a private and personal mode. These pages become moments of reader-response that also replicate to some degree the analytic situation; they also reproduce the inherent power dynamic of this relationship. "Check: am I writing *freely*?" asks Dowrick, in boxed comments on her ostensibly "blank" pages (69).

Some contradictions of self-help journals as guidebooks for free creative expression are inherent. This is a paradox further embedded in the term "self-help" itself; self-help is not self-devised.[15] What is of interest here, however, is not the internal logic of how-to journal practice (nor its legitimation as a technique for accessing or healing the self) but the impact this use of the diary form has on diary writing more generally. Does the self-help diary operate to authorize or undermine other kinds of diary practice? This chapter has been the necessary place to begin thinking about expectations of the genre now: the technology of diary writing as profoundly authentic and authenticating work. Because diary writing is seen as natural and authentic, it accrues an authoritative power in the representation of certain kinds of experience. When contemporary individuals want to present "real" self, and to claim an authentic voice, the diary is invoked as a genre of choice.

The popularity and broadening usage of diary now, the ideas of self that this taps into, are important for framing diary as a contemporary discourse. These ideas reflect a larger shift in self-talk, and in the representation of that talk in generic narrative forms. The step-by-step didacticism of early precursors in the genre, like Progoff's highly planned *At a Journal Workshop*, gives way to the broad spiritualism of texts like Dowrick's *Living Words* or Cameron's *The Artist's Way*. These texts, energized by the scripts of therapeutic culture, in turn symbolize the growing reach of therapeutics in general.[16] As a cultural moment, the rise of the how-to diary is significant, and the discourse of self-help that these texts engender in turn tells us about the genre of contemporary diary writing at large. How-to diaries make visible underlying myths and assumptions of the genre: the form as a vehicle for uncensored access to individual experience, or as an artifact designed to capture representations uniquely devoid of artifice or intent. Moreover, an emphasis on diary narrative as a privileged mode for accessing the authentic self, as a practice that disciplines the self into honest

3

The Ethics of Being There and Seeing

Thomas Goltz, Paul McGeough, and the Journalist's Diary of War

What after all is the difference between living and reporting life?

Zygmunt Bauman, *This Is Not a Diary*

What happens when the story becomes more than that—when it becomes life?

Thomas Goltz, *Chechnya Diary*

*I*deals of the authentic self and other expectations of the diary (intimacy, privacy, truthfulness) that are key in the how-to journal are also significant for diary writing in other contexts; many of the exhortations about diary in the how-to genre reappear in the diary as a broader cultural phenomenon. This chapter considers diaries by individuals who, nonetheless, might seem to have little in common with the audience imagined by the "how-to" authors of the previous chapter—the melancholy, "weightless" audience of the therapy diary. Autonomous and professional, with a public profile and a ready-made audience, journalists are not the obvious subjects of a discipline of self-help; yet therapy is not far away here. In diary publications made after the work of war correspondence has concluded, Thomas Goltz and Paul McGeough use diary to make various ethical and moral dilemmas visible. They focus on their experiences, on what they "missed," or were compelled (politically, stylistically, ethically) to leave out in dispatches and stories filed at the time of events. Kept alongside the work of their professional journalism, the published diary allows Goltz and McGeough to draw readers geographically and temporally distant into the intensity and immersion of daily life as a war correspondent. Indeed, for war correspondents like Goltz and McGeough, the diary might seem to be the ideal form through which to unfold and explore the limits and complexity of the journalistic profession.

Flexible and mobile, the diary has links to the mode of journalistic work, enabling the documentation of information in the field and stabilizing the opportunity for verification through reference to chronological time, to place, and to informants. Here is the source material for stories filed to news desks and other media outlets that constructs the parameters for public discourse and political feeling "back home." In keeping with contemporary uses of the form explored in this book, the diary is also conceptualized here as a literary document and as one destined for a public readership. Indeed, both Goltz and McGeough describe various work editing their diary accounts to best represent the ethical and moral standpoint they wish to convey. The diary is thus a practical choice (a form that allows for contemporaneous documentation), but it is also a rhetorical device that allows for personal material to be positioned (and consumed) in a particular way. Crucially, the diary has significance as a *document*. Its presence signals that here is the source material, the actual field notes of the journalist at work.

The authority of these accounts thus derives from their claimed closeness, temporally and geographically, to experiences on the ground and to diary as the mode that verifies and correlates to this lived experience. As publications, they are part of a larger shift to personal narrative and private experience in the construction of public discourse, to what Gillian Whitlock has called the "requirement to speak more personally in these times" (*Soft*, 132). As war diaries, however, Goltz's *Chechnya Diary* and McGeough's *In Baghdad* are specific examples of a changing genre,[1] and they are literary texts that negotiate strategically with the expectations and assumptions of genre. They are diaries that reach out to their intended audiences, inviting them into the private side of war correspondence by revealing what goes into crafting the public copy media audiences consume in another context. Indeed, like the diaries of other professional writers,[2] journalists' diaries draw self-consciously and strategically on assumptions of diary writing as private, personal, and "unrehearsed," and they do so with a technical and professional skill. As Whitlock observes, journalists who write autobiographically often "draw on and enhance" well-established professional reputations: "These autobiographers need no introduction, for their names, voices, and/or faces are often familiar" (*Soft*, 133).

Given the urgent issues of ethics, truth, and authority that attend both the public role of the journalist and situations of war and conflict, autobiographical narratives open up space for reflection on and by the journalistic subject and for a consideration of the journalistic profession. "How is it made personal, to what effects?" asks Whitlock of the surge in memoir by journalists from the Iraq war zone (*Soft*, 133). The question also directs attention to genre. There is a mass of autobiographical and media "product" coming from journalists in places like Iraq, and it is jostling for authenticity. How does genre amplify or change the effect of the personal in the production and consumption of auto-biographical writing? When journalists publish diary, questions like this come sharply into view.

Writing the Reporter

There are precedents for personal, self-reflexive forms of journalistic engage-ment: Joan Didion, Ernest Hemingway, Michael Herr, John Pilger, Ryszard Kapuscinski, and Tom Wolfe among others famously employ personal voice and memoir forms in crafting journalistic accounts. In his manifesto for the movement of literary nonfiction known as "New Journalism," Wolfe empha-sizes the need for journalism to compete with the novel and for journalism to acknowledge that, just like the fiction writer, the journalist *works* with raw material, shapes it rather than merely conveys it. Significantly, for Wolfe this was to be accomplished by a change in the journalistic voice and persona, a shedding of "understatement" and neutrality: "This had nothing to do with objectivity and subjectivity or taking a stand or 'commitment'—it was a matter of personality, energy, drive, bravura . . . style, in a word . . . The standard non-fiction writer's voice was like the standard announcer's voice . . . a drag, a droning" ("Birth," 45). Norman Sims in his introduction to a 1995 "best" collection of American nonfiction also indicates that at least some of the appeal of literary journalism lies in its ability to situate the reporter as a character in the account: "Standard reporting hides the voice of the writer, but literary journal-ism gives that voice an opportunity to enter the story" (Sims and Kramer, *Liter-ary*, 3).

Entering the story can be inferred as a key motivation for journalists who shift away from traditional journalistic formats and into the flexible generic space of memoir and autobiography. In this chapter, I acknowledge a tradition of personally inflected journalistic writing, but I look specifically at when and how diary narratives feature in this production. That is, I explore what this means given the specifics of genre in the dissemination of personal accounts. In doing this, I concentrate on editions of journals and diaries published not by an editor or family member but by the diarist. Such an approach responds to the increasing volume of diaries published by an author during their lifetime (a recent phenomenon) and to the diary as a distinct autobiographical form—that is, a literary form with specific rhetorical effects.

Journalists who publish diary do so for a number of reasons, and one of these may be a publisher decree, something Goltz responds to directly, as I discuss later. Another might be form: the diary adapts well to the kind of "field-work" a war correspondent must perform. "Originating from the idea of one who writes in a journal, or diary," observes media scholar Barbie Zelizer, "the term 'journalist' initially connoted someone who systematically kept a record of certain happenings within a specified time frame and who tended to make that record public" (*Taking*, 21). Rachel Cottam acknowledges that "journal" is a term often used for diary but that it is used also for newspapers and magazines; both diary and journal "are derived from roots meaning 'day,' but only rarely is a diary written daily" ("Diaries," 268). Linked to a formal capacity of the genre is a discursive effect; dailiness is a key rhetorical mode in both diaries and journalism, something that is often used to distinguish diary from other genres of autobiography or journalism from other forms of cultural history or public record and a distinction that in both cases is used to confer value. That is, "daili-ness" is connected not only to a mode of production, one from which both journalism and journaling may diverge to varying degrees, but to a delimitation of scope and significance. Both journaling and journalism, especially in "daily" contexts, have frequently been seen as inferior or "temporary" modes—forms that benefit from shaping into something "proper," as history, memoir, or fiction.[3]

In contemporary contexts, dailiness retains an ambivalent relationship to news and information. The advent of twenty-four-hour news channels and an increasingly "speeded-up news cycle that emphasizes immediacy and live reports over accuracy, on-the-ground reporting and substantial information" (Wall, "Blogging," 111–12) means dailiness acquires both a new value and a new ten-sion. Bill Katovsky, discussing media coverage of the Iraq conflict in particular, observes that "television's intense wall-to-wall coverage was offset by its dizzy ephemerality. Complexity and substance were sacrificed for the searing images, a burning Iraqi tank or inspiring sound-bite from an exhausted Marine taking a breather from shoving another artillery round into a smoking howitzer" (Katovsky and Carlson, *Embedded*, xvii). Immediacy is both a value and an anxiety. Moreover, the effect of competition within an increasingly syndicated media, the global reach of new information technology and its accessibility to everyday citizens, and the advent of transformative modes of information production have meant that it is foreign news that is most often sacrificed to "insular and parochial perspectives" (Bickler, "Reporting"). This shift replicates a broader transfer in attention "away from serious issues of policy to personality journalism and headline grabbing trivia" (Bickler, "Reporting"). In framing news as entertainment, or "infotainment," networks seeking to fill voracious news cycles favor graphic and attention-grabbing footage, the kind of sensorially violent images Goltz refers to as "bang-bang": the explosions, bodies, and physical and material carnage of conflict in faraway places (*Chechnya Diary*, 6). Deborah Leith observes that contemporary journalists face specific ethical challenges: "Perhaps journalists and photographers have now become unwitting participants in war, not because they carry weapons as [Ernest] Hemingway and Winston Churchill did, but because advances in telecommunications have meant that their 'real-time' reportage of events in a war zone can affect the course of the conflict" (*Bearing*, xxiv). This context for the contemporary journalist gains further complexity in the now iconic figure of the embedded reporter. In *The First Casualty: The War Correspondent as Hero, Propagandist and Myth-Maker from the Crimea to Iraq* (2003), Phillip Knightley recounts a sinister anecdote in his chapter "The Deadly Video Game"—on the Iraq conflict of 1990–91: "True, there could not be a return to the days of the First World War when an officer on the staff of the British general, Sir Ian Falconer, summed up the military view of war correspondents—a properly run country did not need them. 'It simply tells the people what it thinks will conduce to winning the war. If truth is good for winning the war, it tells them the truth. If a lie is likely to win the war, it tells them a lie'" (483). During the first Iraq conflict, Knightley notes there was a determination among the media to resist "managing" by the military, and to intervene in the propagandist politics of the U.S. government: "But this was a battle it could not win—even if it had summoned the will to do so" (484). The effect of embedding journalists with troops during the second Gulf War produced a new kind of reporting, but there were also new ethical concerns. For most commentators, the close relation between journalist and soldier that characterizes embedded scenarios is inherently compromised. Katovsky articulates this critical issue in his introduction to the anthology *Embedded: The Media at War in Iraq*: "how critical can the press be when these troops are also . . . my protectors?" (Katovsky and Carlson, *Embedded*, xvi). The appeal of the embedded report, however, matched growing ethical concerns: "The war helped television news," explains Katovsky. "Internet traffic soared. Weblogs proliferated. Newspapers printed special war supplements. The public was granted front row seats in [a] media multiplex" (xviii). At the center of this massive coverage, the embedded report represented a highly desirable commodity: a perspective on the ground and from the front line.[4]

The ethics of the reporter in a zone of conflict is a key concern for the journalists whose diary publications are the focus of this chapter. Both Goltz and McGeough recount experiences complicated by their professional status;

they negotiate with an ethics of being there and seeing that is founded in witnessing, and they contest a media filter that prioritizes only the most "entertaining" or visceral stories over the "ordinary" hardship of citizens and participants on the ground. That they use diary to do so is the focus of this chapter, which explores how genre can draw attention to ongoing tensions between public and private knowledge, to what a journalist is, and to what personal narrative can (and cannot) do.

Being There: *Chechnya Diary*

Though the publication of a trilogy of diaries based on foreign correspondent postings and personal missions to regions of the Caucasus has drawn attention to him as a diarist, Thomas Goltz is by profession a documentary journalist. A citizen of the United States, Goltz refers frequently to his farm in Montana, though he has spent nearly a decade reporting in Turkey and nearly as long again in and out of neighboring regions like Azerbaijan and Chechnya. For Goltz, living and reporting in these locations is linked to a personal ethical methodology: "History as Contact Journalism. If you don't get bumped around a bit (as in blood sports like football and ice hockey), you have no business talking (or writing) about a place like Azerbaijan and indeed, the Caucasus as a whole" (*Azerbaijan*, xi).

Getting "bumped around a bit" is the subject, in different ways, of each of Goltz's diaries. *Azerbaijan Diary: A Rogue Reporter's Adventures in an Oil-Rich, War-Torn, Post-Soviet Republic* (1998), *Chechnya Diary: A War Correspondent's Story of Surviving the War in Chechnya* (2003), and *Georgia Diary: A Chronicle of War and Political Chaos in the Post-Soviet Caucasus* (2006) are accounts that Goltz has formulated through living and traveling with the people he reports on. He spends time with freedom fighters, oil barons, presidents, as well as with ordinary citizens; he is entertained by a "strange collection of hosts . . . that most tourists could never be privy to" (*Azerbaijan*, 9). Contact journalism is a methodology for getting to the heart of the action, getting closer to the real stories, and it is the moral framework around which he constructs his experience and around which he will ultimately frame a transformative disillusionment with his profession. In the meantime, he takes risks for the story, he puts himself on the front line, and he eagerly positions himself as a key witness:

> "Okay," I confessed. I am here illegally. Just like I have been the illegal witness of every one of your disasters . . ." "God," said the colonel, rolling his eyes and

smiling in spite of himself. "You have violated every rule we have!" "That's right," I said, returning the KGB colonel's stare. "Someone has to write your history." (*Azerbaijan*, 438)

In *Journalists under Fire: Information War and Journalistic Practices* (2006), Howard Tumber and Frank Webster argue that "frontline correspondents are major players in the mediation of war. The reporters who put together the 'whys' and 'whats' can be crucial in the war effort. This is why they are subject to perception management from all sides, from the combatants themselves, from politicians, and from their own organisations" (5). The compromised position of the journalist, especially in contexts of limited and highly managed information, is a recurring concern in commentary about foreign correspondence; indeed, it is a founding concern of reporting and journalism in general. Goltz's advocacy of himself, therefore, as a self-styled "rogue" reporter who will stop at nothing to obtain the facts has a certain appeal and it is also an authoritative claim. A recurring motif in the diaries, this self-representation is one that Goltz also reflects on directly in prefatory material, for example, in the introduction to *Azerbaijan Diary*:

> The "scholarly reader" may take issue with the first-person style of writing and the virtual lack of academic-style footnotes. The reason for the paucity of reference to "others" is that I have seen far too many examples of bad sourcing in the press and in scholarly articles on Azerbaijan to believe anything not witnessed by me (or by someone whose honesty and integrity I can vouch for). (xi)

Throughout this self-reflexive preface, Goltz oscillates between claiming authority based on experience ("those of us who lived through the chaos and violence of the region in the post-Soviet era") and professional mandate: he is a journalist intent on "differentiating fact from fiction" (xi). These objectives are at once linked and in conflict. He has imagined *Azerbaijan Diary* as "a sort of annotated diary, a journey of discovery on which the reader was invited to travel with the writer as his or her imperfect yet enthusiastic guide" (xi), but he also has "the arrogance" to proffer this account as a definitive one. Indeed, he positions it as a corrective version and recommends to "reporters, editorial writers, and, ultimately, scholars of the period and place that they take the time to wade through this opus before furthering the promotion of 'facts' based on repetitive errors" (xii). Goltz is a commando witness, a member of what he calls "the informational shock-troops" on the ground committed to getting the record straight

(*Azerbaijan*, xi). In part, his diary publications become so important to him because they allow for the presentation of factual correction and for the representation of detail otherwise ignored or trimmed in the curtailed frame of news reporting. In *Azerbaijan Diary* and the third volume of his "trilogy," *Georgia Diary*, this is the dominant motif, and Goltz takes pains to emphasize in these works that he is both journalistic authority figure and trusted compatriot abroad—elsewhere in the preface to *Azerbaijan Diary* he likens himself to the protagonist of the wry and socially perceptive political humor cartoon *Doonesbury*. However, if *Azerbaijan Diary* and *Georgia Diary* are essentially interpretable as a kind of travel journalism inflected by unfolding contemporaneous crises in the region, *Chechnya Diary* offers a different register for thinking both about the situation of the foreign correspondent and for the representation of that experience in diary.

Goltz has a special fondness for Chechnya; he considers it part of "his patch" (*Chechnya*, 61). In February 1995 he is on assignment: he has "accepted—no, pursued—a contract with ABC's *Nightline* to sally forth to Chechnya at war to create a one-man documentary on 'the Chechen Spirit,' made on the basis of my unique ties, language ability, and cultural connectivity" (16). The remote western Chechnya village of Samashki, however, is an unprepossessing location for covering the Russo–Chechen conflicts of the mid-1990s. When his illegal Chechen guide leads him there unexpectedly, Goltz at first fears he may have been kidnapped; there seems no other reason to be in the town. Nonetheless, he shoots "generic B-roll footage" of smashed-up houses, shattered furniture, and stoic villagers (84). His objective is straightforward:

> My plan was to spend a few days in the town, get to know some folks, go out on a
> few missions, and then get out while the place was obliterated. In the best of all
> possible worlds, I would accomplish the getting out while the obliteration was
> taking place. In the television trade, this is called collecting "bang-bang." (6)

Samashki is disappointing on the conflict front, and a "pretty weak brew compared to what was going on in Grozny a mere twenty miles away" (84), but Goltz stays—partly because he only has a "makeshift" Russian-issued press pass, a fact guaranteed to irk the local bureaucracy and to make traveling difficult, but mostly because he unexpectedly finds what he has been looking for in Hussein, commander of the local resistance: "With a jolt I understood that the man standing in front of me was exactly the sort of vessel I needed to explain the essence and nature of the Chechen spirit" (90). Goltz explains the documentary to Hussein, and he is self-conscious about sounding cliché. Nonetheless, he voices his desire: he wants this documentary to motivate American audiences to support the Chechen cause. Hussein forecloses on this idealism and offers up a corollary motive: "You want to build a career on this experience" (92). Hussein's charge is an indictment: it casts Goltz as a media mercenary, and Goltz frets about this. After all, his presence in this war zone derives from a market pressure and not just a personal philosophy for capturing "real" detail. Audiences—and importantly, news editors—desire footage from the thick of it. Goltz is alert and compliant to this demand. He has timed his visit to Chechnya to "coincide with Genocide Commemoration Day of February 23–24 because I was sure it would make good television" (104). He needs the tense ethnic rivalries between Chechens and Russians to erupt so that he can capture on film the "bang bang folks at home find so very entertaining." Has he really "bought into the idea of war as entertainment" (123)? Goltz wants to refute Hussein's charge, but finds he cannot.

The Chechen resistance fighter Hussein is a moral and narrative center of *Chechnya Diary*. The frontispiece photo is of Hussein and his family, and in his acknowledgments Goltz thanks, "at the top" of his list, "Hussein and his extended family, who invited me into their lives during a brief period of extreme confusion and duress. I doubt any will ever see this work" (ix). This poignant dedication, preceding the gung-ho bravado of the opening narrative, signals the seriousness of Goltz's project, and its complexity. Admitting that he had "sallied forth" with "an overly romantic view of Chechnya and the Chechens, . . . how this little people could rally their resources to fend off the overwhelming force of the might of the Russian army" ("Conversation"), in Hussein he found the noble figure he desired: "a farmer defending his home" (*Chechnya*, 90). But the urgency of Hussein's plight and the daily reality of the village's defensive endeavors, the basis of Goltz's story, become discomfiting. Goltz finds his own presence in the conflict zone—and his reasons for being there—edging ineluctably closer to something other than that of witness:

> Waiting for some shell to fall close enough that I get a good, solid "bang" but hopefully far away enough that I don't die in the process. Just the people who have been looking after and feeding me and washing my boots after a hard day's slog through the mud. Jesus Christ. I am worse than the usual casual voyeur of the death and destruction of strangers. I actively want the death and destruction of my friends because if it does not happen I do not have a story. (104)

In *Chechnya Diary*, Goltz is concerned with sharp ethical questions: "Are journalists perfectly neutral vessels who only see and record? Or does their very presence at critical moments make people act differently than they would have had the journalist not been there at all? What happens when *the story* becomes more than that—when it becomes *life*? When does the observer affect the observed?" (12). The question, as much ideological as it is philosophical, cuts to the heart of his growing ambivalence and unease with the professional guise of war correspondent. After all, Goltz tells his reader, he has "sallied forth" with not just a romantic view of Chechens, but also of his own potency in this zone: "This is common to many journalists, young and old, namely, the belief that the article you will write, that the television program that you shoot, will be so effective that the viewer, that the reader, will stand up and shout, 'Stop! Stop this war! Stop this madness!'" ("Conversation"). But it is a kind of naked, naïve idealism he resisted using on Hussein and the kind of romanticized image of the benevolent and effortlessly effective reporter that he wants to reject, even as he acknowledges its purpose: "Maybe this is the pretense that you have at a certain point as a journalist, because otherwise it would be almost impossible to do your job in these extremely difficult circumstances" ("Conversation"). He wants to discard a construction of the war reporter as "neutral vessel," and he wants to problematize the assumptions of journalists as witnesses, but to do so is to risk his self-perception as an ethical subject. "My contact with Hussein," writes Goltz "has led me to ask a number of uncomfortable questions of myself and others involved in journalism, especially in areas and times of war and crisis" (*Chechnya*, 11). For Goltz, *Chechnya Diary* provides both an opportunity and a problem: to work through the "uncomfortable questions" of war journalism and to atone for unforeseen moral consequences of his professional role. Meeting Hussein is a narrative turning point after which Goltz finds himself increasingly "slipping" over the "unspoken line" between correspondent and "comrade" (99). A growing sympathy for the rebel cause, combined with a parallel disenchantment for the values of news media, impels Goltz to reposition himself in relation to the story. "I was out," he writes. "I was alive. I had my tapes. I had my story. No. *Our Story*. That was my part of the bargain" (143).

"To survive is to be allowed the opportunity to bear witness," says Chris Daley, and it is also "an atrocious privilege" ("Atrocious," 182). The atrocious privilege of the journalist is that his or her survival is far more likely than that of the subjects reported on: "We foreign correspondents wing our way into ghastly situations and report on them, and just leave and move on to the next assignment with no respect for the aftermath," observes one of Goltz's colleagues from the BBC (*Chechnya*, 220). For Goltz such a position has no longer become tenable. He returns to Chechnya determined to follow up on the rebel story and to finally secure the right attention for the cause: "It was the logical, and now funded, follow-up assignment to my original, almost-award-winning story on Samashki. It filled me with inexplicable dread" (220).

In Chechnya, Goltz travels with fellow journalists, but he is out of sync. When a colleague sees smoke on the horizon and is furious at missing an opportunity for footage, Goltz feels "sick at heart" (*Chechnya*, 160). He drinks, and frets: "What has happened to *my people*?" (165). He stumbles across incriminating information about the Russian high command, evidence of war crime interference at Samashki: "*That is news. Not without bodies*, say all the editors I petition. Vodka that night. Buckets of it" (179). When he finally makes it back to the village, he learns of a particularly brutal attack that coincided with his departure from the country. For befriending the American journalist who suddenly looked like a spy, Hussein and his family had been exiled. In his diary, Goltz reflects on the situation:

> The foreigner, meanwhile, remains blissfully oblivious to the impact of his very presence in the small community in the small country at war, and particularly, the impact his presence has had on the life of the expelled leader because the foreigner was only there observing. Yes, that was it. The foreigner was not an actor; he was merely observing, and thus innocent of any crime, hurt, or fallout. Not. It was all much more like a real-life, warped paraphrase of the Heisenberg chaos theory about the observer affecting the observed. (249)

For Goltz, confronting the consequences of his presence and absence in Samashki, experiencing the aftermath, is overwhelming, and the illusion of benevolence by the reporter in the foreign conflict zone is exposed as devastatingly inadequate. Ultimately, the transaction he wants to make, impelled by his sense of inclusion, is revealed as empty.

Unfolding events for his reader in a diary account is a sympathetic way to show this kind of story and it is authoritative. Goltz is clear: he has worked on his manuscript, readying it for publication to the point that he was "embarrassingly close to being seven hundred days overdue in submitting" (*Chechnya*, xii). *Chechnya Diary* is not a simple artifact of his experience; it is a carefully crafted construct that trades on the ability of diary to re-create for a reader the experience of ethical choices Goltz has made day to day. In a discussion of the internment diary of Peggy Abkhazi, Laurie McNeill attributes the lack of popular success for the narrative to its natural scope as a diary, which is to identify its limited effect as a story. "Writing originally in diary form," argues McNeill, "Abkhazi could only narrate what she was experiencing in the moment. She therefore could not shape her story to include pattern or purpose; writing without the benefit of hindsight she could not know what kinds of events could matter for a narrative of 'history,' both public and personal" ("Performing," 89). The diarist's perspective of immersion is a generic feature of the diary form, creating a sense of immediacy in the narrative and supporting perceptions of diary as a form that is less self-conscious in its construction than other modes. Though McNeill suggests this lack of narrative construction might be a problem for certain diary texts, Lejeune argues that this quality, what he calls "the feeling of *touching time*," may also be the "thrill that helps readers put up with and even appreciate many things that would be imperfections from a classical literary point of view" (209). However, as Hope Wolf has argued, immediacy is a powerful rhetorical gesture, one privileged above all for its implications of "innocence or purity" ("Mediating," 328). That is, diurnal forms like diary are primarily valued, as Wolf puts it, for "a diminutive temporal lapse between life and writing" (328). The immersed perspective of the diarist is seen to confer greater authenticity, even where such accounts are inevitably limited narratively.[5]

Wolf 's observations on the significance of immediacy, particularly in letters and diaries and particularly in wartime accounts, go some way to explaining why Goltz does agree to publish a clearly crafted, undated, carefully self-reflexive and thematic account of war correspondence as a diary at all. That is, in both how he positions himself, and so his reader, and in how he unfolds the story, diary enables a representation of the subject *enacting* their choices. Like Abkhazi, Goltz represents himself as immersed in his story, with no sense for where the narrative is going, for what will matter. Unlike Abkhazi, Goltz achieves this through deliberate effect.

Nonetheless, this effect of diary is not one Goltz says he would have chosen on his own, a reminder that, as Whitlock also observes, such narratives are "highly marketable commodities" and subject to processes of commercial production (*Soft*, 135). Further, here we see versions of experience that move through genres and extend and recycle the initial report and the "life" (and lives) at its center. In various appearances to promote the publication of *Chechnya Diary*, Goltz reflects on international relations, on journalism, and on writing personal narrative. Providing a forum to promote his political views on Chechnya and the Caucasus in general, these public performances also allow Goltz to intervene in his audience's perception of his text, which he does to contest its generic nomination as diary. That is, Goltz claims that genre is an imposition, one of a series of problems tied to the production of a publication: "I would never have chosen the word diary for either the Azerbaijani book or the Chechen. They were both imposed upon me" ("Meet"). Considering Goltz has cemented his reputation as a "Caucasus diarist" with the publication of *Georgia*

Diary (2006), such an assertion is disingenuous. Yet what is Goltz rejecting by claiming that he would not have chosen "diary"? After all, genre is a social agreement that not only works to shape or name content but to position readers and audiences in certain ways toward the completed text. What does diary mean here?

Chechnya Diary, like Goltz's other diaries, is a hybrid text. It contains accounts of dreams, moments of retrospective reflection, excerpts from the memoirs of his peers and from scholarly reports. Sometimes he indicates futures yet to un-fold, such as when he nods to the ethnic tensions that will bubble up in the area after 11 September 2001. Sometimes italicized passages from what seem to be the original diary are included. This structure heightens the sense of *Chechnya Diary* as an amalgam—part autobiography, part reportage, part social and political commentary, but not strictly a diary at all. But what is a diary, strictly? Part of the problem here is that the form is both clearly recognizable as a generic mode even while it also elides simple definition as a textual artifact. Both con-temporary and historical diaries routinely confound any "hallmarks" of diary form to the point that capaciousness, mutability, and hybridity in the diary genre are perhaps its most powerful traits. Rosenwald, attempting to untangle the issue in his "Prolegomena" to *Emerson and the Art of Diary*, observes that the difference between diary and other forms of autobiographical narrative, and even between diary and its "nearer neighbors of authors' notebooks," is "more often a *felt* distinction" (6). Such feelings are clearly subject to cultural, social, and historical shifts.

Without eliding the ways in which Goltz's text is or is not a diary in a "pure" sense of the term, it clearly acts like one, it is usually interpreted as one, and it is named as one. This is important. That is, it becomes increasingly clear that Goltz's resistance to genre is not structural, a sense of false ascription (to the ways in which his version of diary might yet leak or flex past already very fluid definitional boundaries) but ideological. Encapsulated in the designation "diary" is a move that Goltz says he wants to reject: the privileging of the Western journalist at the center of a story about conflict elsewhere. The subtitle, "A War Correspondent's Story of Surviving the War in Chechnya," only exacerbates his problem:

> Without joking, I said absolutely not. This is not a book about me, rather it is about me but it says it already in the title, *Chechnya Diary*, which you've imposed upon me. We've got to get something that is a little bit more resonant, that says something more about the book. What about "The Story of a Massacre and Its Aftermath?" And the marketing people said, no. ("Meet")

On one level, Goltz's concerns demonstrate an obvious point. Books need markets, and genres designate audiences; that authors may have little to do with either of these ends is hardly a revelation. Goltz admits he was late in submitting the manuscript, and that this robbed him of bargaining power, but there is also a more urgent issue at stake. He desires his account to capture the lives of hitherto marginalized others—the Chechen people—but he wants somehow to reduce his role in this representative act. He is concerned about the authority genre confers and its jurisdictions:

> The subtitle misses the entire [point] and it shifts the emphasis to the vessel or to the recorder, namely the journalist, the war correspondent, as opposed to the event. I wanted, and I fought for having the word "Samashki" in the subtitle. I wanted and fought for having the word "aftermath" in the subtitle. I wanted and fought for having the word "massacre" in the subtitle, like, *Samashki: The Story of a Massacre and Its Aftermath*, thus moving the emphasis away from the journalist. But the marketing people had their way. ("Conversation")

In various news media, Goltz has tried to tell and circulate his story of Chechnya. For various reasons, these circuits have proved elliptical. *Chechnya Diary*, then, becomes a talismanic project, and Goltz cathects it with redemptive and ameliorative power. "I have been working on *our* book of war," he writes, "as some sort of testament or at least reminder of human foibles and frailties but also devotion" (285). For Goltz, diary is not a structural or textual object that he can take up or move away from, but an ideological problem. It is a consequence of marketing, but also of the story he has to tell. In his public discussions of his text, Goltz presents diary as burdensome: an imposition that narrows the focus back to the author and in this case reinscribes Western privilege. Nonetheless, in his narrative and in his oeuvre, he accedes to the conventions of the genre and takes up and benefits from its strategic possibilities.

In some ways, Goltz's resistance to diary reveals a lingering prejudice attached to the genre as an inadequate mode for telling public history. In another way, Goltz reveals his uneasiness with a market that demands a Western body at the center of the story, and he tries to show some of the consequences of this presence—to make the aftermath part of the story. In both cases, Goltz reveals the diary to be a capacious and hybrid mode, but also a distinct form and a provocative one. Paul John Eakin, in *How Our Lives Become Stories: Making Selves*, notes that a characterization of biography as "bloodsport" acknowledges that the genre "does possess the potential to harm its subjects; text can harm a person because the person–property axis runs both ways" (172). So Goltz's earlier conceptualization of journalism as "bloodsport" (*Azerbaijan*, xi), like Eakin's, acknowledges the dangers inherent to professions dependent on representing others, while his sense that it is only through being close enough to the action, close enough "to get bumped around" (xi), that the truth can emerge tells us about what feeds this impulse. For Goltz, the diary provides an alternative to journalism, and is a mode in which his story and that of the Chechen people can travel to powerful audiences in the West. But the problem remains that this story must travel through him.

Seeing: *In Baghdad*

"This is not a journalistic work," writes Garry Leech in his author's note to *Beyond Bogotá: Diary of a Drug War Journalist* (2010), "but rather the personal story of a journalist's search for meaning in the midst of violence and poverty" (xi). William L. Shirer's foreword to *Berlin Diary: The Journal of a Foreign Correspondent* (1941) sets out a similar mandate: "The kind of job I had appeared to be giving me the opportunity to set down from day to day a first-hand account of a Europe that was already in agony and that, as the months and years unfolded, slipped inexorably towards the abyss of war and self-destruction" (v). Diary accounts signal something particular about the composition of a published account, and more significantly, about an author's position in relation to it. Like Shirer, Norwegian journalist Åsne Seierstad takes up a role as witness, a position complicated by her professional role as much as it is a product of it: "For a hundred and one days, from January to April 2003, I tried to record what I experienced in Baghdad" (*Hundred*, 1). *A Hundred and One Days: A Baghdad Journal* (2005) is composed from the "snapshots, glimpses from the war" (3) that Seierstad files as a war correspondent. "My greatest advantage," she says, "was that I *was* there. My eyes were there, my ears were there" (2). Her readers, however, "see only the outcome; the articles say little of how they were first conceived or what has been left out" (1).

For these journalists, autobiographical narration is not about extending or reshaping the parameters of reporting (though this is also a consequence) but about claiming a subjective and authoritative stance to tell their side of the story, which may also be about advocating on behalf of those whose stories have not yet been adequately told through the news media, or by the journalists themselves. "No story contains the whole story," explains Seierstad. "This is just one fragment of many and it gives a fragment of the whole, not more" (*Hundred*, 3). For the Australian journalist Paul McGeough, telling more of the story is also the driving motivation for his 2003 diary publication, *In Baghdad: A Reporter's War*, an account he produces for publication very quickly. Indeed, as he recounts it, as soon as McGeough walks in the door of his New York apartment, he "had dinner[,] and then disappeared" into his study for three weeks, working "round the clock—pushing out chapters under the door for the dead-eye reckoning" of his wife's "red pen" (*In Baghdad*, 291). As a diary, *In Baghdad* can respond very quickly to both the personal urgency McGeough feels in relation to his recent experience and to the demands of a voracious and fickle market. The genre also conveys something about the nature of the experience: here is the exhausting all-hours regime of reporting, writing, and sending copy that McGeough has just performed during his stint reporting in Baghdad, and through the account of which his audience can experience some of its relayed intensity. However, this publication also signals that the journalistic work has not been comprehensive. *In Baghdad*, like similar accounts by other journalists, is a supplement to what has already been said in the news media, and it reveals that this venue is both compromised and partial. In addition, it demonstrates that the personal is both marketable, a commodity that extends the life of the reporting experience, and missing in journalistic discourse within conventional frames. Though McGeough is already a recognizable figure as a correspondent, his publication of a diary account allows him to access audience in a different way. Positioning this account as the inside story to a professional output elsewhere allows him to establish an individual ethical stance in relation to the events and politics he has already reported on, and this is crucial in establishing a market for this work. It is also important for supporting the kind of journalistic subjectivity McGeough wants to claim. This is the reporter as witness.

Like Goltz, McGeough wants more than to simply report: he frames himself in relation to the event of reporting, to the personal subjective experience of being a reporter and seeing the conflict in Baghdad. And while McGeough also articulates his sense that, for various reasons, news audiences have missed crucial information about life in war-torn Baghdad, a promise to tell more about the Iraqi experience "on the ground" cannot be separated from an invitation to show more of the reporter as he goes about his work in this space. McGeough belongs to a cohort of foreign correspondents experienced in modern conflicts of Central Asia and the Middle East; he has been a frequent guest at "the hell-holes of the world" (*In Baghdad*, 12). Like Goltz in *Chechnya Diary*, McGeough develops the diary as a mass-market product; his accounts are edited, crafted, and composed with publication in mind. Editing his diary enhances its readability and heightens a dramatic effect of following events over time. Ultimately, however, it confirms that diary is a distinctive rhetorical device for this kind of story. This is all the more important for McGeough, as his diary exists within the bounds of another dominant contemporary discourse, one that both energizes and complicates this textual production: "the war on terror."

Where Goltz is subject to the whimsy of international news—forced to justify his presence at the site of an obscure, localized conflict—and at the mercy of its ebbing market interest, McGeough has a highly desirable commodity to sell. This very powerful context for personal narrative, one that Whitlock has explored closely in *Soft Weapons*, demonstrates a moment for life writing in which personal stories become strongly enmeshed in broader political concerns. Indeed, McGeough's previous publication, *Manhattan to Baghdad: Despatches from the Frontline in the War on Terror* (2003), opens with a first-hand account of the September 11 terrorist attack in New York. Yet "People Are Crying in the Streets" is slightly out of place with the "despatches" that follow—it is not the chronological starting point for the narrative, though it is clearly the ideological one (*Manhattan*, 1). Indeed, the first two parts of the book are concerned directly with events in Afghanistan, an account that commences in July 2001. For fellow foreign correspondent John Martinkus, the seams are too obvious: "At first glance this book looks like a quickie bashed out to take advantage of the looming war in Iraq and to cash in on the coincidence that the author—taking a break from his day job covering wars for the *Sydney Morning Herald*—happened to be in New York when the towers came down" ("Slap," 12). As an attempt to give some coherence to the imprecise locations, various battlefields, and nebulous contexts of the "so-called war on terror," and as a "very good rundown of the pre-existing conditions, conflicts and events of the past year and a half in disparate conflict zones," Martinkus, himself the author of a memoir of reporting in Iraq, welcomes *Manhattan to Baghdad*. However, he also voices a lingering suspicion: this is a disjointed text, a collection of vignettes from a range of locations that, "but for their being woven together by the common thread of the US reaction to September 11 . . . probably would not have got into print" (12). There seems little doubt that Martinkus is right. Life narrative tracks sites of unrest and spikes at moments of global interest. As Kay Schaffer and Sidonie Smith tell us: "at this historical moment, telling life stories in print or through the media by and large depends on a Western-based publishing industry, media and readership. This dependence affects the kinds of stories published and circulated, the forms those stories take and the appeals they make to audiences" (*Human*, 24). Life narrative is a cultural practice that reproduces and sharpens broad contemporary concerns about individual ethics, and particularly during times of conflict and unrest, life narrative is timely. Crucially, "at any historical moment, only certain stories are tellable and intelligible to a broader audience" (Schaffer and Smith, *Human*, 32).

For Martinkus, McGeough's coverage of events in *Manhattan to Baghdad* is suspiciously convenient, a narrative too aware of its own potential currency and that cynically trades on the kind of interest critics like Schaffer and Smith identify. Such concerns are not allayed by McGeough's next foray into personal narrative: *In Baghdad: A Reporter's War* follows its predecessor closely, picking up in Baghdad, days before allied strikes commence and precisely where the *Manhattan to Baghdad* narrative concludes. But where the dispatches of *Manhattan to Baghdad* weave connections among disparate geopolitical locations and chronology, *In Baghdad* documents twenty-eight consecutive days in the besieged Iraqi capital. *Manhattan* makes fresh a bulk of already published material with a strategic narrative structure; *In Baghdad* performs a different rhetorical move. "McGeough's account," comments one reviewer of *In Baghdad*, "tells a very different story of the conflict than the sanitised official version offered by the Bush administration and the British and Australian governments" (Fazio, "Paul"). And it should. This is, after all, a diary, and *In Baghdad* is chronological and sequential, a classic diary form. An entry for each of the twenty-eight days of allied strikes on Baghdad beginning in March 2003 mimics the daily rhythm of McGeough's reporting for media outside Iraq. This effect of dailiness is a vestige of form, but it is also crucial in establishing the gap between what is re-ported and what is experienced; there is a difference between what is reported "daily" and what the reporter experiences each day. This effect is heightened throughout *In Baghdad* because each daily entry also commences with an excerpt from the relevant "filed" report and that then precedes (and demarcates) the "diary" account. The effect is of an official and unofficial record—journalism and journaling—side by side.

In some ways, the kind of boundaries Martinkus says he wants to guard between the public aspect of the war correspondent and the personal life of Paul McGeough appear to be made clear here. However, a demarcation of where the foreign correspondent ends and the person (and the personal) begin also becomes a textual strategy. Smith and Watson, in *Reading Autobiography*, note that even in the most traditional of autobiographies the "I" is a compli-cated representation (61). In choosing two narrative voices, McGeough simul-taneously produces different and competing autobiographical "I's": there is the "real" or historical "I" (the Australian journalist and the body at risk), the narrating "I" (the professional journalist), the narrated "I" (the journalist as hero), and the ideological "I" (the humanitarian compromised by professional obligation). In the various "I's" that McGeough inhabits, the tension between the historical "I," who has a professional obligation to report in this context, and the ideological "I," which reveals the impact of humanitarian discourse on journalists' self-perception, is taut. His sense of this tension is apparent in the choice of narrative structure as well as in the form: a desire to tell two sides of the same story and to represent a multiple and shifting construction of the war reporter in Baghdad finds resonance in the generic mode of diary.

In Baghdad also draws on generic associations of the diary in its content: as would be expected in this kind of work, McGeough brings into view a particular and intimate construction of the war correspondent. For example, he includes material that may be regarded as banal: an e-mail apology to his wife for being "ratty" while stressed about deadlines and coping with lack of sleep (54); her wifely admonishment when, carried away with excitement (and machismo), he fails to wear his earplugs during missile strikes (117). On-the-spot political analysis is supplemented by images of home: "The tension and the anxiety spread well beyond Iraq. In Perth, in Western Australia, my mother was working what a friend calls her 'heavy duty' rosary beads" (24). It is apparent that McGeough chooses to include his role as husband and son in a diary narrative of reporting from Baghdad for distinct reasons. These interludes are gently mocking, portraits in miniature of the worrying women in McGeough's life, but their invocation here is strategic: he draws attention to his distance from their concerns—a difference exacerbated in the war zone. The "cockroach infested and litter-strewn corridors" of the Palestine Hotel display the limits of a world far from the feminine, motherly, and wifely boundaries of "home"—this is distinctly a "reporter's war" and a journalists' world: "Walk the corridors of the Palestine at night and you entered a journalists' world. You might find a French party—real wine in real glasses in a real war—while in another room you'd see the pained expression of the creative process on deadline. Not far away, you'd hear invective screamed at a failed piece of vital equipment; or from another room maybe, just maybe, the strains of a Bach prelude" (39). Here is the private aspect of the war correspondent. These mundane inclusions are a contrast to the professional "filed" journalism, which is lacking in these reminiscences and anecdotes. McGeough's inside report promises the reader access to the domestic world of the foreign correspondent. A diary account in this context is a valuable commodity, satisfying the desire for closer and more intimate and more detailed accounting of "behind-the-scenes" material than has been a feature of media coverage in this conflict and trading on the assumptions of immediacy and authenticity that are attached to the genre. Moreover, getting closer to McGeough's day-to-day experience holds the seductive promise of also getting closer to the "truth": diary particularly taps into a desire for alternative articulation about experience, for information beyond dominant political and partisan rhetoric.

As a professional journalist, McGeough uses diary rhetorically to signal his authenticity and agency apart from this persona. Yet he also wants to reveal the complexities of reporting war, to reveal something about the strategies of the war reporter. Ultimately, the journalist is represented as a compromised figure. There are "behind-the-scenes" machinations, for example. So, in order to get a visa from the Iraqi Information Ministry, he spends "a bizarre couple of hours as a 'seeker of truth,' during which I rendered much of what I had written for the *Herald* into mush that would be acceptable to the regime . . . the 'dictator Saddam' now read as 'President Saddam' and lines like 'After Saddam's brutal suppression of the Shia in Karbala . . .' became 'After Saddam restored law and order in Karbala'" (*In Baghdad*, 21).

The compromises of the reporter during wartime are ostensibly well understood. Personal narrative, therefore, simply contributes more to the story. This point is illustrated in this diary through an anecdote about McGeough's fellow correspondent, the American journalist John Burns. In an entry for "Day Thirteen: Wednesday, April 1," McGeough records that Burns has disappeared from the hotel and that the circumstances are suspicious: "Across the world," writes McGeough in the following day's diary entry, "readers of *The New York Times* would have been puzzled by the absence from the April 2 edition, for the first time since the start of the war, of a report from Baghdad by John F. Burns. But we decided we would keep the story of his predicament quiet; we would watch it play out a bit, before families and foreign desks were informed" (*In Baghdad*, 146).

As the record of events as they unfold, the diary offers a different context through which to piece together the flows of information from the war zone of Iraq. For McGeough, the diary is a chance to work through ethical compromises, and inevitably, it is also a mode through which to justify such choices to his audience. It also allows McGeough to more carefully define and present a role as witness. An account of the fieldwork of the war correspondent becomes part of a personal legitimation for being there and witnessing:

> It's during such moments, spent standing on a median strip waiting for an unknown ride in an unknown city in the middle of the night, that you sometimes wonder about this job. Why? And as I looked at Jon Lee's chiselled features and

at dark-haired Caroline buried under her photographer's swag, and I was filled with an overpowering sense that somebody from the outside world had to be in al-Shuala this night; someone had to be bearing witness. (*In Baghdad*, 90)

This act of witnessing is also replayed in the narrative structure of *In Baghdad*. In a radio interview, McGeough explains:

You kept your sanity by, well one of the things I've done with this book is to separate it into two, so that it's the two stories in the one book because it's very important to remember that we were there by choice. The Iraqi people didn't have a choice and anything that happened to them was infinitely worse and infinitely more shocking than anything that might happen to us . . . for me it was important to separate out what was happening to us as journalists, as a professional exercise, so that it didn't overcome what was happening to the Iraqi people. Because I think the story had to be the story of the Iraqi people. (Loane, "Interview")

Long-standing associations of the diary with surveillance are energized here—McGeough uses his publication to document and, crucially, to *show* how the eyewitness reporter obtains the intimacy and detail that underwrites his stories. This is also a space for self-scrutiny. McGeough expresses a desire to use his diary as testimony for the Iraqi people—he wants to "witness." In doing so, the diary is the evidence for his ethical and moral responses in Baghdad. For example, when the hotel's power supply fails (as usual) one night, McGeough chooses to sit in darkness: "I could have jumped up immediately and kick-started the generator on my balcony, but I thought the darkness might be useful. I felt rocked to my soul by the little fellow I'd seen in the hospital today, Ali Ismail, and by the circumstances of the children in the other wards" (*In Baghdad*, 163). This is also an insight into the therapeutic uses of diary for the journalist. "Such moments," he observes, "can be excruciatingly painful; but they can also be very focusing, and, for me, they often precede one of the best ways of coming to terms with horror, grief and indifference—writing about it" (164). McGeough makes it clear to his reader that he is using his diary not only to monitor the situation in Iraq (a role for the diary as logbook or field book) but also to monitor himself for feelings of impatience and inhumanity, to reframe the dislocating and traumatic experiences of his time here. He wants to justify his ethical clarity and humanitarian intent, and the diary is a strategic and highly persuasive form for this kind of representation, one that readers find authentic as a generic frame.

Hot Copy

When Alex Vernon considers the war historian Paul Fussell's statement from *The Great War and Modern Memory* that "the further personal written materials move from the form of the daily . . . the closer they approach the figurative and the fictional," it is to support Fussell's claim that diurnal forms of autobiography like diary are the "most faithful record of the individual's experience" (Vernon, *Arms*, 23). For Vernon, memoir and autobiography are less authentic and less transparent in their representation of events because they cannot escape "the necessity of fiction" (23). Contrasted to the diary as a daily record, the memoir is evidently retrospective; "written after the fact, even if by authors with perfect memory, their very structure is an imposition on the actual events" (23). The key effect here, however, is the quality of immediacy in diary forms, what Wolf, in her discussion of the appeal of eyewitness and other first-person accounts in military documentary and anthologies, has argued is tied to dreams of "hotness": "hyperbolic immediacy aspires not to approximate the experience, but to erase the temporal gap entirely" ("Mediating," 327). Indeed, for Wolf, the emphasis on immediacy not only instates an unworkable condition of "innocence or purity" on the diary text but also risks "discouraging the production of more obviously mediated, but still antagonistic, forms of life writing: accounts that stand back and critically reflect on what has happened" (329). Wolf is critical of the sense, visible in statements like those by Vernon (and Fussell) that the "ordinary" record of war experience provided by soldiers or civilians, of which the qualifying feature is "being there," is one in which aesthetic qualities are necessarily eclipsed (or rendered irrelevant) by the proximity of the experience. A desire for "immediate" and visceral accounts is relayed structurally by media and publishing corporations as a strategy for market share, and this preference can ultimately come to obscure other kinds of experiences, ones that may indeed be more or less aesthetic, or more or less "sensational" (in the most sensory meaning of the term) but nonetheless relevant and authentic.

Do journalists' diary accounts come closer to approximating the productive hybrid space Wolf envisages, where both "emotive and antagonistic" reports can emerge? ("Mediating," 335). As Whitlock has closely explored in her analysis of journalists' memoirs from Iraq, the reporter in the context of personal narrative occupies a performative space in which new autobiographical subjects and genres are emerging (*Soft*, 149). As diarists, McGeough and Goltz engage with the "hotness" and immediacy of diary form in conveying experience, and they negotiate with the opportunity to construct and represent an authoritative interpretation of the journalistic identity that feels authentic. As Goltz has made clear, the diary as a form for publishing a personal account of reporting war is significant in creating access to markets and publishers, and McGeough also uses diary as an alternative to mass journalism, and perhaps also memoir. Documenting the life of the reporter as he goes about his daily business in the foreign conflict zone, McGeough is able to make visible the mundane and banal work of reporting—he shows himself endlessly sifting information, hunting for a balanced point of view, looking for Iraqi voices, and struggling for a humanitarian position. Using diary, then, is McGeough's narrative solution to the compromised position of the war correspondent, and he makes use of a formal as well as generic promise of the mode as self-surveillance. The memoirist, even if he does not take the opportunity, must negotiate with a generic reflectiveness of the genre as public history (Whitlock, *Soft*, 135). The diarist does this too, though the focus can perhaps more easily shift to experience as it unfolds, in the creation of a fluid space for representation that oscillates, sometimes seamlessly, between private and public, political and personal. In this way, Goltz and McGeough use diary to offer something more personal about events in Chechnya and Iraq. They want to tell more of the story than their previous reportage has allowed, and they want to reveal more about the journalist in this location. Lawrence Rosenwald says of reading diary: "A single entry is like a single sonnet; it may be a single literary gesture, aimed accurately at a reasonable and commonplace desire, revealing nothing of the gesturer but a reasonable and commonplace end and the power to achieve it. A *sequence* of entries will reveal not only power but also character" (*Emerson*, 17).

Here the diary appears self-consciously, as "evidence and testimony" for an experience of war reporting that is being explained further, and more intimately, than before.[6] This is journalism invested in telling the "ordinary" and "personal" story, the "real story," and it is through diary that Goltz and McGeough position an intention to reveal a more intimate account, quotidian and mundane, to produce a more personal commentary on a professional assignment and that will also then draw attention to the individual behind the journalist. That is, journalists' diaries provide a form for confession and witnessing that supplements (and also undermines) what is often framed as the objective, neutral, and unengaged ideal of reporting that mainstream media still largely promulgates.

Being there and seeing is a privilege, and it is an enterprise fraught with risk—physical and ethical. Narrative from the proximal site of such conflict is a valuable and highly sought commodity. Both Thomas Goltz and Paul McGeough use diary to respond to growing public concern about journalism as a practice, to negotiate an emphasis on individual knowing and independent credibility in telling news, and to fulfill a desire for transparency in their professional practice. They use personal narrative to represent a conflicted professional "I"—the fractured self of war, the traumatized witness to conflict, the exhilarated eyewitness to history. Part of the effect is structural: diary narrative allows for the reader to see the self in process, as it unfolds and changes over time, and it allows for the representation of contradiction and discontinuity in subjective experience. Ultimately, diary allows Goltz and McGeough to re-inscribe their own particular experiences in reporting on and responding to war, and it allows them to challenge or sometimes renew certain stereotypes of their profession.

In turning to autobiographical modes to reflect on, intervene in, and revise the journalistic profession, war correspondents also seek access to ways of negotiating the trauma, ethics, and grief that emerge out of personal contact to zones of conflict and disarray. For journalists like Goltz and McGeough, diary represents the prospect of amplifying a professional persona, of making visible the ethical and moral dilemmas of war correspondence that mainstream news media elide or ignore and of achieving and projecting a viable personal voice. Yet this production is also in tension with an economy of circulation in life narrative. McGeough and Goltz are authorized as journalists to speak, and they use their role to promote and validate their personal reflections. The diary allows them to move into a realm of representation that is frequently absent in the hot copy needed for a voracious news media cycle; here is the backstory to personal and ethical choices made on the ground that inform the reporting circulated "back home." The need to reassure a sceptical public of the authenticity of the journalistic subject, the need to provide an individual perspective in a time of media saturation and competing alternative coverage, the working through of an individual sense of ethical responsibility derived from being there and seeing are just some of the concerns war correspondents explore and make visible in their published diaries of war. However, and particularly concerning to Goltz, this kind of production also poses new ethical dilemmas. When journalists step into the role of life narrators they are again part of an industry, and they must sell product if they are to be heard.

War correspondence and its expression in diary open a space from which to consider the complicated production of authorized information in the formation of public knowledge. This is also about identifying how a historically marginalized or trivialized mode for self-representation is being renewed and re-energized. The diary, particularly as a genre for representing war and conflict, taps into broader contemporary concerns about authenticity and representation that are explored throughout this book. For journalists, however, the diary is a specific mode and a method for exploring and making visible ethical issues of reporting from sites of conflict and trauma that allows for the representation of the fractured and ambivalent self of the reporter who must work from within these zones. Diary publications by contemporary journalists embody powerful tensions in personal writing now, and they draw attention to the specifics of genre in transactions of the personal in this context.

4

The Intimate Appeal of Getting Closer

The Diary as Evidence and Testimony
in Nuha al-Radi, Riverbend, and Suad Amiry

> Please Vera, take the carrot cake with you, Lamia and I are on a diet . . .
> Please take it away otherwise we'll eat it in one go. We've both gained
> so much weight during this curfew.
>
> Suad Amiry, *Sharon and My Mother-in-Law*

*W*hat accounts matter when narratives of war and testimony circulate? Whose voices are listened to in the exposition and imposition of political debate and analysis? Who intervenes in the impersonal cartography of "lines on maps" and makes human the story of war and conflict? "Autobiography," argues Gillian Whitlock, "circulates as a 'soft weapon.' It can personalize and humanize categories of people whose experiences are frequently unseen and unheard" (*Soft*, 3). A "soft weapon" can intervene and reshape the personal, allowing it visibility and agency within the political sphere, but it can also be "coopted," becoming complicit in the "careful manipulation of opinion and emotion in the public sphere" that constitutes modern propaganda (3). In such contexts, attending to the flows and transits of life writing is also about being conscious of genre: "Genres of life narrative," says Whitlock, "and various ways of imagining the self autobiographically become emergent, dominant, and recessive" (16).

The diaries in this chapter are soft weapons, but they are also more than that. That is, in the production of life writing that Whitlock and others have identified as now flowing from the Middle East, the diary is a particular current and it must be attended to on its own terms. As I argued in the previous chapter, publishing diary allows the journalist a special privilege: to reflect on what makes a "good story," to negotiate an ethics of reporting war and conflict, and to offer a supplement to both a public image and a professional output as a war correspondent. The diarists in this chapter also have war stories to tell, but as Arab women living in conflict zones they lack journalistic authority. At the same time, their perspective "on the ground" is privileged as authentic; it is appealing to audiences in the "West." Moreover, as female diarists, these women enter into a tradition of diary writing that has a gendered history: they speak to centuries of female diary keeping and to the production of autobiographical records that have historically been marginalized, trivialized, and ignored— documents that also have the potential to subvert, disrupt, and contest. The epigraph to this chapter crystallizes this context. In Suad Amiry's diary account of life under Israeli occupation, the polite social ritual of sharing food is meshed to the larger context of circumspection and control that both enforces this occasion (a product of curfew) and makes it necessary (an act of group solidarity and survival). Diaries like these are evidence that private and intimate contexts are thick with political detail and public significance.

Nuha al-Radi, Riverbend, and Suad Amiry, citizens of war-torn locations, are female diarists who have reached a global and transnational audience. *Baghdad Diaries: A Woman's Chronicle of War and Exile* (2003) is Iraqi artist al-Radi's diary account of living through the first Gulf War and the beginnings of the second. In *Baghdad Burning: Girl Blog from Iraq* (2005), Iraqi blogger Riverbend uses an online diary to record the "aftermath" of being in Baghdad during the American occupation in Iraq since 2003 and to reach global audiences both current and belated to the events she describes. Palestinian architect Amiry's diary also begins as electronic media in the form of an e-mail diary from the occupied West Bank to close friends before being published as a book, *Sharon and My Mother-in-Law: Ramallah Diaries* (2003). Such uses of the diary show how the intimacy of the mode can be deployed: these diaries, and this is especially vivid in electronic iterations, represent diarists who are using the form to write back.

As eyewitness diaries from zones of entrenched conflict, the diarists in this chapter have a perspective that is particularly enticing to a public wary of "media spin" about Iraq and the Middle East. Writing in a genre with discursive links to a Western canon of private female experience, this production is also of interest to a transnational readership. Life narrative, as Whitlock says, is frequently "caught up in fantasies that the West likes to tell about itself," yet it is also available as a strategic mode, "an opportunity to talk back, to reflect on rhetorical processes of othering and self-fashioning" (*Soft*, 13). The diaries I explore in this chapter negotiate the interstitial territory of cross-cultural life narrative. Ultimately, the appeal of these diaries as ones that take us into the sequestered and gendered space of a Muslim household (something heavily emphasized in the respective blurbs and marketing material) means that issues

of gender and domesticity that already circle around diary assume new resonance. Here the diary moves around and across borders—real and symbolic—
of war-torn homelands and stereotyped cultural identities. Though public and
rhetorical, in that they actively engage with the prospect of audience (in the
case of Riverbend, literally, through the interactive capacity of her blog site)
and deal with events of historical and public significance, these diaries are
marketed on a promise to represent the private, intimate, and sequestered spaces
of exotic households: they promise to allow Western eyes to enter what are
stereotypically represented as forbidden gendered spaces of Arab cultures and
societies. These are locations that remain resolutely closed to the journalists
McGeough and Goltz, for example.

For Arab women, there is not a long tradition of published life narrative;
however, experiences of women in war zones produce new subjects and new
forms of diary. Here, as elsewhere, issues of gender and domesticity become
urgent as these diaries engage in the work of intercultural communication
across borders and zones of entrenched conflict. At the best of times, diaries are
provocative sites for autobiography. During war (and war diaries are an entire
subgenre), they raise urgent questions about the cultural politics of writing and
draw attention to the significance of personal discourse in this context. As a
form associated with women's experience, diaries are also an important medium
for the expression of female subjectivity, something Harriet Blodgett acknowledges in *Centuries of Female Days*, one of the earliest critical monographs on
women's diary writing and one of the first anthologies to turn deliberate attention
to a marginalized canon of women's autobiographical writing.

Blodgett's perspective on wartime diaries, however, bears analysis. Though
they are a rich and hitherto untapped source of women's diary writing, for
Blodgett these diaries are problematic. That is, valuable because they "show
women doing writing in relation to a major public event," she omits them from
her groundbreaking anthology because they fail a crucial criterion—they are
not private: "The restriction *private*, which is so important to me, does not signify
domestic, but rather *personal*: diaries not written or revised by the diarist for immediate reading by a second party" (*Centuries*, 13). The appeal of the diary, for
Blodgett, is the prospect of seeing "what women might say when free of others'
scrutiny," and women writing during an event of public significance are likely
be self-conscious: "Common sense says that when a diarist has a live recipient
for her words in view, she will have to adulterate her self-expression consider-
ably. She will have to present herself and can no longer just express herself in
terms of a personally acceptable image" (12–13). As a form of life narrative with
strong links to everyday and private experience, the diary is a genre in which

authenticity is a more than usually convincing claim—the form is stereotypically assumed to be both more authentic and more revealing, more naïve and more subjective, than other life narrative modes, and a large part of this conceptualization derives from a sense for diary as "private" writing. Blodgett's early concern for distinguishing between the diary as a "truly private" text, and then, between different states of "privacy," reminds us of what has been seen at stake here: "Certainly, any diarist who does not personally destroy her diary knows that someday she may chance to be read. . . . Nonetheless, although the anticipation of posterity may affect self-presentation, it still allows for some sense of present privacy and therefore potentially for more forthright self-declaration than does the sense of an immediate reader or public audience" (14). For Blodgett, gender is a key consideration here: the private female diarist has an opportunity to elude "self-consciousness," which is also about the "limitations of androcentric language" (13).

In her introduction to *She Left Nothing in Particular: The Autobiographical Legacy of Nineteenth-Century Women's Diaries* (2001), however, Amy L. Wink notes that while "valorizing the private voices of women" is a significant achievement of feminist readings of women's diaries, this perspective also produces a tension in which the "private voice" is located as the "better" and more authentic representation. Such a perspective is essentialist, dividing the public voice from its private self and eliding the complex links in between: "A woman's private self is one aspect of her multiplicity, and to claim her private voice as the "better" representation limits the significance of her public voice" (xiii). Instead, Wink reads for the stylistic choices women have used as a way of exploring subjective experience: "Women's diaries offer us a particularly powerful example of the manner in which women chose to structure their interpretations of their experiences" (xvii). In *Diary Poetics: Form and Style in Writers' Diaries, 1915–1962* (2010), Anna Jackson offers a similar perspective; however, she notes that in the 1980s and 1990s, when the diary began to receive recognition as a mode for "life writing," "the attention was directed away from the diary *as diary*, as generic differences [were] elided in order to focus on content rather than form, on women's lives rather than texts, on *bio* rather than *graphy*" (3).

In attending to the stylistics and poetics of a given diary text and even by subjects who aren't self-consciously literary (unlike the well-known writers Jackson focuses on), the rhetorical authority and potency of diary narrative comes into view. This is to see diary as not merely incidental, or coincidental, but as a literary genre with specific and recognizable effects and the author as an effective agent in shaping and responding to these. Such a perspective is particularly useful when turning to a context where both life writing and diary are relatively new, such as the Middle East. Indeed, Nawar Al-Hassan Golley, observing the entrenched stereotype that neither "discourses on orientalism nor studies of white feminism has been able to dislodge . . . that of an invisible and silent woman shrouded in mystery," argues instead that

> Arab women have been courageous and creative in the lives they have lived and the ways they have written about them. They have played a full part in political struggles and developed many different modes of writing the self. Arab women's autobiographical writings serve as more than a means by which to create images of the self through the writing act . . . they have served as a way to find a voice—whether private or public—through which to express what cannot be expressed in any other form. (*Arab*, xxvi)

As cosmopolitan subjects well versed in the literary canons of the West, diarists like al-Radi, Riverbend, or Amiry negotiate in complex ways the injunctions to femininity, privacy, and intimacy that have so frequently characterized the diary genre. Nonetheless, reviews of these texts emphasize that the diary is still viewed as a very particular form in relation to women's experience and that Arab women must also navigate this if they are to reach the audiences they desire.

Writing Back: *Baghdad Diaries* and *Baghdad Burning*

Commencing as so many diarists do, in response to a situation of crisis and as a way of preserving images and experiences that will soon be "gone," Iraqi artist Nuha al-Radi records that she is compelled "to keep some kind of record of what is happening to us" (*Baghdad*, 10). However, it is 19 January 1991, and "the third day of the war" before she begins her account: "It has taken me that long to realize that the war has actually begun and I am not dreaming it" (10). While the United States and allied forces bomb Baghdad, al-Radi's diary ebbs and flows as the intimate and domestic spaces of her world are reshaped traumatically by the urgency and violence of conflict. She performs wry cultural translations, preserving her insights: "Only we would escape from a war carrying freezers full of goodies. Iraqis have been hoarders for centuries. It's a national habit" (14). Entries recount indignities, absurdities, and dangers. Her Baghdad home has begun to double as a "refugee" hub for various relatives and friends, and she ironically renames it "*Funduq al-Saasa*, or Hotel Paradiso." Days that are conflated or passed over in her diary reveal a flattening trauma in the ongoing situation: "*Days 24 and 25*. I tell you, there is this sameness. Even war becomes routine" (31). Her "guests" have their own individual coping mechanisms, but al-Radi discovers that hers is to write: "Funny thing," she notes, "since the war started I have not been able to read a word, not even a thriller. Instead I'm writing this diary, not something I normally do" (17).

Nuha Al-Radi was born in Baghdad and traveled widely throughout her childhood for her father's job as Iraqi ambassador to Iran, and then India. She went to university in Switzerland and in Lebanon before pursuing her vocation at art school in London. Before the war, al-Radi had developed a reputation for ceramics, and her experience of conflict adds the impetus for a political dimension to her work. For example, *Embargo Art*, a series of sculptures generated from debris and other found material generated by the 1991 Gulf War conflict, is a sharp political statement—a sculpture of "whole families of people made of stone and car parts . . . the heads are painted stones and come off easily, a recognition of the reality that is present-day Iraq?" (*Baghdad*, 109). Alongside her art, al-Radi's diary becomes another means through which to comment on the political landscape; it becomes a parallel mode of intervention. The diary is cross-cultural, elite, reflecting her affinity and experience with Western culture even as it wrestles with her identity as Iraqi and "other": the first ten days of "shock and awe" in Baghdad produce a deep despair—"I don't think I could set foot in the West again. If someone like myself who is Western educated feels this way, then what about the rest of the country?" (19).

For Western readers, al-Radi's diary allows easy modes of identification, even as it complicates the perspective being offered: the new Iraqi anti-aircraft gun makes a sound such that "it is almost possible to fool oneself into thinking that one is attending a Philip Glass–like opera with an overlay of *son et lumière*" (*Baghdad*, 41). The grim Iraqi resilience she sees everywhere reminds her of Peter Sellers in *The Party*, "refusing to die and rising up again and again, another last gasp on the bugle" (47), and "Ma says she feels like Scarlet O'Hara in *Gone with the Wind*" (29). This cultural fluency, she notes, is mostly one-sided: "Sheikha says that the only thing the West knows about us is the fable of *The Thief of Baghdad*" (52). While many entries in the diary reveal a kind of mundane or banal reality, albeit of the most surreal order, some meditate directly on the U.S. president, "Mr Bush." By implication here, those readers who operate within his politics, and under his jurisdiction, are also brought into the frame: "What a brave man, he passes judgment on us while he plays golf far away in Washington" (41). The U.S. president is figured as a direct responder for the conflict in Baghdad—"Bush says he has nothing against the Iraqi people. Does he not know or realize that it is only the Iraqi people who have suffered? It's us, and only us, who've been without water electricity and water—a life of hard-ship" (59). Here, the war diary reaches across cultures with an urgent desire to draw readers into painful and foreign contact zones where they are, by implica-tion, complicit in the damage wreaked by Western occupation.

How do diarists like al-Radi use genre to take up a rhetorical position through which to speak of experience? How does life narrative travel differ-ently to audiences in a particular moment? After all, though Golley notes that women's autobiographical writing is a new phenomenon in Arab cultures, it does not therefore follow that it is naïve or unself-conscious.[1] As Arab women take up genres with entrenched literary histories they engage stereotypes of genre (and identity) and negotiate and mobilize diverse ways of speaking. This is also about form and voice. What does it suggest about the power of diary that it can produce the engagement with an audience in a way that, elsewhere, al-Radi's militant and political sculpture cannot? In many ways, al-Radi is able to acquire an agency as a diarist that she is denied as a political artist. However, the history of diary and its particular relationship to ideas and ideals of privacy remain significant. What are the benefits and what are burdens for the Arab diarist in this context? Al-Radi's diary publication is shaped by her moment of experience, and it is also subject to the cultural and international politics of publishing at the time.[2] However, Arab women are not only accessing osten-sibly "new" cultural forms of self-representation like diary, and challenging gendered (and cultural) ideals and ideas of privacy in this context, but are also active participants in the global technological moment of Internet communica-tion. That is, they are not only writing (and importantly, publishing) diaries but are also taking up new kinds of autobiographical representation such as blogs.

Even in its most public iterations, diary writing is connected to private experience and to unself-conscious (or self-consciously private) representation, and this remains a powerful trope of the genre. For Lynn Z. Bloom, the most evidently "public" form of a diary is the writer's diary ("Inscribing"). However, new contexts for life writing and diary, such as the apparently contradictory public/private mode of the online diary or blog, not only expand the poten-tial for even the "unprofessional" writer to conceptualize and access audience but also make it clear that privacy is a rhetorical position, one with particular potency in online locations. A correlation between privacy and authenticity, between unself-consciousness and truthfulness, however contested, is replayed in online spaces, and contemporary diarists (and their audiences) engage with this tension when they write in this location. In *Soft Weapons*, Whitlock identifies the blog as not only a new technology but also a new genre of autobiography, one that must also be understood as a "potent yet flawed" weapon in cross-cultural engagement (3).

Precisely for such reasons, seeing blogging as a new space for diaristic activity is useful; it shows that while certain conventional rhetorical assumptions about the diary form are being contested, others have evolved or endured. This is not to claim that blogs are simply diaries, a critical position I unpack in detail in chapter 5, but it is to observe that in many cases blogs do function as, or, and this may be equally important, they are *read as*, the diaries of their authors. Because of the kinds of complex rhetorical and self-representative issues they engage, war diaries and blogs are particularly interesting in this regard. For example, *Baghdad Burning: Girl Blog from Iraq* (2005) is the book of pseudonymous Iraqi blogger Riverbend's web diary of the same name.[3] From the outset, Riverbend activates certain assumptions of the diary mode: this is a temporal text "from" the location and experience it describes and it is a gendered form—though it is clear the description is mostly employed ironically, this is a *girl* blog. Though precluding the immediacy available to readers who followed the blog in "real time" as Riverbend posted between August 2003 and September 2004, the book publication of the blog remediates the appeal of diary narrative as a direct trace of writing, a representation from "the moment,"[4] and it makes available the original forward chronological sequence, which is more difficult to access in the digital archive.[5] As in conventional diary forms, Riverbend's blog is first person, mostly present tense, and serially constructed so that meaning is developed through accretion. For example, we learn over time that Riverbend, despite her initial declaration that "all you need to know" about her is that she's "female, Iraqi, and 24" and "I survived the war" (17 August 2003; 5), is more than willing to disclose personal details about her domestic life, her occupation (she was a computer programmer, "before conditions made it unsafe for Iraqi women to attend workplaces," 24 August 2003; 22), and her religion, "about half Shi'a and half Sunni" (22 December 2003; 170). She recounts at length her views on local social and political history, cites statistics, and collects and analyzes newspaper commentary on developing issues. This discourse is always juxtaposed: the complex politics of postwar Iraq cannot be separated from Riverbend's domestic world, something she reflects on and makes overt. "I have spent the last two days ruminating the political situation and . . . washing the roof. While the two activities are very different, they do share one thing in common—the roof, and political situation, are both a mess" (1 June 2004; 270). For readers, the narrative appeals as an insider account, a mundane and everyday vantage on a complex globally inflected political situation. "For more than a year," says James Ridgeway in his introduction to *Baghdad Burning*, "this anonymous 'girl blog' has made the war and occupation real in terms that no professional journalist could hope to achieve" (Riverbend, *Baghdad*, xi). As an alternative to "professional" journalism, Riverbend's appeal is in her experience:

"Once you are into Riverbend," says Ridgeway, "her war becomes your war" (xii). In her foreword to the book, the Egyptian novelist Ahdaf Soueif engages a similar register: "*Baghdad Burning* brings us as close to the war in Iraq as it's possible to be. And 'close' does not mean just knowing about electricity cuts and water shortages, about street battles and raids on homes; 'close' means right inside the heart and mind of a young Baghdadi woman as she lives through the war" (vii).

The appeal of personal narrative in this context is not for better information (as in more detailed or nuanced reports) but for more intimacy. This is why scholars like Derek Gregory contrast the personal or autobiographical perspective to "the world of high politics and lines on maps" and describe it as a narrative that brings "the struggle closer to the lives of ordinary men and women" (*Colonial*, 355). For Gregory, it is personal discourse such as diary or memoir that has the most potential to intercede in the stereotyped abstractions that fuel conflict, to perforate the political stratagems that rely on and perpetrate "indiscriminate categorizations of whole populations" (143).[6] However, and especially in contexts where "objective" information is understood as limited or constrained, diaries in particular are provocative sites for autobiography: they raise questions about the cultural politics of war writing, and they raise issues of genre and problems of ethics and authority that are also about voice and about authenticity. For example, a "close" perspective is highly appealing, but it is also limited in certain ways. Critics of Riverbend's blog routinely question her identity as an Iraqi, and as a female. Her blog is pseudonymous (a convention of online communication), and while her gender is identified (which doesn't necessarily mean it is believed), a query about identity in this context is also a query about authority and experience, about the authenticity of her point of view and the "truthfulness" of her information. In the interactive context of online discourse, Riverbend responds directly to her critics:

> You know what really bugs me about posting on the internet, chat rooms or message boards? The first reaction (usually from Americans) is "You're lying, you're not Iraqi." Why am I not Iraqi, well because, a. I have internet access (Iraqis have no internet), b. I know how to use the internet (Iraqis don't know what computers are), and c. Iraqis don't know how to speak English (I must be a Liberal). (18 August 2003; 6)

Simply choosing a form like the blog means Riverbend contests myths and stereotypes of Middle Eastern "primitivism" and the lives of Arab women.[7] Other parts of her narrative also pre-empt detractors: very early on she establishes that she was born in Iraq but lived abroad as a child for several years, "the reason why my English is good" (24 August 2003; 20). However, her blog also actively challenges other assumptions of authenticity and privacy that have significance for interpreting how contemporary diary narrative now circulates. Riverbend asserts from the outset that her blog is a personal account and its style is a private discursive mode: she intends to perform lots of "complaining and ranting" (17 August 2003; 5). This claim, while reinforcing the personal standpoint of the blog, also directly anticipates her audience, and it articulates how she wants such readers to approach the text. Riverbend's authority is experiential and it is subjective: she is a survivor of the war, "and that's all you need to know" (17 August 2003; 5), at least at first.

An assumption that private diary writing produces a more authentic representation shapes much early scholarship around women's diaries—indeed, it remains an influential stereotype of the genre, even for contemporary readers. Without doubt, the market for diaries by Arab women in the recent past is generated by the desire for authenticity, for privileged access into so-called Arab worlds, that is also signified in a designation "diary." That is, diaries have a particular relationship to knowledge, though this is also paradoxical. Margo Culley says: "as invaluable as women's life-records are as historical sources containing a kind of 'truth' about women's lives not found in other places, we must remember that diaries and journals are texts, that is, verbal constructs" (217). The diaries that are the focus of this chapter represent personal stories, and they are also political and rhetorical interventions by gendered subjects; these women are alert to complex and fraught political and cultural contexts, and they have shaped a voice, and found a form, to both speak of and respond to this experience.

Riverbend, for example, regularly responds to readers, sometimes encouraging them to comment, occasionally defending against criticism. Sometimes she responds to e-mails or thanks a reader for a concerned enquiry. She posts a particularly long entry on 12 September 2003. Just as U.S. citizens are the bulk of Riverbend's readers, so too Riverbend can peer into the "other side"—she has been following the blog of a U.S. solder: "I read his blogs and look at the troops and wonder, could that be him? It's strange to read stories from the 'other side.' I'm glad he's going to be able to go home, safely" (12 September 2003; 59). Riverbend, of course, is already "home"—and it's definitely not a safe place to be:

I haven't been writing these past few days because I simply haven't felt inspired. There's so much happening on a country-wide scale and so little happening

personally. Everything feels chaotic. Seeing what we're supposed to be living on
television differs drastically from actually living it. The moment you hear about
something terrible happening somewhere, you let it sink in, then "take stock"
and try to figure out who you have living there and how you can contact them.
(12 September 2003; 61)

This post, however, apart from being long (not unusual for Riverbend, who
sometimes updates her blogs four or five times over the course of a day) and
containing several updates, also reveals that Riverbend is not only accounting
for her time but is being called to account: "Someone asked me why I didn't
write anything yesterday mentioning September 11. I'll be perfectly honest—I
had forgotten about it until 2pm. I woke up to no electricity, washed up, and
went into the kitchen to help out with breakfast" (12 September 2003; 63). The
blog, despite her assertions and positioning of it as a personal "rantlog" (17
August 2003; 5), is not simply Riverbend's private reflection, nor is it simply her
own perception of her experience; it is responsive, interactive, and shaped by
the questions, as well as challenges, offered by its various (mostly U.S.) readers.[8]

A diarist who "writes back" as a blogger or invites comment further unsettles readers who are concerned with a stable authorial identity or value
"unself-consciousness" and privacy as the hallmarks of an authentic personal
account (or the signifier of a diary). Readers of the blog participate in and to
some extent help create the rhythms and discontinuities that the narrative is
shaped by—that is, Riverbend's "moment" of experience includes her inter-
actions with her blog audience, and the flexible mode of diary records this.
Moreover, responses to the text like those offered by Soueif and Ridgeway, that
frame the narrative for a new, belated readership, make it clear that this account
is primarily valued for how "close" the narrative brings us to the experience of
Riverbend, and an interpretation and presentation of this blog as a diary is
crucial in this. That is, while privacy is no longer an overriding concern here, the
appeal of the diary is connected to its status as a private domestic and private
personal representation, and this remains intact even in new and ostensibly
more public forms like blogs.

Diaries are texts that arouse expectations of disclosure, revelation, and intimacy, and the personal perspective is an empathic point of entry for readers, as
well as a powerful platform for the articulation of what Brinda Mehta calls
"creative" dissidence ("Dissidence"). Indeed, Mehta elsewhere observes that
the enduring construction of diary narrative as private and intimate cannot be
extricated from the long association to women's writing and to "feminine" form
(*Rituals*). Mehta, for example, argues that the "unmediated expression of intimate

feeling inscribed within an immediacy or urgency of experience" that al-Radi
offers in her diary primarily draws power as "a woman-version of the invasion
[that] undermines the self-centeredness of the master narrative" (*Rituals*, 211). A
perceived link between diary and female experience is key here, and Mehta
draws here on constructions of the diary as a feminine form; she cites ideas of
l'écriture féminine, to emphasize her sense of the diary as uniquely linked to "experience as text" (*Rituals*, 210).

Like the restriction of privacy, contemporary critics have challenged the
stereotype of diary as an essentially "female" mode.[9] Yet gender matters when
the "insider" is also an Arab woman—Mehta has observed that stereotypes of
Arab women as "beleaguered" and at "the mercy of the savagery of their men
and the backwardness of their religion" have become resurgent in a "post 9/11"
backlash against Arab cultures worldwide (*Rituals*, 1). The appeal of private
narrative from Arab women plays into the stereotypical registers that Mehta
identifies—these texts promise access to "cloistered" personal spaces. To some
degree, Riverbend and al-Radi both play into gendered stereotypes about diary
writing: Riverbend subtitles her blog "Girl Blog from Iraq" and opens the narrative with a "warning" to "expect a lot of complaining and ranting" (17 August
2003; 5) that ironically recognizes the dismissive way in which women's critical
voices can be received. The mass-market edition of al-Radi's diaries also
emphasizes gender; it is subtitled "A Woman's Chronicle of War and Exile"
(*Baghdad*).

Gendered assumptions about diary play out in other ways too. Mehta says
that al-Radi "documents life under siege through the collapsing of the public/
private divide in which private concerns receive public articulation in the form
of uncensored political commentary and social critique" ("Dissidence," 225),
and *Baghdad Diaries* is notable for al-Radi's willingness to engage with political
discourse. However, this commentary on public politics is informal, juxtaposed
with descriptions of the everyday domestic and other routine activities she is
also urgently engaged in. Lizzie Skurnick, however, reviewing the 2003 edition
of *Baghdad Diaries*, describes the diary as "by turns lyric and heavy-handed,
hackneyed and enlightening" and complains that al-Radi's political insights
lack substance or usefulness because they "gravitate between resentment and
pique" (Review). Emphasizing the difficulty that can follow personal narrative
as it engages with the public political, Skurnick says that "al-Radi's strength is
in the quotidian—not the bombings but the bucket of water she receives on her
birthday." Skurnick finds al-Radi's *Diaries* ineffective as political discourse, the
domestic frame of the narrative failing to convey the complexity of "life under
Saddam." Instead, Skurnick anticipates the possibilities of "our era of embedded

journalists and the Web" in conveying a properly "complex" picture of the region.

The diary is a form in which the mundane and banal, the highly subjective, are anticipated and regarded as authentic. While "everyday life" has more resonance in the public sphere at this time than any previous historical moment, the domestic and the mundane are still understood to be primarily marginal locations. The consequences of living in a war zone, however, mean that every-day life and the domestic sphere can become more overtly (and more urgently) imbued with political meaning. As an Arab woman, al-Radi uses her daily diary to talk back to stereotypes of Iraqi life and culture—to intervene in the "othering" that is a consequence of ideologically inflected conflict. That is, while contemporary diaries (especially online ones) lack the kind of unself-consciousness or isolation that early critics like Blodgett exalt, they nonetheless employ a highly intimate and personal perspective to focus on the private do-mestic and the intimate daily, and they appeal to the reader as a text closer than any other to the author's subjective experience in this zone. While River-bend's blog ostensibly unsettles many of the assumptions that traditionally underwrite a diary text, the response of reviewers and critics highlights the personal and unique nature of her perspective; they vaunt her voice as one that enables intimacy, insight, and authentic connection with her experience from inside Baghdad. Even in new forms, such as blogs, the authority of the diary as a private mode, as a particularly personal genre, continues to shape expectations and responses to a life narrative even though the parameters and particularities of these assumptions have evolved or changed. Moreover, while expectations about diary as a private and feminine genre may in part enable certain narra-tives to circulate more freely—and the blog as diary is an example here, because it can easily be marketed as a unique "alternative" to other kinds of information and as an insight into the "private" culture and experience of an Arab woman—genre can also impose limits on how this narrative is interpreted, particularly in terms of its perceived capacity to convey a political viewpoint. This is some-thing Skurnick, for example, illustrates when she denigrates al-Radi's diary as appropriately personal, but lacking information: "Her news is as secondhand as anything on the BBC" (Review).

Writing Borders: *Sharon and My Mother-in-Law*

"The tremendous international success enjoyed by Suad Amiry's *Sharon and My Mother-in-Law*, which has already been released in several languages," says John Collins, "speaks to the reading public's desire for a more human account of the

Palestinian predicament than is typically provided in the corporate media"
(Review, 1). What Collins calls the desire for a "more human account" also
drives a thriving industry in life narrative. Moreover, while contemporary audiences might desire access to "other" experiences and lives, this is not always a
fair exchange. Sometimes Riverbend's cross-cultural fluency, her grasp of
American idiom, and even her technological access work against perceptions of
her authenticity—she does not fit with stereotypical expectations of the Middle
Eastern woman. Susan Stanford Friedman, describing teaching *Baghdad Burning*
to her undergraduate women's studies students, notes that "they are surprised
that there are any computers in Iraq at all, let alone a Muslim woman who is
clearly more modern than they are in computer literacy and her use of the
blogging medium" ("Futures," 1708). Suad Amiry is also a cosmopolitan subject, educated, technologically literate, and invested in audience. Amiry's diary
publication, *Sharon and My Mother-in-Law*, composed from diary entries and
e-mails, spans a period of eleven years (1981–92) in Ramallah, during which
Amiry "loved, worked, fell in love, married and acquired a mother-in-law" (ix).
This generic marriage plot, however, is juxtaposed to the political: Amiry is a
Palestinian resident of the West Bank, and the mother-in-law of the title, reluc-
tantly evacuated from her home in central Ramallah, stays with Amiry during
the 2002 Israeli siege of the city.

Like Riverbend, Amiry claims an "ordinary" perspective: this narrative is
concerned with the mundane and the domestic and so with the politics that has
inflected each aspect of everyday life for these women and their families in these
places at these times. Here "Sharon" (the incumbent Israeli Prime Minister) is
as significant a presence in Amiry's everyday life as her "mother-in-law"—and
equally as intrusive in Amiry's "private" life. Moreover, Amiry "makes strategic
and effective use of hegemonic gender constructions, playing the role of the
'hysterical' or 'crazy' woman in order to exert power in an interaction with
(male) Israelis" (Collins, Review, 1). Using diary, a stereotypically female genre,
is also part of this strategy. There is a therapeutic impetus here, too:

> Writing my personal war diaries . . . started as a form of therapy . . . late in
> the evening, I would often sit down and send e-mails to friends and relatives
> who were anxious to know what life was like for me during those terrible times.
> Writing was an attempt to release tension caused and compounded by Sharon
> and my mother-in-law. I hesitantly shared these thoughts with some intimate
> friends. (Amiry, *Sharon*, viii)

Compared to the blog, e-mail is a closed network. Amiry's "hesitant sharing"
in this context is the product of a desire not to worry or concern her friends,

balanced with a need to tell what is happening to her and her life. As a publication, the intimacy of this exchange is communicated by its fashioning as a diary. What is the significance of diary in this version? Is it simply a convenient nomination for a chronologically spaced narrative? What happens to the unique value of diary as "trace" once it has been organized and shaped for publication?

Contemporary diaries shift focus from the moment of inscription and intention to the capacity of diary to do and be certain things in the world. "Diarists," Friedman notes, are typified by a "personal rhetorical stance," and this stance is strategic ("Futures," 1708). As a blogger, Riverbend "writes openly for a virtual public," but she also retains the personal perspective and authenticity of the diarist, and this is very significant in the uptake and reception of her account (Friedman, "Futures," 1708). For Amiry, diary writing is also an activity crucially linked to politics (as it has been for diarists in the past). Daily living in Palestine is a litany of absurdity and "senselessness"—a diary is a useful method to document such experiences, and it also has rhetorical power. After all, any movement through the heavily regulated zones and borders of Ramallah requires careful daily negotiations, and Amiry uses her diary to record these experiences and also to reconcile them. When a young and "easily rattled" Israeli soldier repeatedly demands Amiry stop "looking at him" during one routine border crossing, she ends the standoff and eventually averts her eyes. In her diary, she contemplates the response she wanted to give, one that could not safely be articulated at the time:

> Fucker, I thought to myself. So easily irritated by a stare!
>
> I wonder what your reaction would have been if you had lived under occupation for as many years as I had, or if your shopping rights, like all your other rights, were violated day and night, or if the olive trees in your grandfather's orchards had been uprooted, or if your house demolished, or if your sister could not reach her school, or if your brother had been given three life sentences, or if your mother had given birth at a checkpoint, or if you had stood in line for days in the hot August summers waiting for your work permit, or if you could not reach your beloved ones in Arab East Jerusalem?
>
> A stare and you lose your mind! (*Sharon*, 69)

A dangerous and humiliating experience at the time becomes a moment of resistance when recounted into writing; later the incident is even further reinterpreted (and its power dynamic further inverted) as a catalyst for humor when Amiry's husband and cousin contemplate an absurd legal limit for the encounter: the husband in court to defend a wife who refused to stop staring at a soldier.

In the quotidian and documentary perspective of diary, Amiry reproduces for her reader a highly politicized space: the Palestinian West Bank. This is not just a physical space, the endless obstacles to Palestinian movement that are enacted within the "permit-raj" of Ramallah, but also a psychic one. In a location where her dog acquires a Jerusalem passport—guaranteeing unimpeded movement—but Amiry and her car need two different permits to get through a single checkpoint, the absurdity of politics in the everyday recurs. Here the diary acquires power as a narrative strategy—it is an authoritative "alternative" to sanctioned public discourse, and it articulates a perspective not usually permitted in this (literal and physical) space. It is one of those "other ways" that Gregory says are so vital and urgently needed for "mapping the turbulent spaces and times in which and through which we live" (*Colonial*, 12). Indeed, Amiry herself explains that she has written her diaries in order to "step out of the frame and observe the senselessness of the moment," and that doing so is a "valuable self-defense mechanism against the Israeli occupation of our lives and souls" (*Sharon*, ix). As a diary, this text intervenes in those processes "set in motion through mundane cultural forms and practices that mark people as irredeemably 'Other' and that license the unleashing of exemplary violence against them" (Gregory, *Colonial*, 16). That is, here diary is a distinctive narrative device that not only is methodologically suited to the kind of narrative and experience Amiry wants to represent but also secures certain rhetorical effects. Reviewer Nomi Morris, for example, approves of "Amiry's approach, to chronicle the stuff of daily life, rather than to pontificate on weighty issues," an approach that has also been successful with her global readership ("Israeli," 18). Nonetheless, while Amiry's diary frequently challenges distinctions between the domestic and the political, the private and the public, a set of restrictions is also implied here: "Being a female writer interested in the 'mundane' aspects of life perhaps also helped—no big politics and no preaching" (Amiry in O'Connor, "Human," 3). Like genre, gender is part of the complex negotiations a subject must make in representing and accounting for their experience:

> Yossi stood still; like all men, he didn't know what to do with a crying woman.
>
> I could see that he was capable of handling Palestinian demonstrators, rebels, stabbers, terrorists. He could handle bombs, dynamite, tanks, fighter planes and submarines. He was trained to handle them all.
>
> *BUT NOT A CRYING WOMAN.*
> *NOT A WOMAN FREAKING OUT.*
>
> I watched a stunned Yossi walk out of his office. Soon after, he came back with another Marlboro cigarette, another mud (which I drank this time), and a

piece of paper with Hebrew scribbles on it, which he claimed said, "Give this
[crazy] woman her *hawiyyeh*." (Amiry, *Sharon*, 43)

Like Morris, Rachel Cooke finds *Sharon* refreshingly different: it is not "boringly
political" or "highly lyrical"—the "camps" into which Cooke claims books
about Palestine usually fall ("Emails"). In *Sharon*'s detail, Cooke finds an unexpected and seductive "sameness": the narrative attracts her for its nonpoliticized
perspective (a focus on the mother-in-law rather than Sharon), and she is sure
this is why it appeals to other "western ears" as well.[10] Moreover, Amiry is "the
antibook [*sic*] of what most in the West imagine to be a "typical" Palestinian
woman. She drinks, she smokes, she does not cover her hair" (Cooke, "Emails").
Amiry's "difference" reassures Cooke: "In a place where the absurd is a feature
of daily life, it takes a particularly sane sensibility to delineate it . . . I have rarely
met anyone as sane as Suad Amiry" ("Emails"). Amiry's distance from racist
stereotypes of Palestinian women—and so her closeness to American and
Western ones, to "us"—her disavowal of the "political" or the "lyrical" in the
narrative scope, and her focus on daily, domestic routines that transcend a national context endear her to Cooke and ensure that the diary, and Amiry, enter
smoothly into Western literary markets.

The lack of an overt polemic in *Sharon* fits with assumptions about diary
writing in general and the genre itself as quotidian and extraliterary. *Sharon*,
however, is far from a nonpolitical representation; Collins reads the diary for
more nuance than Morris or Cooke will allow. Indeed, for Collins a focus on
the domestic and the daily in this context must be seen as charged with political
significance; the mundane is *the* location of political struggle in the Israel and
Palestine conflict on the West Bank, and the daily negotiation of multiple checkpoints and borders is revealed as detrimental to individuals on both sides, part
of what "closes off the possibility of uncoercive contact between Israelis and
Palestinians" (Review, 2). In short, says Collins, "this perversion of the personal
by the political is Amiry's primary message" (2). For each of these reviewers,
the form of the representation here as a diary is crucial, and Collins in particular
emphasizes this though he also ultimately qualifies his assessment: "Readers
and teachers looking for a book that provides deep historical and political context
will need to look elsewhere, for this is not Amiry's purpose. Given the nature of
the diary form, the choice is entirely appropriate" (2).

The form of Amiry's narrative as a diary is particularly significant for readers
and reviewers, and it seems to confirm that this narrative is not "abstractly" or
threateningly political, indicating something about what writers and readers
seek from the diary genre. That this narrative is, nonetheless and intrinsically, a

political representation does not contradict its status as an "ordinary" and personal account. In discussing the production of personal narrative from Palestine in particular, Cynthia Franklin and Laura E. Lyons offer further context for this kind of representation, and particularly in this location: "Representations of the Israeli–Palestine conflict are notoriously one-sided[;] . . . Palestinians are most often represented through the endless repetition of images of suicide bombers" ("Bodies," xiv). So it is they are excited to discover the 2003 anthology *Live from Palestine: International and Palestinian Direct Action against the Israeli Occupation*. This text is unusual: "The volume's organization insists upon the primacy of Palestinian accounts of life under the Israeli regime and resistance to the Occupation," and it is multifaceted as a "variety and mix of genres . . . diaries, emails, journal entries, phone interviews, essays, statements, eyewitness accounts, photographs, maps" (xv–xvi). Further, the volume pays particular attention to eyewitness accounts: it "includes structural analysis," but "it does not privilege such writing over more immediate, first person accounts" (xvi). Ultimately, whether it is the exigency conveyed by "interviews with ISM or other human rights workers that take place in hotels under siege and under the pressure of dying cell phone batteries," what is key for Franklin and Lyons is that "these eyewitness accounts are resolutely unaestheticized. While they are often quite arresting, there is no sense that they have been crafted to produce their effects" (xvi).

The daily, informal, multiple, and spontaneous genres characteristic of personal narrative are polemical in a distinctly subtle way. Crucially, for Franklin and Lyons, these modes are "unaesthetic," because they appear uncrafted. This kind of narrative is framed as a subversive alternative, a counterbalance to official narratives, and to historical and cultural analysis—narrative fettered by crafting, construction, and intent. It is as a mode that gives access to the kind of "unaesthetic" representation Franklin and Lyons acclaim that the diary is relevant here. That is, the diary is a genre that appears to accommodate for representing unrest or discontinuity that is not easily contained in other autobiographical forms. "Does war create some kind of atmosphere in which the diary, and other 'nontraditional' autobiographical writings, flourish?" asks Jane DuPree Begos, concluding, "it certainly seems to" (70). For Franklin and Lyons, a "nontraditional" alternative to autobiography "proper" is crucial; they attend to diary as a genre in which this objective is particularly close. For example, they discuss a diary excerpt that narrates a quotidian and mundane perspective: "the daily but intolerable navigations through checkpoints that make going to work often an impossibility," and the diary replicates this experience as an account that allows "for no sense of closure." Instead, it serves to "underline the ongoing nature of the crisis" and to reveal a "sense of emergency" that is a daily experience here (Franklin and Lyons, "Bodies," xvi–xvii).

The kind of representation—urgent, ongoing, and daily—that Franklin and Lyons find so unexpected and so important in *Live from Palestine* is characteristic in diary. But is it unaesthetic? In the terms that Franklin and Lyons set, "resolutely unaestheticised" characterizes the eyewitness accounts of *Live from Palestine* because, "while they are often quite arresting, there is no sense that they have been crafted to produce their effects" ("Bodies," xvi). For Franklin and Lyons, only this kind of eyewitness narrative, which is uncrafted, spontaneous, and "unaestheticised," is able to reproduce the "emergency" quality of everyday life in Palestine. It is a mode vastly different from analysis, history, politics, or critique, yet it is powerful and urgent: these stories "serve to expose conditions from which there is no easy recovery" and to reveal "forms of violence that must be stopped" and that are otherwise covered over or obscured in different kinds of representation (xvii).

Is the diary only viable here under the terms that Franklin and Lyons offer? Amiry's account is not a first run or naïve text; it is a composed account, organized chronologically and with a self-aware narrator. A text like *Sharon* derives from the everyday and the ordinary, yet it is also crafted. For example, Collins makes special note of the "diary form" of *Sharon*, approving the genre as the appropriate "choice" for Amiry to reflect on her experience and convey her message (Review, 2). The "unaesthetic" is also an aesthetic goal: genre is deployed precisely to mobilize a realism that depends on the projection of non-literary, uncrafted narrative effect. Amiry and her publishers make use of this.

As diarists, Nuha al-Radi, Riverbend, and Suad Amiry bring attention to an increasingly prominent role of the diary genre and form in the early twenty-first century. In locations distant, ideologically and geographically, from the Western tradition of this mode, al-Radi, Riverbend, and Amiry each reveal the tenuousness of conventional interpretations of diary as private, personal, and marginal. Moreover, each of these published diaries reveal that there is a shift to diary as a flexible description for accumulated, personally orientated material. So al-Radi "updates" her text to better reflect the cultural moment of its circulation, and like Amiry, she finds diary a useful voice to speak across cultures. Riverbend also uses diary to access privileges attached to the form. Furthermore, as a blogger, she mediates with assumptions about diary that emerge freshly in new media contexts. However, each of these diarists also reveals that despite this formal flexibility, the diary is a mode also heavily inscribed with particular expectations and desires. What is posited in the desire to perceive personal narrative as uncrafted, spontaneous, and deeply and thoroughly ordinary is an aesthetics of realism that demands such narrative conceal the trace of construction, manipulation, and selection that must inevitably result from any act of writing, and this has consequences too for the kind of subjectivity these texts shape and represent.

Reading Arab Women's Diary: On Not Being *Anne Frank*

"Ironically," says Gillian Whitlock in *Soft Weapons*, "the power of autobiography to induce empathy across cultures is also its risk" (15). Deploying this insight in a different context, Leigh Gilmore and Elizabeth Marshall observe, "identification is facilitated, even propelled, by life stories, yet it risks short-circuiting an encounter with difference by mirroring the reader's self-image as a compassionate person worthy of being addressed" ("Girls," 686). A desire to not only encounter but also to identify and empathize with the "other" underpins the circulation of life narrative in contemporary times. And of course, while the autobiographical "other" is a figure as likely to be found at "home" as abroad—see the thriving U.S. domestic industry in "misery memoir"—the context of transnational life narrative presents a clear occasion to consider how self-representations from different geopolitical and geocultural circumstances enter into popular frames, to what degree this transit is successful, and for whom. After all, cultural and ethnic differences do not deter readers from comparing Riverbend's Baghdad blog to one of the most famous published war diaries in Western literature, *The Diary of Anne Frank*. Reviewers on the Internet marketplace Amazon.com also invoke Anne Frank to discuss Riverbend: "Iraq's Anne Frank?" asks David Dix, in the title of his customer review, while customer Jalus asserts: "Anne Frank in Baghdad."[11] And when the global editor of *Ms. Magazine* Robin Morgan declares *Baghdad Burning: Girl Blog from Iraq*, in an inside cover endorsement for the published book, "the 21st-century version of Anne Frank's Diary," adding, "we can only hope that this story ends less tragically," she is drawing links between two very different historical figures as well as framing an intertextual relation between a "classic" diary and a very new form of diary, the blog. In both cases, the reference works to authorize and extend the significance of the text and its form.

In certain ways, Riverbend fits an association with Anne Frank—yet, though her Western education makes it likely she has heard the story, she certainly never mentions it. So while using "girl" in her title may indeed be an oblique reference to Anne Frank's *Diary of a Young Girl*, it is also more likely simple pragmatics: as an anonymous online avatar, Riverbend's gender is not necessarily apparent and must be acknowledged. Nonetheless, on Amazon .com, detractors accuse her of being a man: "It also doesn't seem like a very convincing female viewpoint," argues one customer reviewer: "There is a glaring lack of authentic femaleness about it. I smell another 'Diary of Hitler'" (J. Vargo "bibliophile," 22 September 2006).[12] The prospect that Riverbend could be a hoax (misleading in terms of gendered, ethnic, or ideological identity) is discussed by a readership conditioned in these times to be suspicious of imposture. Yet, when the reviewer Jai Singh notices that the "American inflection" in her tone "combined with her anonymity raises questions about Riverbend's real identity," he also notes that these questions are partly satisfied through her use of the diary form ("Blog," 3). That is, the diary allows for the representation of an experience over time and this is authoritative: "Riverbend demonstrates deep familiarity with local customs and traditions . . . She even dedicates a parallel weblog to her Iraqi recipes. If she is a fake she is doing tedious research" (3).

Riverbend's diary is contentious. Her identity as an Iraqi is crucial to perceptions of this narrative as authentic, but online this cannot be substantiated in any conventional way. As an authoritative interpretative frame, then, the association with Anne Frank is useful as an intertextual reference that links to an ideal of girlhood culturally disparate readers can identify with.[13] Nonetheless, this association can also work otherwise. When the reviewer Lizzie Skurnick, for example, invokes Anne Frank in a comparison to the Iraqi diarist Nuha al-Radi, she does so to find al-Radi lacking: "Anne Frank's literary executors can rest easy: those seeking an insider's view on despotic regimes will be unmoved by Nuha al-Radi's *Baghdad Diaries*, which chronicle the travails of an Oxford-educated, upper-class artist living under Saddam Hussein" (Review). The inconsistences of this kind of cross-cultural and cross-historical association are here mobilized as critique: for Skurnick, al-Radi is the wrong kind of subject — not confined enough, not deprived enough or young enough, and not enough at risk — "while she discusses the talk of robberies, kidnappings, and rapes, her news is as secondhand as anything on the BBC," concludes Skurnick.

The Anne Frank diary is the canonical war diary. The story of a thirteen-year-old Jewish girl who, while hiding from the Nazis in an attic with her family, kept a diary documenting the ordeal as well as her awakening sense of self-identity, is part of popular cultural memory of the Holocaust. In her discussion of *The Diary of Anne Frank*, Victoria Stewart notes a "key image" is of Frank as a "basically uncomplicated figure with whom we can all identify" (*Women's Autobiography*, 85). Part of this identification has to do with genre. The diary is a locus where desires about Frank, about the Holocaust, and about trauma can cluster;

it is also where particular anxieties are revealed. So Stewart spends some time working through ways in which the diary as a genre exists in tension with ideas of private documentation and public history. She notes that Frank may have been "writing with a direct view to publication" and that to this end, there are experiments with form: Frank reflects in her diary on its likeness to the "detective story" and wonders about the future significance of the record for history. Stewart argues that, in view of these things, Frank self-consciously amends her style. Thus, "her diary defies the usual definitions of that form"—that is, as an unself-conscious (private) document (Stewart, *Women's Autobiography*, 91). However, for Stewart the issue is not about a "violation" of form but a loss of authority. She notes that textual and other inconsistencies in the Anne Frank *Diary* have "been used as a means of questioning the diary's authenticity by Holocaust deniers" (91). Ultimately, Stewart finds Frank's diary a "fragile text to bear the weight of critical apparatus or critical interpretation. . . . Frank's diary is always complete in itself, as a piece of Holocaust testimony, and always partial and deficient as an historical document" (109).

Apart from observing an ongoing tension between the diary as history and testimony, it is evident that as a war diarist Frank embodies a series of qualities. In the Anne Frank story, the spheres of good and evil, innocence and corruption are clearly established. Alexandra Zapruder notes the powerful mythology that has become embodied in Frank's diary: "not only as a document that could shed light on a facet of the history of the Holocaust but as a symbol, capable by its intimacy of rescuing the girl; by the resonances of her voice, rescuing her generation; and, by its seemingly dominant theme of hope for humanity, rescuing all of us in the process" (*Salvaged*, 7). This Anne Frank is "the most innocent and tragic of victims, not an adult, but a child, and not a survivor, but a martyr"—her qualities of innocence and youthfulness are embodied in the diary as artifact (4).[14] Zapruder says that "while adults' diaries have long been depended upon to yield useful information . . . the diaries of children have been reduced to rescuers of meaning or evokers of emotion" (11). The myths of innocence and transparency that attend cultural conceptions of childhood intensify in the marketing and reception of children's war diaries—while the adult is considered with suspicion, the child is idealized as a vessel for truth.[15]

In such a context, neither *Baghdad Burning* nor *Baghdad Diaries* is comparable to *The Diary of Anne Frank*. (Perhaps for obvious reasons, no review I have found draws the Jewish Anne Frank into correlation with the Palestinian diarist Amiry.) These diarists are not children (even when they strategically are "girls"), and as representatives of cultures and ethnicities constructed as "other" to the West—as enemies in the "war on terror"—neither are they on the "right" side.

Invoking Frank, then, is to facilitate access for a Western audience, reminding readers of an existing cultural register for interpretation of war diary that affixes a moral value and a horizon of expectations. Embodied here is the ideal of an innocent (unself-conscious) narrator recording from the heart with abandon. This is a powerful myth of diary in this context and an ideal that shapes the marketing and reception of war diaries—even those by adult women in cultural (and technological) contexts very different to the Frank story.

Canonical expectations make cross-cultural transits of Arab women's diaries into Western markets a complicated process, for all these appear to offer an authentic and original insight into unknown worlds. War diaries by Arab women enter Western markets as evidence and testimony, and they confront expectations established by earlier and very different narratives. During war, diary allows individuals to represent kinds of experience that may otherwise go unremarked. Are these diaries an effective mode of political intervention? Whitlock has observed that personal narrative can be all too easily coopted into political frameworks, subject to fashion as much as the "soft power" of media spin or political propaganda (*Soft*, 54). Al-Radi, Riverbend, and Amiry lack the professional authorization or publication networks of journalists like Goltz and McGeough, yet their diary-narratives of invasion and insurgency are powerful, and sought after by readers eager for authentic contact with an exotic other. Offered in the familiar form of the diary, these narratives offer unsettling reports that must simultaneously draw in and differentiate a disparate readership. Both historically and discursively the diary is associated with the domestic and the private. However, in the reception of these war diaries by Arab women we see that their capacity to draw readers into this sphere is limited in various ways.

Contemporary diaries by women in the Middle East alert us to the ongoing tension between diary as personal testimony and as a historical document. In these diaries the traditional gendered and domestic associations of the diary assume new force and resonance. However, by reading these three Arab women's diaries together it is possible to see their very different histories as texts caught up in cross-cultural engagements and battles for authenticity that have broader implications for autobiographical self-representation and personal writing now. As autobiographical fashions ebb and flow, the diary again and again surfaces in contexts where authenticity, intimacy, and ordinariness are urgent concerns.

5

Sex, Confession, and Blogging

The Online Diaries
of Belle de Jour and Abby Lee

> One of the main (social) functions of a journal or diary is precisely to be
> read furtively by other people, the people (like parents + lovers) about
> whom one has been cruelly honest only in the journal.
>
> Susan Sontag, Reborn

The back cover description of *The Mammoth Book of Sex Diaries: The Ultimate
Collection of Sex Blogs* (2005) makes its premise very clear: "These compelling
journals of the most intimate kind come straight from the hottest blogs on the
internet. Where people once confided in their diaries, more and more of them
are now writing blogs—web logs—updated daily and posted on open sites for
the world to read." An imprint of British publisher Constable & Robinson, the
Mammoth "book of" series is a long-running and popular series of themed
anthologies. Published in paperback, and aimed squarely at a mass-market
audience, the series is devoted to various kinds of "genre" literature: true crime,
fantasy, erotica, and adventure, for example. *The Mammoth Book of Sex Diaries:
The Ultimate Collection of Sex Blogs* offers two different genres, one very old, and one
still emerging, and links its collection under the theme of sex. The editor of *Sex
Diaries*, Maxim Jakubowski, however, draws mostly on the diary in framing the
content of the anthology as well as the motives of a reader who approaches it:

> as human beings, we have an unerring curiosity to read what goes on in others'
> minds. How often have we wondered what a close acquaintance might be writing
> in his or her diary? About you? About others you know? About events which
> both of you might have been involved in, of a public and private nature? . . . the
> Internet has changed all that . . . a blog is strictly speaking a web log. A diary or
> journal that anyone can write and publish online, and which is therefore visible

to all and sundry . . . these are real people and they write about their lives, their sex lives, with total abandon. No taboos, no restrictions by the so-called rules of society. (Jakubowski, *Sex Diaries*, vii–viii)

In 2005, and particularly in a print-published format, the blog is still a relatively marginal form. A link to diary in the title of this collection of blogs, then, does two things: it establishes a "new" genre in relation to an old and familiar one and it deploys certain stereotypical understandings that serve strategic and rhetorical ends. While critics have problematized the association, something I consider later in this chapter, the blog as diary has a very clear and popular appeal, one that finds particular energy in a context such as that described by Jakubowski, as the intimate disclosure of an individual sex life.

The sex blogger, disclosing personal and intimate detail, fits into a tradition of diary as private self-expressive writing. Doing so over a period of time, and locating this discourse in the everyday—the back cover description of *Sex Diaries* invites the reader to "discover the daily thoughts and adventures of a stripper, a web cam girl, a prostitute, a dominatrix, a high-school student" among others— allows for certain formal parallels to be drawn to conventional forms of diary narrative. However, linking diary to this kind of writing is not just a matter of form, the resemblance or not of online diaries to a print diary tradition, but subjectivity. Tapping into a contemporary aesthetic for immediacy and transparency in representation, these blogs also claim and register their authenticity through an association to the genre of the diary. For example, a nonliterary style characterizes the popular and pulp genres of the Mammoth imprint, but it is also a mark of the blog/diary's authenticity and one that is not necessarily tolerated in other autobiographical modes like memoir. Derided in the press as badly written, narcissistic, or banal, this kind of narrative appeals directly to readers seeking the "real" and/because unvarnished story, and a status as diary confirms this expectation will be met.

The sex blog is an example of a context in which the diary has been particularly visible as a generic designation, and this is in contrast to other kinds of blogging where diary has been distanced or rejected as a narrative description (Bruns, "Practice," 11). This chapter considers why and how this might be; it is interested in how subjects have used blogs as diaries (and a context in which blogs are more often assumed to *be* diaries) and the significance of this. First, however, the next section briefly considers some of the debate over what a diary is in relation to the blog as a way of establishing both the discursive context for the consideration of sex blogs that follows and identifying a particular set of concerns that energizes and potentially reforms the diary in this location. As a coda to this chapter, I also discuss the concept of the digital manuscript as a way of broadly engaging with the theoretical and critical possibilities of diary in a mode of online self-presentation like the blog.

The Diary Blog

In *Private Chronicles*, Robert A. Fothergill discusses at length some of the difficulty for settling on a definition of the diary:

> The trouble with efforts of definition is that the Pepysian format—which I suspect is most people's unconscious norm—is continually sliding away on all sides into its many kindred forms. Surrounding the diary, at various points of the compass, lie meditations, letters, anecdote collections, occasional essays, rough-drafts, chronicle histories, commonplace books, and many more examples of more-or-less regular, more-or-less private writing. (3)

For Fothergill, a historical multiplicity of diary forms means that rather than as a set of formal rules, it is more useful to conceptualize diary as a distinctive rhetorical stance. He states: "In general let it be agreed that a diary is what a person writes when he says, 'I am writing my diary'" (3). Andrew Hassam contributes to what is an ongoing debate over definition when he suggests that "the diary norm is attached to the word *diary* and exists as a cultural paradigm or model separate from diary writing as a practice" (*Writing*, 18). What Fothergill sees as mostly a matter of intent, Hassam considers in terms of effect: "The norm that we use to gauge the degree to which a work may or may not be a diary is sustained by a cultural concept, that is, as a paradigm shared by a certain community of readers" (18).

What is significant in each of these perspectives is the sense that expectations about diary are culturally based; interpretations of the form reflect prevailing social conditions and historical perspectives. This is borne out in critical discussion of the diary as a historical form. For example, Felicity Nussbaum notes that the seventeenth century "marks the historical *proliferation* of the serial autobiographical text," the result of important social, cultural, and historical shifts ranging from increased secularization to new communication technologies to formative ideas of the private individual ("Toward," 131). In this the diary is categorically a private text, one where resistant subjectivities can be articulated and new philosophical ideas of the self as discontinuous, multiple, and shifting find formal expression (133). Roger Smith, however, notes that the diary in the

eighteenth century becomes the "outward sign" of an individual's commitment
to the values and expectations of a community ("Self-Reflection," 56). Uses of the
diary at this time reflected a culture in which, like the "refinement of manners,"
keeping a diary was perceived as the indication of a socially responsible person
(56). The diary is here not only seen as the discursive signifier for a certain kind of
self but as a mode of representation and as a style that becomes associated with
a realist and authentic mode of address. Rita Felski observes that eighteenth-
century realist authors used the confessional style of diary and letter precisely
for these reasons: they allowed an author to replicate "as far as possible the
patterns of everyday speech . . . an attention to realist detail, was able to inspire
strong identification in the reading public, as evidenced by the reception of
such texts as *Pamela* and *Clarissa*" (*Beyond*, 102). Paying attention to the social,
historical, and cultural place of diary draws attention to how the "self" is positioned in relation to the discourses available to it and to how these discourses
produce the self in return.

In the twenty-first century, the diary as blog responds to the unique public/
private juxtaposition of online spaces and to a cultural moment that values and
commodifies the first-person personal in a multitude of ways. In tension with
more clearly retrospective or literary modes, like memoir, "immediate" forms
like diary and blogs are valued for their perceived more-realistic-because-less-
figurative representation of self. That such immediacy is itself a construct does
not necessarily lessen the appeal of this narrative; "closeness," authenticity, and
intimacy are qualities promoted by both blog authors and others who seek to
market this work, and a nomination as diary is one way in which they signal this.

In tandem to rapidly evolving technological modes, life narrative scholars
have been interested not only in new digital forms of self-representation but in
the experience of self produced when life itself shifts into online and virtual
spaces. Whether through e-mail, blogs, web browsing (and the personalized
data caching that results), social media, or virtual online communities, for rapidly
increasingly numbers of individuals the Internet is an aspect of everyday life,
one that offers opportunities for self-expression, or for self-assimilation. While
modes of self-representation and engagement in online contexts are highly
diverse and rapidly changing, some recognizable or relatively stable genres
have emerged. For example, in "Blogging as Social Action: A Genre Analysis
of the Weblog," Carolyn R. Miller and Dawn Shepherd observe: "there is strong
agreement on the central features that make a blog a blog. Most commentators
define blogs on the basis of their reverse chronology, frequent updating, and
combination of links with personal commentary." However, while the "syntactic
and formal features" of blogs elicit agreement, it is "when bloggers discuss the

purpose of the blog, its function and value as social action involving rhetors and audiences, that the nature of the generic blog becomes problematic" (Miller and Shepherd, "Blogging").

As a feature of Internet communication since its inception, the digitally native blog or weblog is a distinctive online mode and one that makes discursive links to certain forms of life narrative and that prioritizes the first-person point of view. Sidonie Smith and Julia Watson, for example, note that the blog is a form of online expression that most clearly resembles older and written forms of life narrative because "on them users write extended personal narratives and update them regularly, airing deeply personal experiences and thoughts" (*Reading*, 183). Indeed, one of the ways in which users and critics have frequently considered the blog is as a form of the diary. This is the effect of certain structural convergences (such as chronological ordering, dated entries, and a present-tense perspective) as well as a perceived rhetorical resonance to forms of personal and autobiographical writing. So while Miller and Shepherd argue that it is important to consider diary as a separate but related mode to the blog, they also note: "it is the diary's personal perspective that makes its relationship to the blog so recognizable."[1]

In various ways, considering blogs as diaries appears to be a common-sense assumption; for others, as Viviane Serafty observes, the idea is rather more alarming: "The concept of online diaries and weblogs usually arouses mild disbelief among listeners, for whom the mere idea sounds oxymoronic. In social representations, diaries are first and foremost intimate writings and making them available online therefore appears to raise intractable privacy issues; diaries are believed to be basically private documents that should never get public exposure" (*Mirror*, 1). Amid a proliferation of uses for the blog, from punditry to advertising, politics to journalism, self-creation to self-faking, seeing a blog as simply a diary is no doubt an excessively reductive exercise. Critics like Julie Rak call for caution in conflating blogs with diaries, though she also finds useful discursive parallels: "Blogging relies on the conceit (however transparent) that the blogger is who s/he says s/he is, and that the events described actually happened to her/him personally. The performance of blogging is based on the assumption that experience congeals around a subject, and makes a subject who can be written and read, even when the discourse that appears to support this subject undermines it" ("Digital," 166). Rak notes that critics who have attempted to address the question of online diaries tend to do so within a framework that needs to contain what appear to be "transgressions" in the diary as an online form. That is, such critics believe they are always seeing a translation between forms and that the "paper diary" is the genitive of an online version that exceeds its origins. Rak argues for the need to "begin with an assumption that weblogs are not a continuation of diary in a new form" (170). A difference between "natively digital" and "digitized" forms (Rogers, *Digital*, 9),[2] however, does not preclude a rhetorical synergy between the diary genre and online modes. In the blog, it is possible to trace assumptions and expectations that have also been applied to the private and print diary, and which nonetheless have become refigured in unexpected and provocative ways. This is not to argue that the blog is simply a diary, but to pay attention to the ways in which discursive constructions of the blog draw on and reshape diary for particular ends. Rather than an attempt to "subject" blogs "uncomfortably" to a "print tradition of diary writing" (Rak, "Digital," 171), this is to interpret (and problematize) how, why, and *when* "diary" appears as an appropriate term for personal writing in the online environment. Quite apart from the difficulties in defining what a diary is, or is not (and so whether a blog is, or is not, a diary), diary is not simply a convenient or nostalgic moniker applied "uncomfortably" to personal representation online but is a distinctive ideological and rhetorical position from which to speak.

In a time where memoir has become *the* dominant autobiographical genre (Couser, *Memoir*), it is interesting to speculate that diarists who use blogging as a platform for life narration might do so because it allows them to eke out a territory marked off from some of the specific provocations or controversies of the memoir form. This is not to say that diarists or bloggers escape the inherent instability and problems of self-representative acts—far from it—but to note that they enter into the dialectic of autobiographical narration differently: the blogger is afforded different interpretations, scrutiny, and deprecations than the memoirist, and they draw more strongly on understandings, assumptions, and expectations of the diary in doing so. Of course, not all bloggers are diarists. In this chapter, I am interested in bloggers who do engage rhetorically with expectations and assumptions of the diary form (and who do overtly position themselves as online diarists). These bloggers shape an audience response that draws on the discursive history of diary forms and positions the blogger in a particular way to a dichotomy of public versus private knowledge. That is, as a form of new media that "remediates" (in the terminology developed by Jay Bolter and Bruno Grusin) the older technology of the written diary, the blog offers new ways of exploring how diary genres may have evolved and changed in response to contemporary contexts. For example, Abby Lee and Belle de Jour use their blogs as public platforms for the dissemination of personal "private" material, and these narratives are positioned to attract a wide and influential readership; indeed, they enable their respective authors to secure book and other media contracts. The diary-ness of these blogs then is less a matter of formal resemblance to certain forms of the diary than to the rhetorical position of the narrator (and the audience) in relation to the content. That is, rather than an intention to keep material private, or *unpublished*—which is what Couser, for example, understands uses of the diary to signal[3]—bloggers trade on the stereotype of diary as personal or secret information, and the blog becomes a recognized forum through which such material can then be authoritatively disseminated. The use of diary here, and a self-conscious position as online diarist that these bloggers employ, signals that this account is authentically an aspect of the blogger's private life, and deploys the titillating prospect of revelation and exposure that "diary" stereotypically inspires.

Sex Blog: *Intimate Adventures* and a *One Track Mind*

Not all blogs resemble or invoke conventional diaries, though some blogs are more likely to be read as diaries than others.[4] Blogs have emerged in connection to journalism, forming constituent parts of online newspapers or magazines and fulfilling an opinion or editorial function familiar from print media. Some blogs are fictitious, part of cross-platform marketing strategies, or they are satirical or otherwise misleading as an ostensibly "nonfiction" form. However, even in such diverse contexts, blogs signal a more intimate and self-reflexive kind of self-narration than other forms—for example, as punditry over investigation in the context of journalistic platforms. Crucially, and particularly in juxtaposition to the various forms of new media it both intersects with and evolves alongside of, the blog is distinctively a *personal* mode. In this chapter, I look at blogs that are overtly personal and that further signal and emphasize the personal as a focus and intent in a promise for particular kinds of content. Abby Lee's blog turned "blook" *Girl with a One Track Mind* and Belle de Jour's mini-franchise of blook, books, and television series based on her blog, *Diary of a London Call Girl*, are popular examples of what feminist critics have often anxiously identified as the spectacle and sexualization of culture in online spaces (Barker, "Editorial," 1). That is, they are sex blogs, a form that Kaye Mitchell says is a relatively new genre, though one that derives from and intersects with the erotic memoir, and both are less "new genres or new phenomena" than "the latest developments in a long history of popular, public representations of femininity, romance and female sexuality, that is, mass produced texts which are intended for mass consumption" ("Raunch," 12).

Sex blogs use new technological forms to continue a longstanding cultural obsession with the private and intimate lives of individuals, an obsession that in contemporary culture seems to have advanced exponentially (or rather, more visibly and more publicly). For example, Kenneth Plummer describes this shift as a dominant cultural moment in his mid-1990s sociological work *Telling Sexual Stories*:

> Tell all about your sexual behaviour, your sexual identity, your dreams your desires, your pains and your fantasies . . . tell, tell, tell. An intimate experience, once hardly noticed, now has to be slotted into the ceaseless narrating of life. If once, not so long ago, our sexualities were shrouded in silence, for some they have now crescendoed into a cacophonous din. We have become sexual story tellers in a sexual story telling society. (5)

For feminists like Mitchell, however, the potential of a breakdown in taboo around the articulation of sexual experience and an attention to its complexity, an exhortation to "tell, tell, tell," is in tension with a postfeminist rhetoric that instates sexual narration as a conservative mechanism through which sexuality remains "the secret" and woman remains reduced "to her sexual activity, whether as sexual object or sexual agent" ("Raunch," 23). Moreover, the ascent of technology in a discourse of sexual storytelling has particular effects. Indeed, despite the fact that blogs and memoirs of female sexual experience are routinely "garlanded" with the "rhetoric of liberation and empowerment," Mitchell says that

> such blogs and memoirs are expressive of a continuing anxiety about female desire and female sexual pleasure—as, paradoxically, both socially disruptive and, somehow, inconceivable; despite their "newness," these narratives participate (often unwittingly) in various extant and historically well-established discourses around women and prostitution, chastity, modesty, pornography, romance and objectification. Above all, both blogs and print memoirs are symptomatic of a persisting belief in sexuality as the truth of identity. (13)

While Mitchell identifies the memoir as a key mode here, the blog is a form of autobiographical discourse more frequently associated with another genre in which secrecy, identity, and truth have also been considered paramount: the diary. That is, not only do Abby Lee and Belle de Jour take up the first-person and personal perspective of the blog, but they also actively construct this space as a diaristic one. Indeed, both blogs are named as the "secret" account of their author's private or concealed sex life—Abby Lee's feminist-inflected sexual adventuring is relayed as the private personal life she conceals from friends, family, and coworkers, while Belle de Jour details the world of the "callgirl" sex

worker whose identity is hidden (as protection for clients as much as herself)—
and the generic designation of "diary" works to enhance and authorize these
claims. Moreover, Abby Lee and Belle de Jour refer frequently to what they
are doing on their blog as "diary" writing, and this is also a visible part of the
publishing strategy behind monograph editions of each blog: in Abby Lee's
case, her blog acquires the subtitle "Diary of a Sex Fiend" in its print published
format.

As the nominated genre in which these blogs are constructed by their
authors, critiqued by the media, and offered to an audience, the diary has a
metonymic relationship to the gendered ideals of secrecy and liberation that
are also in play here. Indeed, while Mitchell defers to "erotic memoir" as the
best broad nomination for sex blogs that describe a wide field of interrelated—
professional or personal—sexual activity, sex bloggers themselves, as Audacia
Ray shows in her interview-based study of sex blogging, *Naked on the Internet:
Hookups, Downloads, and Cashing in on Internet Sexploration* (2007), tend to describe
their writing as diary. This is also a significant feature of the marketing of these
blogs once they become print-published commodities: diary is used to identify
a formal quality of the narrative, something about its organization and register,
but also to confirm that this narrative is authentically an aspect of the blogger's
private life. Given that these are blogs ostensibly detailing aspects of their
authors' sex lives, this is particularly significant. Diary blogs trade on the titillating prospect of revelation and exposure, of secrets and scandal, that "diary"
has long been associated with, and this is a generic expectation that publishers
have also used strategically.

The *Intimate Adventures* of a *One Track Mind*: The Sex Blog as Diary

Online diaries have multiple roles to play in the circulation of narratives of
sexual experience and "adventure" online. In the case of callgirl or escort blogs,
the sex blog contributes to a broader cultural fascination with the private world
of sex work (Bernstein, *Temporarily*, 12), and it is a useful marketing tool. For
example, Seattle sex blogger "Mistress Matisse" uses her blog *Mistress Matisse's
Journal* to discuss her life as a dominatrix and to link to her professional website
for clients. British blogger Belle de Jour also uses her blog to talk about life as a
professional sex worker, but she insists her blog is exclusively a "diary" and
"not a site to drum up business" (*Diary*, "mercredi, novembre 12," 12 November
2003). Both Belle's professional and personal identities are disguised on her

blog. On the now deleted blog *Diary of a London Callgirl*, Belle links to a selection of blogs by sex workers and sex bloggers. She articulates a politicized perspective on prostitution: she writes a letter to *The Times* concerning a series of murdered sex workers, but she has to make do with publishing it online ("vendredi, décembre 15," 15 December 2006). Erudite and evidently well informed, however, Belle usually stays away from direct social commentary, positioning herself instead as a witty expert dispelling myths of the profession to an audience she constructs as middle class, prurient, and misinformed: "In a world of twelve-year-olds in sexy boots and nans in sparkly minidresses, the surest way to tell the prostitute walking into a hotel at Heathrow is to look for the lady in the designer suit. Fact" ("dimanche, novembre 2," 2 November 2003). She reflects back a pop culture obsession with the "working girl," demoting "Julia 'sexless' Roberts" and promoting "Elizabeth Hurley" in casting for "women who are not working girls but should be" ("samedi, novembre 22," 22 November 2003). She explains the processes of applying to an agency, getting promotional shots, and "blurbing" her escort persona as well as the expectations of a working date. She details an expensive underwear obsession. She has a boyfriend. This is the everyday world of Belle de Jour, and the quotidian aspect of call girl life and its representation online is a political gesture that speaks to a desire to intervene in marginalized and heavily stereotyped identities of erstwhile "private" professions like sex work, as well as to contest dominant conservative constructions of female sexuality. Doing so in a pseudonymous diary links Belle to a tradition of scandalous female secret-keepers, and it energizes the implications of diary as a form intimately associated with domestic and private sphere experience. And Belle's blog is perhaps more interesting in this context because it eschews many of the interactive functions that blogs conventionally promote: since 2003 Belle's blog has had no comment function, e-mail address, or author profile.[5]

Rescinding interactivity mutes one of the more commented-on distinctions between online communication and offline modes—the potential for direct engagement and responsiveness with an audience—while Belle's own absence as a "live" responder on the blog contributed to parallel debates over the authenticity of her persona. In these discussions, the prospect that anonymous authors can construct gendered identities through the successful deployment of narrative voice and generic form (here, notably, the diary) becomes a central issue. Noted for her positive account of sex work as well as the "cool eroticism and ironic detachment of her writing style," a perceived incongruity between Belle's literariness and her occupation fed from "fears about the disembodied nature of cyberspace to position her as doubly inauthentic: as a writer posing as a prostitute, and as one who misrepresents the reality of sex work" (Ferreday,

"Writing," 274). As Feona Attwood elaborates, the anxiety was not only that Belle's writing was too intelligent for her profession but that her style was essentially masculine: "Belle's approach to sex (particularly paid sex), by turns lusty and matter-of-fact, could not be read as authentically female" ("Intimate," 8). In a paid opinion piece for *The Guardian*, British madam Cynthia Payne agreed with the critics, deriding Belle's ability to quote literature to clients as improbable and arguing:

> I've never met a working girl who has kept a diary. The girls I knew were not proud of it. Most were unmarried young mums struggling through life, and they certainly didn't advertise what they did—it was their terrible secret. I think the only person who would write a diary like this about prostitution is somebody who intended to have it published, and in all likelihood somebody who had this published wouldn't be on the game. Also, it sounds so male to me, like a man trying to fulfil a fantasy for other men. But it leaves me cold. ("Belle")

In this kind of critique, "working girls" are resolutely uneducated and ignorant, and though Belle is herself under suspicion in this comment from Payne, in many ways she only reinforces such class stereotypes because Belle is not the kind of "working girl" with whom Payne is familiar. Though she does advocate for the rights of sex workers (notably, in her commentary on a series of murders of street-based prostitutes in 2006), Belle is also insistent that she is a "high-class" escort, and her narration offers attendant detail that allows her to establish her considerable agency in the decision-making process around both clientele and services, something that is not as readily available to sex workers in other kinds of circumstances.

The debate over Belle's identity, however, reveals more than deeply ingrained social and class prejudice. On the sex blog, anonymity becomes an argument in two directions of belief: secrets are both validated (the author is anonymous because this is so real) and unsettled (the author is anonymous because this is a fake). Because online identity is notoriously unstable and available for imposture, the diary itself becomes an important signifier in the need to sway audiences toward the first belief: that here are secrets that would, if revealed, compromise the author in real life. Indeed, despite a concerted media effort to unmask the London blogger, something Attwood evocatively terms "the hunt for Belle" ("Intimate," 7), the author revealed her own identity in a newspaper interview five years after her blog had commenced and after having successfully remained anonymous through two subsequent book publications and a television miniseries. It was a feat surprising not only for the amount of time she had successfully eluded her tabloid pursuers but also for the revelation, as Debra Ferreday wryly notes, that she "turned out to be exactly what she claimed to be: an educated, middle-class woman in her thirties who had worked as a prostitute in London" ("Writing," 282).[6]

Unlike Belle de Jour, UK sex blogger and pseudonymous author of *Girl with a One Track Mind* Abby Lee was unable to conceal her offline identity as her sex blog gained attention and notoriety in the press. "By night she worked on Harry Potter, but by day . . . ," announced journalist Anna Mikhailova in an exposé that described the erstwhile assistant film director's sex blog as "an erotic version of Bridget Jones" ("Revealed," 3). On her blog, Abby Lee (Zoe Margolis) reflected on the experience:

> Today this blog is three years old. What started out as a private place for me to express my thoughts and vent my feelings has now developed into something I never, in my wildest dreams, imagined . . . I've always done a yearly round-up of blog posts on this date; today is no different, barring the fact that this last year has been the oddest I have ever experienced. What was once my private life has now become public, in its most literal sense. I've been proud that my writing crossed into the book medium this year; I've been gutted that I lost my anonymity in the process. ("Three," 1 January 2007)

The sex blog intersects sharply with conventions for the representation and expression of female sexual experience in public. Indeed, unlike Bridget Jones,[7] whose sexuality is decidedly secondary to her romantic bumbling in Helen Fielding's series of novels, Abby Lee's "blog-turned-book" is perceived as decidedly transgressive by journalists like Mikhailova and as part of a worrying new wave: "The most explicit in the female 'erotic odyssey' genre sparked by Belle de Jour, *The Sexual Life of Catherine M*, and *Diary of a Manhattan Call Girl*" ("Revealed," 3). For Mikhailova, it is also clear that the "commercial value" of both the sex blog genre and Abby Lee's installment "depends on readers believing it is the true account of a sexually liberated woman," and she observes that "the blog quickly gained cult status . . . the book went to the top of Amazon's pre-ordered paperbacks charts" (3). An authenticity that appeals to the market, however, is also a sign of moral decline: "With such a shameless interest in sex it is no surprise Margolis has gone to great lengths to try to conceal her identity. Her name does not appear on the electoral roll and her phone number is ex-directory" (3). While Ferreday observes of responses to Belle de Jour that "particularly problematic is the way in which 'shame' is naturalized as an inevitable and detrimental consequence of being outed as a sex worker"

("Writing," 285), Mikhailova's construction of Abby Lee as similarly "shamed" establishes that for women, sexual narration is inherently risky ("Revealed"). Such risks might seem to be exacerbated through genre: the sex *diary* directly negotiates with a prospect of titillation, unmasking, secrets, and taboo. Jakubow-ski emphasizes just this kind of assumption in his anthology (*Sex Diaries*), and it is an expectation routinely made visible in popular culture and other uses of the diary form. Ultimately, Abby Lee's status as blogger and the different conditions of discourse online means this narrative negotiates awkwardly, and detrimen-tally, to expectations of genre that are familiar (though potentially equally re-strictive) in conventional diary modes. That is, while a nomination as diary functions to encourage or attract readers of the blog, and especially when it circulates in a print-published version, a sense for the blog as simply or only a diary also becomes a way for critics to question its functionality and to demand certain limitations in its production. The sex blog draws discursively on diary conventions and stereotypes and the outcome of this is not always to the blogger's advantage.

The sex blog turns on a very particular promise: that a "real" life and identity is here concealed in order to disclose intimate material. Anonymity, however, is both a promise and a problem. In *The Mirror and the Veil*, Serafty notes that while some online diarists provide their actual names, thus appearing to affirm "one's name" as "both a sign and a guarantee of one's identity" (92), many bloggers use pseudonyms or remain anonymous. This convention, "con-trary to appearances . . . does not really go against the trend to greater self-revelation. For one thing, pseudonyms are often accompanied by pictures that add the density of corporeity to the diaristic text" (93). In the same way that the design and layout of the blog are interpreted as components of the blogger's self-representation, pseudonyms may be chosen in order to "actualise some of the psychological traits the writer cannot vent anywhere[;] . . . the self-chosen names or pseudonyms may become significant metonymies of the self" (93). Functioning as a context-specific layer of identification, the pseudonym also serves a more conventional function in emphasizing that the author perceives risk attendant in the publishing of this content. The pseudonym draws attention to the blog as a location for narrative that may be too dangerous or scandalous to admit to by proper name but it has also been seen as a ploy to generate interest in the concealed author, or, conversely, it opens up the prospect of hoax.

In *Naked on the Internet*, her autobiographically inflected and interview-based survey of "hookup" culture and pornography online, Audacia Ray notes that an "overwhelming majority" of women she interviewed about their blogging had also kept private journals in the past (94). For Ray, it was "no surprise" that many of these bloggers were "the journal keepers of yesteryear," but she is surprised that many continue to maintain a separate (she specifies "handwritten") journal. Noting that a private journal and a public blog might thus be seen as "complementary" practice, Ray cites an interview subject who rejects such a conventional separation of spheres: "I want to rip myself wide open and live as genuinely as possible, so private diaries are not my thing" (94). As a form that seems to hybridize the conventional diary, that appears to shift a private practice to a public stage, blogging has been idealized as a powerful and liberating space for the articulation of individual experience.[8] For Ray's sex blogger, making the private public is a declaration of politics and a claim to authentic subjectivity and self-representation; diary blogging is situated as the mode through which the subject can represent what would otherwise remain concealed. Indeed, a perception that this is private writing done in public, rather than modestly hidden in a parallel and private diary, is the key persuasive appeal of this form, and Ray argues that pseudonymity is an important condition for women who blog about sex precisely because it is also linked intrinsically to their desire for safe self-exposure: "For many women, blogging about sex is, paradoxically, as much a solitary pursuit that's solely about them as it is a public confession that needs an audience to flourish and grow. Either way, women's sex blogs are a personal and political space for both their writers and readers alike" (98). Indeed, Ray observes that women are more often associated with sex blogs, though she also notes that while writing about sex in general is seen as a low cachet activity online, women in particular are viewed more disparagingly when they blog about their personal sexual experience: "Writing and thinking about sexuality is seen as an easy way to get attention and not at all a noble pursuit, and most of the people who blog in detail about sexuality and their personal sex lives are women" (*Naked*, 100).

Seen as both a common female pursuit and a derided or inferior category of writing, the sex blog has much in common with a historical location of personal diary writing, which has long been associated with domestic and "trivial" discourse and with female authors. Nonetheless, for women who kept diaries historically, the genre was also understood to enable a resistant and subversive position in relation to dominant discourse, deploying what Nussbaum identifies as the openness of the form to "a series of coterminous and contradictory subject positions" ("Toward," 129). The fluidity of diary thus allows for the subject to try on or reciprocate the ideals of subjectivity available in their historical moment: "individuals construct language," says Nussbaum, "but the individual—rather than being the source of his or her own meaning—can only adopt positions within the language available at a given moment" (131). In her witty and cosmopolitan persona, as much as in her perceived "masculine" approach to sex and intimacy, Belle unsettles certain stereotypes of sex work and challenges persistent taboos around the articulation of female sexuality and its narration by women. Her online diary is a representation of empowerment and agency in her life as (an admittedly, elite) sex worker, as much as it is also an "ironic" reflection on the impossibility of this given the cultural and social condition of women's sexuality in contemporary culture (Ferreday, "Writing"). How does the determination of an online sex blog as a diary influence how an audience responds to this blog? How does this use of diary affect and draw on uses of the diary elsewhere, historically and in the present?

One of the key ways in which contemporary blogs and diaries connect is through the mode of confession. As sex bloggers, female diarists are enmeshed in powerful discursive tropes to do with personal narrative. For journalists like Mikhailova ("Revealed"), a narrative like Abby Lee's is confessional because it is an admission of both shame and guilt, and her upholding of a blogging convention for pseudonymous authorship only strengthens these suspicions. However, Irene Gammel observes that "while women have transgressed into the public domain with their personal stories, their sexual expressions are frequently read by the media and public as confessions" (*Confessional*, 1). Confession has a long history and association with women's voices, and particularly within contemporary content where autobiographical narration has had a central role in feminist consciousness-raising. However, Rita Felski articulates the central tension of the mode when she asks whether confession is "a liberating step for women, which uncovers the political dimensions of personal experience, confronts the contradictions of existing gender roles and inspires an important sense of female identification and solidarity" or a redundant ideology of "subjectivity-as-truth which feminism should be calling into question?" (*Beyond*, 86). Reflecting a dominant perception of women's sexual self-narration as transgressive (and confession as shameful), such a stance also fails to understand the emerging codes of ethics and authorship that anonymous blogging operates under. Armadeep Singh, for example, considers how pseudonymous blog authorship functions within an ethical code, one in which authenticity is prioritized over identity. That is, as Singh argues: "It is not simply the case that these writers are using pseudonyms (or eidolons) to protect themselves from prosecution (or, for that matter, honor "challenges" and duels). Rather the eidolon always draws attention to the imagined private author writing behind the veil of the public persona" ("Anonymity," 28). In contrast to the historical situation, where literary anonymity was ostensibly a puzzle to be solved, blogger anonymity "reminds[s] us of the porous boundaries between public and private, and suggest[s] the rebirth

of an author-figure asserting a desire to write, and be, in both worlds at once"
(Singh, "Anonymity," 34). Indeed, responding to the exposé, Abby Lee (writing
under her real name as Zoe Margolis) explains the apparent "great lengths" of
her anonymity, and claims not shame but liberation as her motivation. Her
online diary was

> a place where I could write, with complete honesty, about the most erotic and
> emotional events in my life . . . The reason I wanted to remain anonymous was
> to ensure privacy for myself and others, not because I have any shame. It's 2006
> for goodness' sake—is sex really that big a deal? If one good thing could come
> out of my losing my anonymity, it would be the hope that my writing might
> help to challenge old-fashioned, sexist views on female sexuality—an ongoing
> battle and one I would be happy to be part of. ("Sex," 34)

The potential for authentically "everyday" and ordinary kinds of experience to
be represented, the space to establish resistance to imposed subject positions,
and for intervention in what may constitute "historic" moments in the future—
through opening up the margins of who may participate in what is written and
kept—are what critics have always valued about the diary. Heightened desires
for authenticity in what is perceived as an increasingly mediated and inauthentic world also privilege modes of representation like blogs as new spaces for
the unmediated representation of self. In cyberspace, utopia seems close: "All
users are free to enter this world of the mind on equal terms and express themselves without limitations . . . the workings of power and conditions of access are
bypassed" (Paasonen, "Gender," 27).[9] A key assumption about personal narrative online is that such content is (deliberately or inadvertently) confessional,
an assumption heightened by the choice of online users to assume a degree of
anonymity.[10] Typically pseudonymous, disclosing intimate and often controversial content, sex bloggers create spaces where exhibition and voyeurism co-
exist, and where the appeal of the diary blog as a stereotypically confessional
mode is foregrounded and eroticized. While critics like Margo Culley remind
us to "remember that diaries and journals are texts, that is, verbal constructs,"
and as such, include "questions of audience (whether real or implied), narrative
shape and structure, persona, voice, imagistic and thematic repetition" (*Day*,
10), much of the attraction of diary narrative for readers still lies in the promise
of access to a less guarded or constructed articulation of personal experience—
to what may be secret or private, and thus to what is "more real."

The diary is historically associated with the production of secret and confessional discourse. In the eighteenth century, says Nussbaum, "among those who
were the most prolific diarists were individuals with secrets to tell, especially

women and dissenters ("Toward," 134). Thus it is that one of the pleasures for
reading diaries, as McNeill observes, "may lie partly in their potential for
confession: readers expect self-exposure and the telling of secrets" ("Teaching,"
27). This prospect is heightened and energized online. For McNeill, the blog is
distinguished by the possibility of an interactive reader and a context where
"though active and intimate . . . participation remains virtual and disembodied.
The confessor stays behind the 'grille' of the Internet, allowing the diarist—and
the reader—the illusion of anonymity necessary for 'full' self-exposure" (27). In
his work on the topic, Peter Brooks has shown that confession is linked intimately
to context; certain occasions or situations are more likely to produce confessional
discourse than others. One of these contexts is the courtroom, where an expectation for confession may even produce false claims: confession, whether volun-
tary, compelled, or coerced, is inherently problematic (*Troubling*, 3). The online
environment also negotiates with expectations of confession in particular ways.
Assuming a deliberately confessional stance—writing self-consciously as a
diarist—can be an authoritative gesture, one that asserts that "the blogger is
her own audience, her own public, her own beneficiary" (Miller and Shepherd,
"Blogging"). However, there are limitations here too: on the sex blog, confession
is both volunteered and already assumed, and a construction of this as diary
space further shapes this as a generic expectation.

For the sex blogger, diary may seem like a good generic choice, a better discursive fit, for example, than for the citizen journalist or even the war blogger.
That is, as I remarked earlier, not all bloggers take up the typically personal
rhetorical stance of the diarist. In "The Practice of Newsblogging," Axel Bruns
notes that while "the uses of blogs are many and varied," there are two "special"
types: the "newsblog" and "the traditional blog-as-diary approach" (11). The
newsblog is linked to journalism and the dissemination of information; the
personal blog "is more like a 'traditional' diary" (11). Seeing certain kinds of
blogs as online diaries and others as journalism or punditry raises, among other
issues, questions of authority. As I have been arguing in this chapter, sex bloggers
who state an intention to reveal highly intimate, ostensibly private content can
establish a personal subjective position as "diarist" as a way to signal this. What
is afforded in taking-up of the diary as a rhetorical position for self-representation
in this context, and what is lost? Online diarists respond to a sense of the blog as
a democratic and egalitarian mode, one that, like the diary, enables subjects
outside of the "grand narratives" of history and social progress to achieve voice
and representation. As sex bloggers, Abby Lee and Belle take advantage of the
blog as a space for play, transgression, and subversion, yet they also reveal this
space as conditional—Abby Lee's attempts to voice a feminist orientation and
Belle's desire to retell the experience of sex work underlie their sexual storytelling

online and are both facilitated and undermined through their use of the diary as the nominated (or acquired) rhetorical choice for this articulation.

Coda: Digital Manuscript

The diary online draws new attention to the impact of technology and form in writing the self, indeed, to the role of technology in shaping the *experience* of self. Media theorists in particular have been determined to establish for the blog its own specific theoretical and critical scope, arguing, for example, against "meta-phors" of "journaling or journalism" to describe blogging as a practice (Dean, *Blog Theory*, 44). In this chapter, however, I've wanted to establish that diary has a role in understanding and interpreting the practice of blogging, even if this is at times a seemingly conservative or limiting one. That is, while blogging may indeed be more usefully understood as "a medium" of communication, as Jodi Dean argues in *Blog Theory: Feedback and Capture in the Circuits of Drive* (2010), content cannot be divorced from (or understood purely in relation to) form. Belle de Jour, or Abby Lee, adopt and deploy a diaristic voice that is also rhetori-cal, and the blog enables them to perform this voice in a new and volatile com-municative context.

As for the other diarists I have considered so far in this book, diary functions here as a personal mode that is also a public form. Moreover, both Abby Lee and Belle de Jour release print-published editions of their blogs, and though these are not necessarily accurate as reproductions,[11] it is in this format that links to diary genres are solidified or made overt. As bloggers, however, Abby Lee and Belle de Jour must also negotiate actively with the conventions and limitations of autobiographical disclosure in this context. Abby Lee's online published response to accusations that her blog is "shameful," for example, is part of her blog narrative and not paratextual to its production, and this open-ness and responsiveness of the medium is significant. Rosenwald argues that, "in a sense, the diary is a manuscript not accidentally but essentially; if we think of a manuscript as a text in a fluid state, a diary is a manuscript by necessity. During the life of the diarist, the diary remains unfinished and open; something can always be added" (*Emerson*, 12). Is it useful to see the blog as a digital correlate to the print manuscript?

What possibilities are associated with the technology of the Internet diary and with the conditions of authorship it both invites and contests? The blog appears to unsettle the conventions of privacy, pen, and paper privileged in the how-to diary, for example, and to supersede and revise the economic rationalism of the publishing house. The blog is a "self-published" and open form that also appears to bypass the implications of revision or loss that necessarily attend the publication of a print diary. Lejeune, for example, exhorts the Internet as a potentially superior location for diary:

> Why is the book the point of reference? For the past century it has kept diaries in shackles. Real diaries, infinite and deliciously chatty, are condensed and cut down to fit into these Procrustean beds, leading to tortured expectations about "style" and "depth" . . . On the Internet, the diary can finally breathe, stretch out on a chaise lounge, and relax . . . the website is a garden with pathways, crossroads, and viewpoints; it turns time into space without shrinking it. (*On Diary*, 316)

The prospect of the blog as first draft or digital manuscript is, of course, paradoxical. While the seamless possibilities of the word processor and the interactive consequences of the network should undermine the authenticity of diary in an online context (in which emendation is so temptingly possible), this narrative nonetheless remains authoritative primarily for a status akin to that of the manuscript: as first-run and immediate. It has the same cachet as "handwritten" material, and the same sense of this as untranslatable into proximal forms. Lejeune's unease about diary texts "cut down to fit" is resonant here, as is Whitlock's dissatisfaction with the blog book as "cold copy" (*Soft*, 24).[12] The blog, then, offers a context where interpretable elements that would otherwise be excluded are retained. The print diary, too, is usefully understood as a mosaic or assemblage; there is a productive relationship here to the automedial context of the blog, something I explore in detail in the following chapter.[13] For example, Rosenwald, addressing the reader of a manuscript diary, argues for a consideration of not only content but also "how a volume of the diary is presented *qua* volume, what span of time it characteristically includes, whether it is given a formal beginning or ending; whether the text is immaculate or scribbled over with revision; whether the page is exploited as a unit of organization; where dates are placed relative to the entries they govern; what non-verbal marks accompany the words" (*Emerson*, 19). Madeleine Sorapure notes that blogs are a location for superior "density" and allow for a range of elements to be read in concert ("Screening," 3). As such, the visual choices, layout, and other language of the blog (including the author's choice or not of pseudonym and the pseudonym itself) constitute an interpretable system. Rosenwald also describes this in relation to the diary, employing a metaphor for handwriting: "Like handwriting it expresses rather than describes the writer; like handwriting it can reliably distinguish one individual from another; and like handwriting it can be read as evidence not only of identity but character" (*Emerson*, 18). Like the diary manuscript (or, the graphic and visual diaries that I explore in the following chapter), the blog diary constructs an appeal based on complex breadth and the incorporation of a fluidity and hybridity.

Acknowledging that a diary representation is multiple and flexible, online or off, contests linear or closed interpretations of diary texts. What becomes significant is not the technology through which blogs or diaries represent the self—and the capacity to which they may do this better or less well than each other, or the ways in which they resemble or not each other—than the status of these texts as closer to a manuscript than any other format. The online diary functions generically to signal to the blog reader that this material should be interpreted (whether or not it can be confirmed) as first-run, unmediated, and authentic. The desire to get ever closer to the "original," what Lejeune calls the "avant-texte" (*On Diary*), characterizes the appeal of personal journals and diaries, and this is true for online diaries as well.

I have argued earlier in this book that the blog is a crucial development in uses of the contemporary diary. For example, in Iraq, Paul McGeough must compete with the culturally authentic voices of Iraqi citizens—enabled by Internet technology and the blog—and with the expectations of audiences who have been tuned to live and unfolding coverage on various media "back home." The diary represents a way to tap into and reproduce the "immediate" and immersed perspective of the blog or the live cross, and McGeough takes advantage of this. What is visible in the emergence of the blog, or in the evolution of uses of the print diary, however, is not simply a technological moment but a cultural one. Diary narrative, online or in print, constructs an appeal based on personal, immediate, and authentic representation. The desires that have traveled with diary from its use as a spiritual journal in the eighteenth century, or as a document of "war, imprisonment, or siege" (McNeill, "Performing," 273) in the twentieth century, continue into the twenty-first century and into digital contexts. Bloggers take up certain structural as well as rhetorical strategies by writing diary online, and they remediate the expectations that characterize diary as a genre for authentic and transparent representation of self and experience. Weblogs or blogs are native digital forms that nonetheless negotiate with and contest the assumptions and expectations (and ideologies) of personal narrative genres like the diary. Where the blog is offered as a personal journal, crucial issues of authority and authenticity become visible: a desire to speak autobiographically and personally and to represent diverse personal and individual experience characterizes uses of the diary online as it does in contemporary culture more generally.

6

Graphic Lives

Visual Narration and the Diaries of Phoebe Gloeckner, Bobby Baker, and *The 1000 Journals Project*

Diaries tell the story differently.

Marina Warner, "Chronicle of a Life Repaired"

Has the journal a better claim to represent character? It is after all itself a work. Or rather: it is a series of works, and the claim we can imagine for it is based upon its status as a series.

Lawrence Rosenwald, *Emerson and the Art of the Diary*

*I*n *Drawing from Life: The Journal as Art* (2005), Jennifer New anthologizes a selection of private visual sketchbooks and working diaries of artists: "journals filled with drawings, photos, collages, charts, and detritus taped or folded into the pages" (8). These journals, says New, appealed to her because they were "visual, and that made them more pragmatic, less confessional, and better fit for public viewing" (8). That is, they are a contrast to the kinds of journals New says she once kept: "Rarely visual in nature, they do not even amount to a writer's personal journal. Rather, they contain the emotional stuff of everyday life, a young woman's search for self: some whining and self-pity, a lot of fretting, and occasional joy" (8–9). Rereading her old diaries, New confesses: "their pages makes [*sic*] me squirm" (9). However, while the self-absorbed narration of "there goes Blindly in Love at 19, followed by Depressed and Searching at 24, and Confused about the Motherhood Decision at 31" (9) is an ambivalent pleasure, the parts of her old journals that attract New the most are not prose at all but "the random images stuck into the pages. Usually these are free-floating, loosely folded, and tucked between pages rather than glued. A newspaper photo of a homeless man circa 1991 plants my feet back on the Seattle streets of my early twenties. A tissue-thin bag from a patisserie in Aix falls out of another book, and a cream-filled cake blooms in my mouth. But I did not so much as mention the pastry or even the shop in my written entry for that day in France" (9). These souvenirs and keepsakes compose a parallel layer of New's journals that retains the privacy or mystery she feels is embarrassingly stripped in prose. For New, the diary composed of images and souvenirs resists a certain distillation because the visual mode is a more open symbolic register; meaning has not been decanted into text. Both "opaque" and "able to shed light," visual diaries thus offer a particular kind of encounter: "The appeal of visual journals to outside viewers," says New, is "the opportunity to see how a person operates" (10).

To see how a person operates, to experience how they *see* the world, is also one of the pleasures of the visual diary modes I consider in this chapter. Bobby Baker's *Diary Drawings: Mental Illness and Me* (2010) and Phoebe Gloeckner's *Diary of a Teenage Girl* (2002) are artist works by individuals who are professionals in their fields, and they are also autobiographical representations that use the form of a diary to represent and narrate personal experience. As such, these texts belong to a category of contemporary life writing that has been gaining significant critical and popular attention in recent times. That is, they fit under the broad definition offered by Hilary Chute and Marianne DeKoven as examples of graphic narrative: "narrative that does the work of narration at least in part through drawing" ("Introduction," 768). The final text I consider in this chapter is also a graphic narrative, though it deviates from the narrative mode of Baker or Gloeckner in that it is collaborative and multi-authored. *The 1000 Journals Project* (2007) is an art project that foregrounds a visual register and uses diary as a methodology to collect, shape, and produce a range of experiences that become a new way of thinking about form and autobiography in the contemporary moment. Here too is an inducement to self-representation that is connected to a powerful contemporary ideal of the authentic self: the self as a creative subject.

As diary texts, each of these works engages in very specific ways with a discursive history of the genre that is lodged in understandings and expectations of the diary as a material and visual object. The diary is a literary mode with a special relationship to concepts of embodiment, materiality, and spatial representation that have also been significant in theorizing graphic styles. In discussing the contemporary rise and significance of graphic life narrative in various forms, something they term "autographics," Gillian Whitlock and Anna Poletti have observed that here "text is approached for texture; for the 'strange alchemy' of word and image on a three dimensional page" ("Self-Regarding," v). The diary plays into such confluence by drawing into view its own significance as an object that is in connection to an ideal of embodiment and materiality of self. Lawrence Rosenwald, for example, advocates the diary scholar pay attention to "not only the words but their incarnation and format," and so to the kind of book the diarist buys, their use or not of the whole page, their sketches or crossing-outs, as well as the presentation of the handwriting itself; in short, the critic must consider "what non-verbal marks accompany the words" as much as they must respond to the words themselves (*Emerson*, 19). That is, extratextual inclusions and other devices (such as whether the diary is a book or not) mean diary is a "thick" mode, one in which textual content needs to be read alongside and as part of an assembly of other material and narrative choices. This is particularly evident when the diary itself is conceptualized and presented as a visual form.

Observing that extratextual as well as textual elements of a diary manuscript must be read in concert, Rosenwald uses a comparison to handwriting as another interpretable system that "can be read as evidence not only of identity but also character, by a reader knowing the conventions within which the writer operates" (*Emerson*, 18). Of course, the diaries that are the subject of this chapter are published texts: they are crucially different from the complex engagement required by a manuscript diary, though in both cases, a need for attention to an assemblage of elements is a common link. In connection both to diaries and to visual styles in general, however, handwriting—and the association with materiality and embodiment it implies—is an important aesthetic and figurative trope. Chute and DeKoven identify handwriting as a key element in "the rich extra-semantic information a reader receives" in a published graphic narrative (particularly, comics) ("Introduction," 767). As Rosenwald advocates in relation to reading diaries, this is an element that demands attention for the ways in which the *texture* (and not simply the "text") of such narrative must be part of its interpretation. Indeed, Chute, returning to the idea of handwriting in her introduction to *Graphic Women: Life Narrative and Contemporary Comics* (2010), argues that a key symbolic of comics in connection to handwriting is that it carries, "whether or not the narrative is autobiographical, what we may think of as a trace of the autobiography in the mark of its maker," and she makes an explicit connection between this quality and the genre of diary: "That the same hand is both writing and drawing the narrative in comics leads to a sense of the form as diaristic; there is an intimacy to reading handwritten marks on the printed page, an intimacy that works in tandem with the sometimes visceral effects of presenting 'private images'" (10). Chute's observation on the significance of handwriting in relation to the graphic narrative relies on a context of direct transcription, wherein "the subjective presence of the maker is not retranslated through type" (11). Yet many graphic artists mediate the handwritten

through the digital—cartoonist Alison Bechdel used a word processing function to create the distinctive "handwritten" font in her award-winning comics
memoir *Fun Home: A Family Tragicomic* by "writing" in an illustration program.[1]
What is significant here, then, is not necessarily the handwriting itself, but the
context of organization of material *by hand*, which, in comics, is a visible part of
the narrative: "What feels so intimate about comics is that it *looks like what it is*"
(Chute, *Graphic*, 11). For Chute, while comics call insistently to their "crafted-
ness" and to an origin as "handmade," the form is nonetheless more powerful
because it is "invested in accessibility, in print" (11). What is so alluring and provocative about the mode of comics is thus partly its unique status as handmade
yet mass-produced. However, unlike other modes in which the structure and
frame of presentation has significant bearings on both meaning and interpretation, comics cannot be "'reflowed': they are both intimate and *site specific*" (11).

Unlike comics, published diaries are often detached from their context of
production. Indeed, Philippe Lejeune remarks that he once published an article
"showing that diaries lost three quarters of their meaning once they were put
into print, as well as organizing an exhibition of original manuscripts as 'psychic
fingerprints'" (*On Diary*, 286). For Lejeune, who defers to the manuscript and
private diary in most of his work, the diary is the most "fundamentally" autobiographical of forms, and materiality is essential in this: "Like those texts
which artists call a 'single-copy edition': it signals by virtue of its paper, its ink,
its spelling, and its script, and many other aspects, while the printed text only
captures words, and often very few words. To publish a journal, then, is like
trying to fit a sponge into a matchbox" (47). The loss of material entailed in the
publication of manuscript diaries encounters new contexts with the advent of
online diaries, where, though the medium may tempt revision, the first draft is
ostensibly the one posted and made available to its readers—the "manuscript"
is online and visible. This sense is emphasized in the book version of blogs,
many of which are careful to indicate their status as an exact reproduction,
though this a highly limited claim given the loss of hyperlinks, flash animation,
and other technology that cannot be reproduced in the printed medium.

Diary scholars have long been attentive to the different specificities and
reading practices that are mobilized depending on whether one is reading a
manuscript or a published diary, and in simple terms, printed diaries have
usually been considered as a compromise in the representation of the manuscript original. Judy Nolte Temple, theorizing what scholars ought to do when
faced with examples of the diary genre that challenge or exceed expectations of
the form—"those from nontraditional writers, that may not appear to be diaries
at all" ("Fragments," 76)—observes that the general public of diary readers has

become familiarized to a version of diary limited by the conventional standards of a publishable text. "What scholars, including myself, do to diaries in the name of love and/or promotion," muses Temple, "has both gained acceptance for our field of study while at the same time delaying the inevitable face-to-face meeting between readers and actual diaries" (77). "Actual diaries," then, are texts that frequently fail the standards of literary narrative and organization, the criteria of "plot," "character," and "setting" that Temple observes are "right out of high school freshman English" (77).

Suzanne L. Bunkers, detailing the complex process of editing and composing manuscript material that goes into the published format, also observes the process ordinarily entails more elision than inclusion and just as frequently demands an editorial structure that must sacrifice original context for qualities of rhythm and coherence ("Whose"). Unlike comics, or even in more clearly textual modes such as fiction or memoir, the reproduction of diary in the form it is produced by the diarist is rare. Even when more complete versions of a diary are made available (Bunkers notes as particularly fascinating the examples of the Virginia Woolf and Anne Frank diaries), extratextual material may remain subsumed. But, what of diaries such as those Cynthia A. Huff considers in "Textual Boundaries: Space in Nineteenth-Century Women's Manuscript Diaries," where extratextual material such as newspaper clippings, death notices, or other inserts becomes inseparable from the written narrative, providing a deliberate context to incidents that may otherwise be unspoken or glossed in the diarist's actual narration? What of the fragment diaries that Temple encounters? Except in the case of artist's diaries, the genre is not usually considered a visual mode—a "more complete" edition is the one that simply includes more textual/written content. And though not diaries in which the representation of "image" is a primary concern (as is the case with diaries that *are* reproduced for their visual content),[2] these texts nonetheless have a material incarnation that is part of the representation of the diarist's self.

The loss of texture that occurs when handwritten and otherwise hand-assembled manuscripts are translated into print can to some degree be reimagined in encounters with diaries that do take (and reproduce) "thick" or visual as well as textual modes of presentation. The online diary is one of these, and so too are the diaries I consider in this chapter. As narratives reliant on and predominantly composed in images, they retain both the aura of looking "*like what it is*" (Chute, *Graphic*, 11) and the intimacy of a visible and material authorial "trace." Such uses make it harder for editors or publishers to dissociate the text's printed edition from its original composition and so prompt editions that respond to the need to reproduce the text as the diarist intended and composed it. That is, unlike other published diaries, which critics have argued lose meaning in printed mass-circulation (Lejeune, *On Diary*, 286), the graphic diary is a form that retains (and circulates) access to the texture of the original artifact. Visual uses of the diary thus negotiate with a ubiquitous state of loss and presence, of mediation and original (a condition of representation, not only form) that approach the site-specific and intimate quality that Chute finds in comics: the image (and not just the text) must be reproduced *as it was made* for the text to make sense.

Phoebe Gloeckner: Childish Form and Girlhood Diary

In recent years, graphic life narrative has become a significant autobiographical form, and graphic memoir in particular has emerged as a distinct and popular genre. The popularity of graphic memoir, however, has not obscured its provocations, particularly given that the genre has mostly been taken up in long-form comics formats: cartoon styles of illustration are hyperbolic, understood to be distorted, exaggerated, or conflated, and even when autobiographical, as also whimsical or escapist. The use of a conventionally nonrealist style to represent an autobiographical experience is part of what has proved equally troubling and compelling, for example, to readers of Art Spiegelman's graphic memoir *Maus*, where cartoon mice narrators render a real-life intergenerational holocaust testimony.

Comic book forms may seem unlikely counterparts in the exploration of the complex epistemological and ontological questions genres of memoir and autobiography raise. Rocco Versaci, in *This Book Contains Graphic Language: Comics as Literature* (2007), notes that popular opinion of the comic book has often been of this kind: that its "conventions of broad humour, excessive emotion, physical action, and large but digestible conflict" have been seen as "elements that do not easily lend themselves to the study of the delicate relationship between our inner and outer lives" (36). However, comics forms also have unique properties to offer the life narrator, not the least of which is, as Versaci notes, "a more flexible range of first-person narration than is possible in prose" (32). While this capacity is surely also visible in more experimental literary prose memoir, in which multiple narrative perspective and literary metaphor and allusion are actively deployed, it is in comic books that such possibilities are considered innately part of the genre, and indeed, as part of the *medium*. "As a representation of what Will Eisner calls a 'special reality,'" says Versaci, "comic book memoir explores issues of autobiographical writing in ways unavailable in prose alone" (32).

Michael Chaney, in his introduction to *Graphic Subjects: Critical Essays on Autobiography and Graphic Novels* (2011), also contextualizes the emergence of the autobiographical graphic novel by noting some of the problems of this description as a category—"nearly all the graphic novels studied in this volume," says Chaney, "make referential claims to the author's lived reality and therefore are not technically novels at all" (4)—and he observes that this kind of autobiographical representation both contests an assumed literary status for autobiography and opens up new generic possibilities. The emergent scholarly canon around Spiegelman's *Maus*, for example, has emphasized "the uniquely supple procedures the comics form can make possible for the representation of multiple yet simultaneous timescapes and competing yet coincident ways of knowing, seeing, and being" (Chaney, *Graphic*, 5). In this context, comics *literally* enable new ways of seeing, new ways of being seen, and new ways of representing the self. Chaney's major argument here is that this is a capacity of visual autobiographical representation in general, and of comics style in particular. That is, while photography and autobiography have something of a shared history, Chaney argues: "If printed autobiographies that include photographs highlight autobiography's claims to historical accuracy and self-reflexivity, autobiographies told in the typically exaggerated visual style of the comics, by contrast, complicate those claims, juxtaposing them against autobiography's other set of authorial promises—to portray experience in a manner that is emotionally and psychologically true to the unique, often idiosyncratic perspective of the author-artist" (4). Chute, in her discussion of contemporary autobiographical comics by women in *Graphic Women*, agrees that the comics medium has particular qualities to confer in the representation of certain kinds of experience, and for particular kinds of subjects. That is, Chute finds comics particularly powerful in the context of women's self-representation and particularly prevalent in the narration of traumatic experience.

Given the provocative status of the comics idiom as a nonfiction mode, a tension exacerbated by "the conventional understanding that the system of *drawing* must be inherently more 'fictional' than the system of *writing*," Chute is "fascinated not only by *how* the authors construct narrative in this way but also *why*" (*Graphic*, 6). For Chute, an instability and danger of the comics mode, as a form often understood as "childish" as well as hyperbolic, allows the women artists she explores to position themselves in productive tension to the particularly powerful assumptions and expectations that surround women's visual self-representation in contemporary culture.[3] Irene Gammel, in her discussion of visual and performative diaries, also frames the issue in connection to women's representation in particular: "Given the obsession with the female body in Western iconography, how do women photographers, performers, and painters represent their sexual lives without becoming caught in a web of confining cultural representations?" ("Mirror Looks," 289). Using modes of representation until very recently largely characterized as childish or lacking appropriately "delicate" literary qualities (Versaci, *This*, 36), comics artists instead draw attention to the flexible and subversive possibilities of the visual medium, which in part has to do with the subversion of stereotypes of the comics form itself. For comics artists like Phoebe Gloeckner, who combines comics with the mode of the teenage diary, a connection between genre and form amplifies the already embedded possibility of subversion and reinterpretation.

A symbolic and cultural connection between comics and childhood further means that artists who have used comics memoir to explore and represent non-normative coming-of-age or other developmental narratives may find themselves in particularly provocative terrain. The representation of explicit sexual experience is a feature of the autobiographical comic, and it is a trope that female comics artists in particular have explored in tandem with feminist concerns about embodiment and representation. The ability of "visual-verbal" narratives to express feminist concerns in this context, however, the "affect and effect" of narratives that "put the body on the page, that push against easy consumption," means that this narrative has also encountered resistance in the mainstream (Chute, *Graphic*, 26). For example, Bechdel's representation of sexual intercourse as a young adult in *Fun Home*, as well as the depictions of sex in Craig Thompson's coming-of-age memoir *Blankets*, aroused the ire of a conservative community group when the books were bought for their local Missouri library. The group claimed, however, that their concern did not lie "with the content" itself but with the accessibility of the sexual content produced in its status as images (Twiddy, "Library"). Using a comics mode that is frequently hyperrealistic and narratively concerned with the autobiographical depiction of the sexual experience of a teenage girl, Phoebe Gloeckner's work has arguably trespassed into even more controversial territory. Infamously, Gloeckner's first full-length comics publication, the 1998 anthology *A Child's Life and Other Stories*, was confiscated by British and French customs officials—"their main complaint: a panel of a young Minnie [Gloeckner's cartoon alter-ego], Hello Kitty diary by her side, about to give a blowjob to a much older man" (Joiner, "Not").

The discomfort with which some readers have responded to Gloeckner's visual narration is important in considering how and why images might disturb and confront in ways that prose might not. Gloeckner's publisher, Richard Grossinger, also emphasizes this phenomenon, contrasting the reception of Dorothy Allison's shocking and very graphic (but much lauded) memoir of sexual abuse with responses to Gloeckner: "There's a resistance to something that's drawn that wouldn't exist if it were written. If you're talking about child abuse, *Bastard Out of Carolina* is in many ways harsher than Phoebe's work. If you drew that, you'd be marginalised" (qtd. in Orenstein, "Graphic," 28; qtd. in Chute, *Graphic*, 61). For other interpreters of Gloeckner's work, the focus on troubling content misses the quality of the depictions itself. Discussing the controversial panels of "Minnie's Third Love" from *A Child's Life*, Tom Spurgeon from *The Comics Reporter* observes that "many of the narrative undercurrents were lost on readers because the stories themselves were so powerfully lurid. Each shows people in pain, and children suffering from sexual encounters and violence that are rarely this clearly depicted in any medium . . . if what many readers take away from 'Minnie's Third Love' are the graphic depictions of oral sex, those scenes loom large due to the very deliberate pacing employed by the artist" ("Phoebe"). Spurgeon draws attention to the self-consciousness of Gloeckner's visual choices and to the deliberations in her process. This is clearly a way of defending Gloeckner against the charges of pornography that visual depictions of sex attract, but it is also to distinguish the stylistic, aesthetic, and literary choices the author has made in her representation.[4] That is, these are not images designed merely to shock (though they are shocking) but are carefully employed storytelling devices. And while Gloeckner's visual register is very confronting, another powerful rhetorical choice here is genre.

Composed as the real-life typed and illustrated diary of Minnie Goetze, Gloeckner's second full-length publication, *Diary of a Teenage Girl*, opens with "A Note of Caution to the Reader" to "Please, do never read this unless and until I am dead"—a disclaimer that functions to establish the protagonist's teenage status and worldview—"If you do read on, don't you dare ever let me know that you did or I swear to God I will kill myself or run away or do any number of self-destructive things" (xv)—and the seductive association of diary narrative as a text that both resists and invites reading, something that incurs extra tension here as the secret diary of a teenage girl. Gloeckner, represented by her cartoon alter ego as "Minnie," who experiences the biographical details of Gloeckner's childhood and adolescence, has been quoted as saying that the narrative for *Diary* is about "one-half of Gloeckner's own real diary from 1976–1977 reproduced intact—word for word" and the "other half of *Diary*, while events may match her actual teenage experience—Gloeckner wrote as an adult author, re-forming her former diary's narrative structure" (Chute, *Graphic*, 74). This uncertain status of the work, as both fiction and nonfiction, real and constructed, emphasizes the hybridity of the work as well as its fluid relationship to "authenticity and inauthenticity" (74). The text challenges assumptions of diary

as a strictly documentary or present tense record. Instead, Gloeckner presents
a shifting set of narrative perspectives (visual and textual) that respond to the
diary's ability to represent and show coterminous selves as part of the diaristic
"archive."

Diary, then, includes retrospective narration, in the form of prose "added"
to the published edition, but also as illustrations that capture the adult Gloeckner's process of reading and "re-visualizing" her teenage self. Most of the drawings in *Diary* are composed chronologically after the events described, though
some are also "souvenirs" of the time, such as the original comics Gloeckner
writes as a fifteen-year-old. This shifting narrative perspective (in word and
image) *shows* the author's changing available levels of retrospection and interpretation, a capacity enabled by the unique presence of the visual image in narrative time and the arrangement of the text here as a keepsake diary. Crucially, the
historical and temporal moment of narration (whether by the fifteen-year-old
Minnie or from the adult Gloeckner) is not visible in prose but through image.
That is, "original" as well as retrospective parts of the prose narration are not
distinguished; the diary is focalized in a seamless present tense. However, while
the narration is stable, the visual register is more fluid. For example, Minnie's
first attempts at comics illustration are included in the *Diary*. "A Walk through
the City," captioned "My first comic," shows a naïve and germinal style heavily
derived from the comic artists who most influenced her as a fifteen-year-old,
R. Crumb and Aline Kominsky-Crumb, and it is reproduced chronologically
in the diary: "I just finished my first comic," writes Minnie on Monday, 28
June. "It's just one page but it took me a really long time to do" (121). Though
Minnie says this is her "first comic," it is not the first comic in the *Diary* and it is
not the first illustration in the text. These images are added many years later by
Gloeckner when she crafts the text for publication, and they have a noticeably
different style than the "Minnie" illustrations presented as "originals" in time.
Chute describes this effect structurally as "narratives that sweep in and periodi-
cally substitute for text" (*Graphic*, 74). The effect on narration, however, is also
more complex than simple substitution: throughout *Diary*, Minnie's future self
(one of the key audiences for any diary text) becomes a *literal* presence, and this
is visually rendered in the style of the retrospective illustrations that extend the
account (visual and verbal) kept at the time.

That is, Gloeckner freely admits that parts of her prose are composed
retrospectively, yet it is only through visual idiom that this crafting of the narrative is "visible." The elegant and distinctive style Gloeckner develops as an adult
after years of professional training and practice as a medical illustrator signals
her different narrative point of view to the events of her past, and certainly

these illustrations are more complex and symbolic, self-consciously dynamic in scale and position, and interweaving intertextual and other symbolic images and tropes (one of these is the Hello Kitty diary itself, which I return to shortly). The sophistication of Gloeckner's textual and visual strategies, then, belie certain assumptions about childhood and about genre (as well as gender) that are also evoked and challenged by the status of this narrative as *The Diary of Teenage Girl*. For example, in *Sophistication: A Literary and Cultural History* (2010), Faye Hammill notes that a quality of sophistication is incompatible with the Victorian view of childhood as idyllic and innocent: "In nineteenth-century fiction . . . there was still considerable uncertainty about the precise meaning of 'sophistication,' and also about whether it was something to be admired. 'Unsophistication' was nearly always a term of praise, suggesting that 'sophistication' retained a meaning related to sophistry, disingenuousness, or perversion" (74). Such views extend to contemporary genres and forms, and indeed, an investment in less censored and more spontaneous writing is visible in certain autobiographical modes; diary is the preeminent example here. Gloeckner's *Diary of a Teenage Girl* sits provocatively over divides like literary/ordinary or sophisticated/unsophisticated, and indeed, also straddles a presumed separation between real/fake, authentic/inauthentic that is invoked by genre. Moreover, both as form and motif, the childhood diary has a distinct rhetorical charge in Gloeckner's work. This also has to do with the kinds of claims to readership certain subjects (especially women and children) make. In her energetic rereading of the teenage Russian diarist Marie Bashkirtseff, Sonia Wilson observes that diary genres in particular operate within a strict discursive field. For example, within "the criterion of ordinariness," literary and highly sophisticated diaries like that by Anaïs Nin, or by the young Bashkirtseff, fail certain criteria: "Their diaries are too 'clever' to be authentic, their 'story' of themselves too interesting to qualify as ordinary" (*Personal*, 12). As Wilson continues, "if it is not possible to tidily tuck Bashkirtseff's diary away on either side of the Literary/ordinary divide, it is because what this particular text does is upset the way in which the interface of diary reader and diary text has implicitly been configured" (13).

The tension between representation and reality and the complexity of "truth" already examined in the graphic memoir can assume further layers and nuance in graphic diary. An emphasis on chronological, sequential content that has an "in the moment" perspective means that diary forms can conjure very strongly associations with the personal, the authentic, and the real, and maybe even more strongly than autobiography, with its often overt aesthetic and structural links to the novel. Moreover, uses of the diary by women and children in particular draw on and redeploy very strong historical links to the narration of private life and especially to the recording of female experience. This is something Gloeckner makes very overt in her work, where diary is both record and testimony.

As a genre, the diary intersects with desires for access to women's sexual self-representation, and this is exacerbated and complicated in the context of an adolescent author and amplified as a visual mode. Indeed, critics like Irene Gammel, who have explored visual and performance diaries of women in particular, argue that we should "map" such diaries as "distinctive subgenres in our autobiographical theorizing of the diary" ("Mirror Looks," 291). As in other modes through which women have actively encountered and "strategically negotiated" the representation of their lives in public, the diary has a special relationship to emblems of female existence, such as dailiness, confession, and fragmentation, and women who use this form both assimilate and contest such ascriptions. For Gammel, the visual diary is a distinct way in which women have given shape and expression to their subjectivity and experience, as well as their desire. So, the diary as a recognizable form and historical mode is important here; it is "a serial form of life writing that allows them to represent their multiple selves in their full complexity, producing an interfacing of artistic, domestic, and sexual selves" (290). However, for Gammel there is also a clear distinction to be made; unlike "the written diary . . . visual and performance diaries more powerfully engage the viewer with the women's *embodied* selves in their *physical* materiality" (292).

In Gloeckner's text, then, the diary also has a metonymic status: as the disconcerting symbol of the teenage Minnie's precarious position between child and adult; as a poignant counterpoint to her status as sexually exploited girl in the "laundry room" scene from "Minnie's Third Love" from *A Child's Life and Other Stories* (2000), the Hello Kitty diary also reappears in Gloeckner's second full-length publication, *Diary of a Teenage Girl*. Here an image of the diary is reproduced photographically (indicating a status as "real" object) on the inside front and back cover, which also include copies of the typed "diary pages" that ostensibly make up the rest of the narrative and that Minnie produces over the course of the diary. The Hello Kitty diary is thus a reminder of textual authenticity, a signifier for a manuscript original, and a statement of verifiability in the context of this work as an autobiographical representation. That this is a photograph (and not a drawn illustration) is also significant, offering yet another counterpoint to the hybrid and cross-discursive status of the text in its dynamic visual/verbal construction. In one of the retrospective comic strips that Gloeckner composes for the *Diary*, the Hello Kitty diary also appears strategically, to mark a point in the narrative that both looks forward to future events and positions Minnie in relation to her historical "I," as a diary-keeping teenager engaged in a self-destructive sexual relationship with her mother's boyfriend. This comic strip, "Shopping for a Boat," depicts Minnie writing in her Hello Kitty diary, her pencil at a ready angle, the minimalist cover and stylized Hello Kitty motif (which is slightly different from the cover motif depicted in "Minnie's Third Love" and from the photograph on the inside cover of *Diary*) occupying much of the bottom half of the panel and obscuring Minnie's mouth (*Diary*, 41). The subsequent panel depicts Monroe, the stepfather figure who has engaged in an affair with the fifteen-year-old Minnie, berating her for documentation: "Christ, you're writing in your diary again! Don't you realize that mothers go looking for diaries and that they always find them? She finds that and everything's over" (41). This scene foreshadows the anticlimactic moment when Minnie's mother does find the diary, and not only fails to make anything "over" in terms of the relationship, but spectacularly silences her daughter's account of events by demanding that Minnie marry Monroe (256). Her mother's inability to protect her daughter or to adequately "read" what has happened confirms that it is Minnie's childhood diary, and her own careful documentation of experience, that will be the means through which this story will eventually be "heard." The Hello Kitty diary is thus, as Chute also observes, "a kind of protection, a future promise" (*Graphic*, 77). The diary itself, an iconic symbol of teenage girlhood, acquires weight as a talismanic object that is also a testimonial form. Publishing her "secret" adolescent diary allows Gloeckner to tell a story that both depicts her experiences of exploitation and vulnerability and asserts her authority as the narrator of that experience.

This is something that also functions visually in the narrative composition. Gloeckner includes several versions of the Hello Kitty cover motif, and these differences are both subtle and obvious: the two drawn versions of the cover are minimalist and resemble each other, but the inside cover image is a photographic image of the actual Hello Kitty diary Gloeckner ostensibly kept as a girl. Subtle variances between the drawn versions, and a difference between these representations and the original, indicate that a retrospective narrator can have trouble accurately visualizing exact detail; the images here offer a subtle reminder that memory is at play in any autobiographical narration, even an ostensibly present-tense one like diary. After all, diary, as Felicity Nussbaum has argued, is uniquely available to the representation of a series of coterminous subject positions, and Gloeckner's use of a visual register shows one way in which a diarist's future self is an available speaking position for the first-person narrator. The sophistication of this narrative perspective is belied by both the comics style and a narration of events as the diary account of a young girl.

Taking up the particular power of the visual medium to juxtapose different selves in time, a capacity refracted and heightened by a choice to frame this narrative as a diary, Gloeckner uses the spatial capacity of comics to craft an account that both enacts a specific historical time for the author and enables concurrent postreflection on that experience. In keeping with a tradition of women diarists in particular, Gloeckner uses the open-ended form of the diary to represent and inscribe the shifting subjectivities and roles of the narrator in relation to her own life, something she further makes visible through the visual/verbal retrospective and present-tense narration that both comments on and pluralizes in "words and pictures" an account kept at the time.

Bobby Baker: Illness Diary and the Visual Mode

Unlike Gloeckner's crafted and complex narration in her *Diary of a Teenage Girl*, Bobby Baker's visual diary drawings, arranged chronologically and represented linearly, present a more straightforward diaristic modality and also fit more easily into a ready-made category such as diary comics discussed, for example, by Isaac Cates. Familiar as a learning exercise or transitional form for young comics artists, the diary comic is composed daily or according to a chronological routine and as such "cannot know the future of the 'story' in which they participate" (Cates, "Diary," 211). The diary comic is thus dependent on contingent meaning, and, like other diary forms, is paratactic in its composition, allowing for the representation of a series of events in which no entry point is clearly prioritized over any other.

Although diary narrative has traditionally been understood as less linear or retrospective, as less like "stories," the diary comic further heightens a propensity of the form to prioritize the lyric moment, the heightened emotion, and the fleeting experience. The diary comic is also responsive to certain formal constraints. The diarist is limited to their day, but perhaps also to the amount of paper, time, or energy available to devote to the project. Like the exercise of the diary comic, Bobby Baker's diary drawings are single portraits, the literal illustration of her sense for the defining moment, feeling, or challenge in her day, and they are plot points on a journey through mental illness in which the outcome has not been secured.

Baker has written and published in diary form before. "Performance artist Bobby Baker," commissioned as part of a project to capture the creative process of nine different artists, is a brief account of six months in which the artist documents her process of developing new work. It commences with a familiar and very diaristic resolve: "21 January 2000, Starting this diary is the most wonderful solution to my problems of making new work, the perfect displacement activity. I will write about how stuck I am and then I won't feel so guilty about doing nothing constructive" (32). Baker's style is paratactic and list-like: "must do more Fat Attacking and drink less whisky" (33). The diary is a discipline, a practice to channel her output and to externalize and combat anxieties: "9 February, Consumed by all these titles, problems, questions. The problem is that there are too many problems. Resolve to washing duvets to keep mind at bay" (35). The activity of "washing duvets" is juxtaposed as antidote and buffer to the intellectual strain of creative work; the correlate to this domestic work is that of keeping the diary itself, and this is also symbolic. Baker is an artist who has engaged in multiple and various ways with the idea of an "everyday" and whose highly politicized social commentary draws its politics from the domestic realm of female experience. Centering on food, private spaces, and the business of everyday living, Baker's work is also largely autobiographical, featuring members of her family as well as the routines and preoccupations of her daily life. *Diary Drawings* is nonetheless a departure from work that has characterized Baker as an artist. That is, while still energized by domesticity and dailiness, the paintings made for this collection are, for the artist herself, more "private" than the work of performing: "That is another thing I loved about the drawings, the feeling I didn't have to show them to people" (Baker qtd. in Lightman, "*Diary*," 161).

There is a contradiction here that finds force in the exhibition of Baker's work that precedes the monograph publication. Sarah Lightman, in a 2010 review of Baker's Wellcome Exhibition, observes that while a selection of the paintings are exhibited in the gallery, the rest are "displayed but inaccessible, the original art remains intact, private and protected with page after page modestly housed in their green ring-bound sketchbooks, remaining closed in glass cabinets" ("*Diary*," 161). As a visual reminder of the diary archive that both exceeds and authorizes the displayed or "published" version, the image of multiple diary originals is something of a trope—a widely circulated photograph of the prolific diarist Anaïs Nin leaning on a tower of her diary notebooks in the Brooklyn bank vault she stored them in for safekeeping is an iconic example. Indeed, Gloeckner, Baker, and journal curator Someguy all make reference to the diary archive that lies outside the published edition.[5] Baker's designation of this work as *diary* drawings further engages with the tension between display and concealment that characterizes the curation of an exhibition. Indeed, given the subject here is the artist's own psychic break with her experience of identity and reality, a key audience is Baker's own future self, one who is well and needs reminding or who doesn't want to forget what has been passed through.

A quality of diary, and one heightened in an illness narrative in particular, is its function as a record unsure of its outcome: these images' particular potency comes in part from the prospect that Baker may not recover, that the illness will perpetuate the break or will succeed in other ways of detaching the artist from her reality (there are several depictions in *Diary Drawings* that reveal directly or indirectly that Baker is contemplating suicide). Though Baker is clearly present to introduce, contextualize, and even participate in the selection of her work, the prospect that the outcome could have been different is clear. A diary in this context holds force as a document written into the void, a lifeline whose practice will buoy or carry the author, but which may also be held to speak on their behalf should they not make it through. In her introduction to *Diary Drawings*, Marina Warner explicitly contextualizes the effect of the work to its form as a diary: "hindsight forgets, hindsight alters the fact. But a diary or journal, a daybook as their names convey, gives us back experience in real time. Their immediacy gives them the rush of sincerity: a howl not a sermon, an exclamation mark not a speech, something blurted, something avowed, something admitted" ("Chronicle," 3).

As with the work of other diarists explored throughout this book, Baker's work takes a generic shape that is very important here. That is, unlike Gloeckner, who composes a visual narrative that contains "first draft" comics and text, but also a retrospective narrative that is polished and professional, Baker's paintings are a series of documents that draw authenticity as the embodiment of a moment of creation. Whitlock and Poletti have noted that it is the "fascination with surface . . . that characterizes autographics" ("Self-Regarding," vi), and Baker's diary drawings exemplify an invitation to read for this kind of surface and texture. The careful reader can observe physical differences in different notebook's spiral binding, sometimes cocked, sometimes perfect. A rare smudge is visible on the page of Day 444 (*Diary*, 99), while a change to the handwritten dating system (from days only to weeks) that occurs on Day 418 is a shift further emphasized in new lighter and more precise etch (presumably from a fresh or sharpened pencil), a contrast to the thicker pencil line on the pages preceding (84–85). This available detail adds interpretive weight to the visual images selected for the monograph and provides a visceral engagement with surface and texture for the reader: this is the documentary (visual and verbal) evidence of Baker's daily struggle toward mental wellness, and it is also a material trace of this experience.

In confronting the traumatic incision of debilitating illness into her everyday world, Baker is both resistant to and deeply hopeful of the medical environment she must navigate in order to survive her disease. The paintings are particularly acute in their representation of the health professionals that Baker must interact with on her stays in the hospital and in various group and private counseling contexts, with such provocative images as Baker's violent fantasy of murdering her therapist (Day 6, *Diary*, 23), but also more poignant images, where Baker represents herself as a dissolved, spectral blob in the triangle of patient therapist care (Day 317, 62). The patient in this context is both the subject and object of discourse yet, despite fantasies of control (which are frequently violent), there is little autonomy. Julia Watson, in her analysis of Bobby Baker's *Diary Drawings* as "prosthetic practice," positions Baker's diary drawing as a self-therapeutic but also self-dislocating project, one in which the subject can engage with the disequilibrium of the "human" in the context of mental disruption ("Visual," 39). She also argues that the project "distinguishes itself from both traditional autobiography and written diaries" and instead, by "incorporating both visual media (drawing, painting, photography) and verbal modes (diaristic confession, commentary, epigrams) to chronicle moments of experience not narratable in ordinary words, *Diary Drawings* is a serial automedial narrative" (25). Using formal capacities of diary modes, such as its "ongoing present" and a serial chronology, *Diary Drawings* challenges the humanist subject and the striving for coherence and normativity that characterizes it (39). In Watson's analysis, the diary is kept as prosthesis, but it also acts as a communication mechanism and a means of repetition and control in moments of disorientation.

While in many ways a radical reinterpretation of the artist's or visual journal, and Lightman notes that it must also be understood within the comics tradition,[6] *Diary Drawings* is also an illness narrative, of which the illness diary is a particular subgenre. Employing both structural and formal effects of the diary while also drawing on visual art traditions, Baker *literally* draws attention to the fractured subject who moves through the inarticulability of trauma, finding form for experience and shaping new spaces for subjective and personal expression in the process. The reader of this work is invited into and must participate in the tense daily cycle of coping with (and surviving) mental illness.

Diary Public: *The 1000 Journals Project*

While each are avant-garde and innovative in their own way, Baker's *Diary Drawings* and Gloeckner's *Diary of a Teenage Girl* reproduce recognizable tropes and structures of the diary form. As a visual journal that is also an intervention and response to a new media landscape where ideas of personal writing, audience, and representation are being radically refocused, *The 1000 Journals Project* is a quite different venue for considering the place of the visual subject in contemporary life writing and for the evolution and innovation of the diary form.

As a collaborative art project of the early 2000s, amid the boom and "bust" of Internet technology and web content and the rise of the "ordinary" individual in public discourse,[7] *The 1000 Journals Project* represents an attempt to weave together new and enduring modes of expression and genres of representation. Like the arguably more successful postcard confessional that it predates, Frank Warren's 2004 (and ongoing) *PostSecret*, *The 1000 Journals Project* responds to autobiography as an everyday phenomenon and demonstrates the powerful role the creation and sharing of personal information in public has in contemporary culture. This project also confirms that visual registers have a more and more significant role to play in the representation (and conceptualization) of the contemporary subject, and indeed, that concerns about authenticity and the individual that are endemic to practices of life writing are in specific tension to discourses of visibility and representation now prominent in broader cultural debates about life amid digital technology.

Prioritizing the production of material artifacts, handwritten inscription, and literal cut and paste, at a time when digital technologies have enabled the seamless juxtaposition of hybrid media, *The 1000 Journals Project* intersects with a modern nostalgia for the slower circuits of communication represented in the technology of the book and for the experience of texture and surface offered in collage, graffiti, and embroidery. Composed of diary pages completed by hundreds of participants, *The 1000 Journals Project* also functions as another iteration of the visual diaries that have been explored in this chapter. That is, it represents a particular kind of engagement with diary form and rhetoric, and it negotiates in particular ways with the ideology of the visual and the handmade that also exists in connection to works like Gloeckner's *Diary of a Teenage Girl* or Baker's *Diary Drawings*.

The 1000 Journals Project is the creation of San Francisco artist Brian Singer and is published under his pseudonym, Someguy. Begun in 2000, as a series of blank, hardbound books distributed by Someguy to people he knew or randomly encountered, the project rapidly expanded, eventually prompting Someguy to leave journals in public places, as well as allowing for sign-up over a project website ("The 1000 Journals Project"). Containing a set of rules stamped on the inside cover along with a series number, and a request for completed, "full" journals to be returned to a San Francisco postal address, circulation is voluntarily traced by contributors over a website ("1000 Journals"). However, and despite a quite active element of online engagement, this is not a web project as such—these journals are not blogs. The website functions primarily as the distribution mechanism and tracking device and also as a nexus for the development

of a community. It also ensures the project's ongoing relevance.[8] As Kevin
Kelly describes in his foreword to the *1000 Journals* book, the project "begins
with the oldest peer-to-peer network we have—face-to-face exchanges—and
then adds our second-oldest network—the postal system . . . on top of these two
robust networks of one thousand moving journals, Someguy added the new
global network of the Web, which is able to track and enliven the digital ghosts
of the traveling books" (n.p.). The Internet is a circulation strategy here, but it
is also an ethos. In his introduction to the book publication (which he describes
as an anthology of the "best bits"), Someguy explains that he generated the
project to extend a fascination with public graffiti:

> I've always been fascinated with graffiti, whether scrawled on bathroom walls
> or carved into park benches—anonymous conversations and arguments held in
> public spaces for the world to see. With raw and spontaneous scribblings the
> walls become a forum of sorts, a collection of opinions about drugs, politics, sex,
> war, racism and a healthy dose of drunken poetry . . . I remember walking
> home from work one day, running ideas through in my head. It finally occurred
> to me that a journal was the perfect medium to engage, and, unlike a wall, it
> could travel around the world. (*1000 Journals*)

While Internet technologies have arguably changed how and what we conceive
a "wall" to be (the "wall" of an interactive chat room, a Facebook wall, or a
"blog wall"), in the context of this project, the journal as wall is a metaphor,
invoking a function as a public space. A wall is also a shared and stationary
medium, though not (and this is especially obvious in the context of graffiti, as
well as in online spaces) a static one. In *Graffiti Lives: Beyond the Tag in New York's
Urban Underground* (2009), Gregory J. Snyder posits a resonance in how graffiti
subcultures employ their art to a practice of bricolage: "Graffiti writers transform spray paint from a household product into a tool to create devastating
art" (160). Lacking the context-specific politics of graffiti, *The 1000 Journals Project*
also uses bricolage and collage subversively, deploying everyday or "household"
objects and narratives: diary entries, restaurant receipts, bus tickets, flyers, newspaper cuttings, letter to friends, letters to self, wishes, regrets, biographies, maps.
There is an emphasis overall on visual representation and on materiality—
reproduced in the book are two hand-embroidered pages—sketches, cartoons,
and other visual miscellanea dominate alongside reproduced handwritten notes
and other textual contributions.

The appeal of this project as one intrinsically concerned with material surface and physical texture connects to certain anxieties aroused by the "digital
age," something Kelly identifies and speaks to in his foreword: "Some folks

worry the digitization of our daily lives will make us disembodied ghosts[;] . . .
we'll work, play, shop, and live online, and the real world—the physical world
and all its pleasures—will rot." For Kelly, "nothing could be further from the
truth," yet contributors to *The 1000 Journals Project* demonstrate that part of the
allure in this context is contact with material modes and methods of communication that may seem obsolete. This is a theme, for example, for some of the
interview subjects in Andrea Kreuzhage's 2008 documentary, *1000 Journals*. In
a chapter of the documentary titled "Craving the Physical World," Mitsu
Hadeishi from the Bronx reminisces how journal #278 became significant for
an established group of webloggers. Despite a density of existing interaction and
engagement, and an extensive knowledge of the group's interests and dynamics,
participation in *The 1000 Journals Project* provides a novel opportunity: for the
first time, the group could "see each other's handwriting, the types of drawing
they do, the collages they would do" (Kreuzhage, *1000*). Though regarded by
the group as "old-fashioned" technology, the book in this context, says Hadeishi,
"felt fresh" (Kreuzhage, *1000*). Participation here provided the means for a
register of engagement the group suddenly felt had been missing. However,
rather than a seeming intervention into the "ghost" world of cyberspace, and
despite an emphasis on handwriting and other craft, *The 1000 Journals Project*
replicates a structure of authorship that is more closely associated with online
modes of writing than its physical antecedents in that the project is externally
curated and the individual contributors are not necessarily identified, nor do
they expect to be.

As autobiography, then, the project undermines the referential connection
between text and author that the genre is usually understood to imply. Diverse
in style and content, a majority of the contributors to *The 1000 Journals Project*
nonetheless choose an autobiographical register, or describe an autobiographical experience, motivation, or response. In categorizations Someguy makes for
the online archive of scanned journals on the project website, certain thematic
categories emerge: "relationships" is a theme for 98 entries, "world events"
describes 71 entries, and "advice/deep thoughts" makes up another 248. The
largest category is "Personal/Diary," applicable to 904 of the submissions
(Someguy, "1000 Journals"). Most of the entries, whether clearly autobiographical or not, are read as manifestations of self—the act of autobiography is here
lodged in the activity of inscription, of narrating, reciting, pasting, rather than
in a verifiable correlate reality, rather than through "signature" or "contract"
(Lejeune, *On Autobiography*). For example, the website describes "The Search for
114," a hunt by family and relatives for two missing journals contributed to by
an Australian man who died in a motorcycle accident. Online, as well as in

projects like *The 1000 Journals Project*, autobiography becomes the archival trace of a person as much as it might elsewhere (in the commercial, literary sphere, for example) be the verifiable representation of factual biographical details or articulate self-representation. In the specific context of new media, it's what David Gauntlett, in *Making Is Connecting: The Social Meaning of Creativity from DIY to Knitting and YouTube and Web 2.0* (2011), calls "the presence of the maker in the thing they have made—the unavoidably distinctive fingerprint that the thinking-and-making individual leaves in their work, which can foster a sense of shared feeling and common cause even when maker and audience have never met" (221). Contributors and participants, as well as readers, clearly respond in this way to *The 1000 Journals Project*, and the reproduction of their efforts, as a visual collage in the monograph publication, is an important authenticating layer in this context. That is, an emphasis on visual styling and texture in the journal entries Someguy curates for the publication link this project to a contemporary moment where material and visual objects have begun to acquire (or reacquire) a very high moral and aesthetic value.

Anna Poletti, in her discussion of the online postcard confessional *PostSecret*, has explored how the composition of the "secrets" shared online for that platform also draw authenticity though reference to materiality: in "the recurring presence of handwriting, collage, objects and photographs—the postcards constitute their authenticity as the physical traces of their authors" ("Intimate Economies," 31). Sharing an emphasis on contributions that are clearly hand drawn and made, that bear the physical or literal "trace" of their author, the *1000 Journals* monograph also attempts to reproduce artifacts not usually incorporated into a published text, such as pages embroidered with real thread that allow for a tactile experience. However, ultimately, the mandate for this project is to encourage the reclamation/manifestation of a creative *self*. With Someguy as the curator, the contributors as "artists," and the project as the "museum," *The 1000 Journals Project* is positioned as the model for what an exemplary "creative" self might achieve (in other iterations of this project, this creative self is also, and much more explicitly, a therapeutic undertaking).[9]

In many ways, creative self-making (the self as creative) is the dominant function or aspiration of *The 1000 Journals Project*, and this has connections to genre (the journal and diary as a regime of self-scrutiny, documentation as transformation, and authenticity as visual trace) as well as to those ideologies and technologies of digital and visual culture that enable the project and shape its aesthetic.[10] The visual mode of the diary in this context thus remobilizes the characteristics of "handwriting" and "hand-crafting" that underpin the diary in its comics form, or that are so seductive and compelling as a series of compositions in watercolor. In each case, the diary as a visual mode allows for the representation of a flexibility and fragmentation long associated with the form but that may be subsumed in more traditional modes of print. Indeed, though departing little from the "invisible medium" of the book,[11] these visual life narratives allow for the representation of more fluid and shifting notions of what constitutes an autobiographical subject and how this may be represented, materialized, and embodied on the page.

The Trace of the Author

"One doesn't 'keep' a poem or a letter or a novel, not as one actually writes it," observes Thomas Mallon, in the introduction to his sweeping survey of diary literature, *A Book of One's Own*: "Diaries are *for* keeps: in fact, they are *keeps* (Noun: FORTRESS, CASTLE: specif: the strongest and securest part . . .)" (xi). Mallon's association of diary to the fortified part of a medieval castle evokes Virginia Woolf's famous and equally spatial description of her diary: "Something loose-knit, & yet not slovenly, so elastic that it will embrace anything, solemn, slight or beautiful that comes into my mind. I should like it to resemble some deep old desk, or capacious hold-all, in which one flings a mass of odds and ends without looking through them" (*Diary*, 1:266). For Lejeune, the diary creates an effect depending on its physical medium: the notebook—"sewn, glued, stapled or bound with spiral wires"—will "*scar everything over*, linking it up and melting it together," while the "datebook 'formats' the writing space according to the supposed rhythm of time" (*On Diary*, 176–77). The manner of keeping a diary, a result of its format or method of composition, can determine both how the diarist feels about the enterprise and what the end result becomes. Lejeune prefers loose-leaf pages to "the slavery of the notebook"—the computer opens the possibilities even further.[12] The sense of diary articulated here as "hold-all" or physical repository, as a format that shapes and affects self-representation, underlies a preoccupation not only with *how* diaries are kept but also with *what* they keep. For example, Huff observes that the nineteenth-century diarist Marianne Estcourt makes use of a new trend for blank and lockable diaries to store extratextual items alongside the written account, including newspaper clippings relaying a family tragedy. Loose collections of tracts and devotional poems and other notational material are also filed in the locked volumes: "Such extratextual items push the spatial boundaries of the diary volumes through accretion of additional material that comments, perhaps obliquely, on what the diarist writes and how she defines herself within the social body. As such, these become as much a part of her record as the written diary" (Huff, "Textual," 130).

Certain kinds of contemporary diaries trade on and repurpose the material and keepsake association of the genre: Keri Smith's *Wreck This Journal* (2007) offers instructions for the reader that range from "Add Your Own Page Numbers" to "Cut through Several Layers." The only page of typed text, a discussion of Smith's purpose and aims for the book, exhorts its reader to "Doodle Over Top [*sic*] of This Page and in the Margins," stating, "This is not an important piece of writing, it is merely a texture of sorts that the reader will hopeful view as a canvas," and adding, a few paragraphs down, "Are you reading this? You are supposed to be defacing this page. Please stop reading at once!" In *Wreck This Journal*, Smith ironically defuses the rather more serious engagement I observed in chapter 2 demanded by self-help and how-to journals, though in both cases the diary is imagined as a tool for creating and owning a self-representation and so as the manifestation of a certain kind of creative and self-creating self. Rosenwald, too, captures the significance of the diary as object in his exhortation to pay attention to "not only the words but their incarnation and format"—to the kind of book the diarist buys, their use or not of the page, their sketches or crossing-outs, as well as the presentation of the handwriting itself—but also to "what non-verbal marks accompany the words" (19). The visual diary is an ideal form in which to make such reading (and such content) available.

The diaries that have been the subject of this chapter foreground a visual grammar of self-representation, and the formal capacity and flexibility of diary in this use is responded to and extended. A continuing interest in the diary as a personal mode of self-exploration or identity creation informs this use, which is also a response to a broader contemporary turn toward graphic and visual styles in autobiography in general. A key argument throughout this chapter has related to embodiment and materiality: the diary finds a different kind of expression when it is produced (both by diarist and publisher) as a visual mode. That is, while the manuscript diary has been recognized for its complexity as a textual artifact, one that requires a specific and sophisticated reading practice, the published version is, by comparison, compromised. This condition for the diary changes when the artifact is recognized as part of and essential to the diary's effect: the visual diary signals that the structural composition of the text, as well as its arrangement in parts, is meaningful. Where prose is the main focus, however, extratextual material or supplements may be elided or ignored. Something like *The 1000 Journals Project* restores the texture of a handwritten diary and makes this easily accessible in a public context. In a different way,

Bobby Baker's *Diary Drawings* also reference their existence as material artifacts through a photographic composition that includes details such as the spiral binding of each notebook (in which slight variances occur) and a repeated background of the artist's kitchen table. In shifting degrees of focus, each image reminds us of its origins as a visual work, and as an object with presence in "the real." In her review of the original exhibition of Baker's paintings, for example, Lightman observes that the drawings are hung behind glass, offering the viewer the possibility of "a glimpse of oneself, transposed onto Baker's face and body" ("Diary," 164). Similarly, the framing of images in Baker's monograph *Diary Drawings* means the reader is reminded that they are *looking*—this is a work dramatically located at what Smith and Watson call the visual/textual interface (*Interfaces*).

The 1000 Journals Project also draws attention to the nexus of image and text, but in this diary project the image stands in for a materiality seen as "superseded" in a new predominance of digital interfaces. While clearly offering a particular kind of engagement for the producer in this context, and the opportunity to "see" what others might do in a diary, *1000 Journals* also presents the means for a different way of reading. As a nonlinear text that blends individual perspectives (allowing for excisions or emendations to the "original") and de-identifies the "author" in favor of the "curator," reading this project as life writing is a way of considering how individuals work with, but also around, genres in determining appropriate spaces and means for self-representation.

Uses of the diary as a visual medium call on the genre's discursive roots to illustrated family books, scrapbooks, artist's notebooks, and family albums, and they negotiate with a hallmark invitation of the diary genre as uniquely receptive to individual style and choice in containing and representing an evolving self. Timothy Dow Adams, in his concluding chapter to *Light Writing and Life Writing: Photography in Autobiography* (2000), argues that a dominant interpretation of *graphe* (one of the Greek roots of "autobiography") as "writing" rather than an equally viable definition as "depiction" or "delineation" has meant that "too often, literary scholars have thought of autobiography only in terms of written texts" (225). A broader definition opens up the possibility, as Adams puts it, of taking into account "not only the uses of photography in autobiography . . . but also the larger question of autobiography in photography" (225). Like the photographic texts Adams examines, the diaries that are the subject of this chapter foreground image as the primary register of narration (rather than as an adjunct or "illustrative" supplement). In exploring visual modes for the contemporary use of the diary here, I have also wanted to explore an argument about the kinds of rhetorical styles that are privileged now and to consider why diary finds prominence in this. That is, like many autobiographical genres, the diary is intensively linked to a seductive quest for ever-more authentic and "true" representations. However, the particular nature of the diary form, and enduring popular perceptions about its practice, means that the genre also has a special relationship to contemporary contexts where immediacy, intimacy, and authenticity are particularly valued, and this is again evident in the context of visual and graphic uses of diary.

Conclusion

Appropriately, then, the diary is also a commodity within its author's
power.

Lawrence Rosenwald

What does it mean to speak intimately in public? The diary is a mode of
narrative in which intimacy and interiority are a generic expectation. Alongside
a formal capacity for representation over time, and for dating and other authenticating data to emerge into narrative, the diary is a rhetorical mode connected
to prevailing or shifting expectations of private discourse in the context of self
and experience. The diary is responsive to the dominant cultural conditions that
shape the production of autobiographical representation, but it is also a flexible
genre with its own historical and social tradition, and uses of the diary show
that both readers and authors find it compelling as a form of self-representation.
Ultimately, the contemporary diary shows that certain forms of knowing remain
attached to particular genres. Even in new and very different forums, such as
online, discourse named as "diary" has work to do in the public domain, and
this is attached to hopes and desire for certain kinds of knowledge, to certain
arenas of experience, and to certain ways of self-identification/articulation.

This book examines contemporary uses of diary. It has focused broadly on
diary publications of the last thirty years, and in particular, published diaries (in
print or in new media) after 2000. My focus on "published" diaries has been a
deliberate attempt to consider how the diary form now increasingly functions
as a self-conscious choice for all kinds of writers, and readers. That is, while the
diary undoubtedly continues to flourish as a "private" form (a practice that
evidently and intrinsically underwrites diary elsewhere), in this study I have
focused on diaries that have rhetorical work to do in the public domain and to

describe how this is partially captured through claims to genre. The publication of English-language diaries by Arab women, the diary as it has emerged as a genre on the Internet, as well as how it has evolved into graphic and comics forms, represents a "new wave" in diary publication and production in the last ten years that has created innovative locations and forms of the genre. Contemporary diaries also reflect an uptake as a literary and published genre, rather than as a merely incidental or necessarily naïve one, and this means that the contemporary diary reveals more clearly than before the distinctive rhetorical position of the diary mode.

Like the broad "umbrella" category of life writing to which it belongs, diary is a dynamic site for drawing into view ever-urgent questions about personal story and public history. In this study, I have asked what is particular about diary as a genre and form as it appeals to and is shaped by contemporary readers and practitioners of the genre, and in doing so I have explored how the diary genre has both evolved and persisted in a contemporary social cultural milieu. For example, even though perceptions of the diary as a secret or extraliterary genre are ultimately unrepresentative of the vast and diverse uses of the form historically, examples like the *Big Brother* "diary room," as a shorthand signifier for "unmasked" self-representation, demonstrate that, perhaps particularly in the spaces of popular culture, the diary remains intimately connected to a discursive rhetorical location as "private" writing. It is a perception of the diary that has persisted even in new and very different locations for personal writing. When bloggers use diary as the designation for an interactive, public, pseudonymous, personal discursive venue, they invoke certain stereotypical conventions that not only shape and limit audience expectations but also affect the author's own subjective experience writing in this location. When a journalist publishes a diary account of an experience already represented in other venues and forms, he or she patterns a new audience engagement with this material, one dependent on a particular social interpretation of what the diary is and can be used for as an autobiographical form. Paradoxes and contradictions of diary recur in these spaces. Journalists who claim a naïve persona and an immersed, unfolding style for their diary accounts do so for the rhetorical benefits such a position confers as much as for how the form suits the experience they wish to convey.

In noting that multiple contemporary writers *select* diary because it enables certain generic presentations of self, that it activates certain unique claims around authenticity and truth, contexts emerge where diary has been taken up particularly energetically or urgently. For example, there is a clear spike in the publication of journalist diaries in the years immediately following the Iraq war, but this trend is not sustained.[1] The diary account fulfills a desire for urgent, "hot" narrative; it offers a point of view that is presumed to be mostly unedited, personal, and temporally close to the events described. Perhaps this is why a diary account may lose market resonance as other kinds of reflective and contextualized narrative begin to emerge, such as memoir. Of course, even though a publication trend may lose momentum, the diary account itself remains connected to the allure of the personal perspective, and as an alternative to the "cold" discourse of retrospective political or historical analysis.

Now so widely published, contemporary diaries fail to be private in any conventional sense (of course, historical diaries too exceed this category). Yet this does not sway a claim to the representation of intimate, *private* experience that the genre has always be understood to signal. The diary is framed as a private and interior account, even when the conditions of production belie such perspective. The diary is a thoroughly public form for speaking intimately of private experience, something that partly explains why readers and authors continue to find it so compelling, and for how it functions as a form that promises to bring experience "closer." For contemporary audiences, the personal voice is a central preoccupation, and this has consequences for how particular life-writing genres are circulated, as well as for whether they and their subjects are potentially celebrated or criticized. The personal story as a representation of subjective interiority is a central contemporary mode, one that is also relayed in the understanding that such experience, and its representation, is partly an ethical problem. In her philosophical meditation on place and memory, *Traumascapes: The Power and Fate of Places Transformed by Tragedy* (2005), Maria Tumarkin recounts an anecdote about the Ground Zero site in New York. Drawn to the location, "two young New Yorkers fake their IDs, shake at the thought of being found out, lie, push their luck, do whatever it takes to get to the site—all in order to (and this is where the possible anti-climax might creep in but it doesn't) hand out cold bottles of Gatorade to the exhausted fire-fighters, strike a few conversations and take in the magnitude of the destruction at eye level" (29). Alongside a heroic sub-plot of altruism and sacrifice, it is being "eye level" that is the moving part of this anecdote. How else to measure the shocking inversion of space; here is a superstructure razed to human scale. As a parable, this works in another way too: we want to get close to the things that affect us, to be eye to eye with experience, and if we can't be there in person, we want an account from someone who is. The first-person "I" narrator frames a perspective on events that are otherwise unimaginably vast in historical or cultural scale. It is a perspective that offers a way of seeing that is human sized, as limited as the eye (I) itself, and as contingent on who is seeing at the time.

Contemporary uses of the diary direct attention to sites of tension around personal story and public history; uses of the diary to represent personal experience draw power from embedded associations to knowledge and experience (secret, taboo, inappropriate) that are assumed to be hidden or less authentic in other kinds of self-representative acts. This contemporary state of the genre is underwritten by a persistence of certain traditions in diary and personal writing. In *Technologies of the Self* (1988), Michel Foucault remarks on the use of daily writing for self-reflection in the early Greco-Roman period as marking a "new concern with self" that was also "a new experience of self": "The new form of experience of the self is to be seen in the first and second century when introspection becomes more and more detailed. A relation developed between writing and vigilance. Attention was paid to nuances of life, mood, and reading and the experience of oneself was intensified and widened by virtue of this act of writing. A whole field opened up which earlier was absent" (28). For Foucault, "the examination of conscience" begins with this practice of self-reflection "at the end of the day," and "the letter is the transcription of that examination," it is a form that "stresses what you did, not what you thought," and so it predates confession and also diary: "Diary writing comes later. It dates from the Christian Era and focuses on the notion of the struggle of the soul" (30). The diary is a technology for writing that is also an epistemology of self: its practice is seen to have effects on the diarist's character, and on their experience of life. By the seventeenth century the diary is firmly linked to spiritual ideals of the self: "A sense of self reached its height in the diary, the book written by oneself as a means of self-reflection and self-control," says Roger Smith, noting that during this period "serious Puritans recommended the diary as a discipline for the soul's steady contemplation of its proper ends" ("Self-Reflection," 55). The history of the diary in relation to individual moral conduct has particular resonance in contemporary culture, but this is also transformed and reconfigured in particular ways. The diary as an authentic representation of the interior self, for example, is tied to popular understandings of diary as a mode of self-documentation that *produces* self-revelation. The insistence on privacy, then, which is so important to early critics like Harriet Blodgett, is an edict for unself-consciousness; it is a disciplining boundary for determining if a diarist is representing his or her "true" character.

Authors who use diary to make visible certain private experiences, then, do so within the rhetorical situation that the genre still confers. A central concern in this study has been the way in which diary is still linked very closely to notions of an authentic self and to desires for transparent and unmediated representation of this self and its experience. In *Inventing Our Selves: Psychology, Power and*

Personhood (1996), Nikolas Rose groups diary writing, "group discussion," and "the twelve-step program of Alcoholics Anonymous" as examples of the contemporary "techniques" through which individuals are asked to "conduct a relation with oneself," and he notes that "they are always practiced under the actual or imagined authority of some system of truth or authoritative individual" (29). One of these is confession, which emerges alongside the possibilities for subjective exploration embodied in diary forms.

Given a contemporary emphasis on making visible "conventionally private emotions and behaviours" (Lumby and Probyn, *Remote*, 14), it is significant to observe that the diary is confirmed as a part of everyday life, as a valuable commodity, and as a hybrid, mutable, and popular cultural practice. Moreover, diary is a genre linked intimately to the representation and construction of self in this context. "The sense of ourselves as beings with inner depths" that Charles Taylor has explored, for example (*Sources*, ix), still energizes a contemporary concern with self-expression and self-analysis, and this is also evident in the forms of diary writing that are finding expression in contemporary culture. "The diary," says Sonia Wilson, "is a form of writing that is also a way of living" (*Personal*, 10). An expectation that surveillance will lead us closer to "reality" in representation, that the confessional voice is authentic, that our "true self" is achieved through inwardness, is key here, and these are ideals linked closely with diary practice, both historically and in the present.

In the loosening of conventional paradigms for self-representation, in the broadening of discussion around what self-narration is and can be, the diary is a specific and recognizable form of contemporary life writing, part of the boom in ever-more diverse life narrative modes and forms and a distinctive genre with specific rhetorical and discursive effects. The diary intersects with but is also unique to other forms of autobiographical and self-representational practice. In this book, I have been less interested in defining diary, identifying limits or "transgressions" in its practice, than in understanding what the diary does as a popular and contemporary autobiographical mode. As a methodology, the parameters are therefore inherently broad (if not intrinsically open). For example, a recent spate of television and film production in which young diarists in particular have been featured demonstrates the continuing popular appeal of the diary,[2] even as it also tells us about a continuing association of the genre to lives in processes of formation, behind-the-scenes, and "hidden" knowledge—the lives of teenagers and young people (as well as women) are often framed in this way, and the diary is a symbolic as well as functional mode in this regard. The fact that much of this production is aimed at young audiences, and female ones in particular, seems worthy of further investigation. Ultimately, diary as a genre assumed to convey intimacy, immediacy, and authenticity, continues to emerge strongly in contemporary locations and retains a particular relevance to contemporary subjects and their lives. Questions such as who writes and publishes diary now, for what ends, and in what contexts have recurred throughout this study.

Contemporary diaries are used for acts of witnessing, confession, and therapy that are of central importance now. Diary is a prominent form in the self-help industry, a popular mode for circulating accounts of war and conflict, and an emerging vernacular of the Internet. In contemporary culture, in contrast to its historical position, the diary is no longer a marginal form. Yet qualities associated with this status continue to resound: the diary is always assumed to be more "everyday," "natural," or "intimate" than other kinds of autobiographical writing. It is also positioned as more ephemeral. The diary has a particular relationship to public and popular culture that goes some way to explaining how and why diary forms have emerged so strongly where the eyewitness, the confessional, and the authentic are prioritized in the construction and representation of contemporary autobiographical experience.

Notes

Introduction

1. Technological developments in a range of media have created new contexts for and kinds of diary narrative. For example, a plenitude of diary "apps" have sprung up to feed the growing smartphone market. These are generally modeled on a conventional, or analog, content model, where the individual selects information and enters it into the diary app. Jason Gilbert, however, reports that in 2012 Samsung patented a "Life Diary," a smartphone app that would automatically record such information as what music a user plays, locations where a user has stopped, a user's social media activity, or the weather at the user's position ("Samsung"). Here the diary is foremost a mechanism of surveillance, and it is external to the self—character is read into the rhythm of choices and behaviors an individual makes on his or her device over the course of a day and may overshadow or stand in for a narration based on what the individual diarist might otherwise select as the important or representative events of their day.

2. For example, the intimate representation of self that is both admired and fretted over in the content generated by Facebook users links strongly to certain expectations around diary forms. "IT'S NOT A DIARY! Stop treating it like one," is an exhortation "liked" by 50,363 followers of the Facebook group It's a Status. Not a Diary. Nonetheless, features like the Facebook timeline foreground a chronological structure that creates meaning through accretion: status updates and other material posted by users is gathered here into a fragmented yet serial narrative that bears much in common with diary as it is commonly imagined and produced. Facebook users respond to the repetitive daily and chronological structure (and to the less overt Facebook algorithm of what eventually constitutes this), and many cultural commentators dedicate time to criticizing the banal, irrelevant, and trivial content generated on these sites, which is a familiar critique for diarists too.

3. The potential of social media to function autobiographically has been of interest to various commentators. In a recent Salon.com article, journalist Michele Filgate wonders whether sites like Twitter or Facebook have to come to substitute for the "writer's

diary." For Filgate, "That's one of the biggest reasons why I turn to diaries, and now to fellow writers I can follow online: I want to hear about the ups and downs in a writer's career. I want to know what they're reading and what inspires them. I want to know what's going on in their lives."

4. Rosenwald remarks that "the myth of the diary as a secret text" is remarkably strong (*Emerson*, 10). The diary implicitly promises a tantalizing glimpse of secret or private life. This is something that is visible in marketing or reviews, for example, around diary publications by persons of public interest. Even banal examples prove the point: "The great celebrity romance of Richard Burton and Elizabeth Taylor is intimately captured in his newly released diaries," announces a celebrity gossip headline (Merkin, "Richard"). The companion piece dispenses altogether with subtlety: see Fallon, "Richard Burton's Sexy Diaries: 13 Juiciest Bits." Diaries intersect with powerful desires for the "true" story, for the unmediated account, and for the most authentic version.

5. A search of the online catalogue for the Internet book marketplace Amazon .com shows a steady increase in sales for titles containing "diary" (excluding calendar forms) over the last fifty years. For example, 2,024 diary texts were published during the decade 2000–2009, but already 2,152 diary texts correspond to publication during 2010–14. (This includes titles scheduled for release in 2014; search conducted on 19 November 2013.)

6. Critics who attempt to define diary as a set of formal characteristics tend to refer to dated entries as a defining feature. Lejeune proposes a definition of the diary as a "*series of dated traces* [série de traces datées]" and argues that "the date is essential. The trace is usually writing, but it can be an image, an object, or a relic. An isolated date trace is a memorial rather than a diary: the diary begins when traces in a series attempt to capture the movement of time rather than to freeze it around a source event" (*On Diary* 179).

7. Mallon says: "The secret-keeping adolescent diary is, or certainly has been, a pre-eminently female genre. We are still not likely to give boys diaries at Christmas" (*Book*, 210).

8. Neil Genzlinger's 2011 essay for the *New York Times*, "The Problem with Memoirs," memorably opens with the line "A moment of silence, please, for the lost art of shutting up," succinctly replaying the broadly disparaging tone that has characterized popular critique of certain autobiographical genres as irredeemably narcissistic and self-absorbed.

9. *Second Life*, invented in 2003 by Linden Lab, is a virtual world where Internet users interact, trade, and participate in activities that ostensibly mirror the complex engagements of life offline. Linden Lab introduced an online version of *Big Brother* to its *Second Life* users in 2006 ("Big Brother Enters Virtual World," BBC News: Entertainment, 6 November 2006, http://news.bbc.co.uk/2/hi/entertainment/6122140.stm).

10. Annette Hill and Gareth Palmer take it as evident that "performance is crucial to an understanding of the series, for the selves that were created for the cameras were entirely there for effect" ("Big," 253). Sam Brenton and Reuben Cohen, however, while

also acknowledging that audiences "overwhelmingly believe that people overact for the camera," observe that the fascination of the program also lies in the prospect of a break between performance and real: amid the display of "gaudy, demonstrative selfhood" viewers search for the glimpses of "false and real selves" that are interplayed (*Shooting*, 51).

11. For example, some UK versions of *Big Brother* made psychological counseling directly available through the diary room, emphasizing the function of this space as one for disclosure and unburdening, for "real" and authentic discourse within an otherwise artificial and contrived context (Brenton and Cohen, *Shooting*, 93).

12. Brenton and Cohen report that, contrary to popular opinion, viewers of "docusoaps" and reality shows are deeply suspicious of the nature of the behaviors "captured" and that the "real appeal is waiting for the mask to slip, in moments of stress and conflict, revealing the concealed 'true self' or 'real face' of a contestant" (*Shooting*, 51). In this "pornography of the performing self," pleasure is in the opportunity to "exalt the carnival and grant it exclusive attention, as the viewer waits for masks to slip and real persons to show themselves—and, on occasion, their real breasts or pecs" (53–54).

13. Rachel E. Dubrofsky uses the term "therapeutic surveillance" in her detailed analysis of the concept of surveillance in the service of the therapeutic on reality-based television dating shows *The Bachelor* and *The Bachelorette* ("Therapeutics").

14. For example, this is something Philippe Lejeune discusses in various essays throughout *On Diary*. Suzanne L. Bunkers (who is also a diary editor) is another innovative scholar on this topic. See Bunkers, "Whose," for a useful starting discussion of the key issues and debates in thinking about editing and the diary manuscript.

15. Julie Rak's exploration of book publishing and memoir in *Boom! Manufacturing Memoir for the Popular Market* (2013) offers a further context for the condition of the contemporary diary as a published mode: nonfiction of all kinds has enjoyed a resurgence in recent years, and though memoir remains the dominant and most recognizable form in this, modes like diary no doubt benefit from the expanding market and correlate production emphasis that has become geared toward autobiographical narrative in general.

16. Paul de Man asks: "Can we not suggest that the autobiographical project may itself produce and determine the life?" ("Autobiography," 920).

Chapter 1. A Public Private Self

1. Though they note that James Olney has explained it in greater detail, Smith and Watson also explain this term in *Reading Autobiography* as a simple etymology: "In Greek, *autos* signifies 'self,' *bios* 'life,' and *graphe* 'writing'" (1).

2. Nonetheless, Fussell also argues that diary may not necessarily be the most useful representative mode, citing the example of Lillian Hellman, who claimed her copious diaries had failed to capture all that she later identified as significant or meaningful. The

diary, for Fussell, can only attain the "significances belonging to fiction" as it moves to the mode of memoir: "For it is only the ex post facto view of an action that generates coherence or makes irony possible" (*Great*, 336).

3. Anna Jackson's recent study *Diary Poetics* explores aesthetics in relation to artistic uses of the diary form. The authors whom Jackson discusses, however, take a literary approach to the diary, as they do to all their writing, though they still express a sense that the writing in this form is different, and somehow parallel or germinal to their other literary work. The aesthetics of diary that Jackson finds does not contradict this perception but demonstrates that the diary is still essentially regarded as a nonliterary or supplementary mode. The exception here is Anaïs Nin (whom Jackson does not include in her study), who frequently expressed a sense that her diaries were a public and literary work. Nin's documented difficulties in convincing audiences and publishers of this perspective, however, is also meaningful here, something Elizabeth Podnieks explores in her detailed chapter on Nin's diaries in *Daily Modernism*.

4. Nonetheless, the circulation of a low-quality amateur photograph is far more common (and economically viable) than the circulation of "unliterary" diaries. See Judy Nolte Temple's analysis of the fragment diaries of "Baby Doe" Tabor ("Fragments") or Laurie McNeill's discussion of internment diaries in "Performing Genres" for a discussion of this issue in specific contexts.

5. The Christian sacrament of confession is a compulsory admission of transgression made by the confessant to God and is set up as a moment of unmitigated communion. However, it is also an articulation intercepted by the confessor, the anointed interlocutor, though within this holy trinity any utterances are assumed to exist in sacred repose. However, as Foucault argues, far from being a private communion, the confession was invented as a mode of discipline, a means of policing the congregation and of disseminating standards of normalcy (*History*, 60). In *The Will to Knowledge*, his first volume in *The History of Sexuality*, Foucault notes a "metamorphosis in literature" in which "we have passed" from narrating the heroic or the pleasurable, tales of "bravery and sainthood," to a fixation on the individual: "To the infinite task of extracting from the depths of oneself, in between the words, a truth which the very form of the confession holds out like a shimmering mirage" (59). The confession is thus implicitly linked to the "bringing to light" of hidden truths, flaws, or transgressions.

6. The ubiquitous, and mostly decorative, lock and key that adorns many mass-marketed blank diaries is one of the multiple subtle ways in which the diary is gendered as feminine. "To write to one's 'secret friend' on all the ordinary days of childhood is not seemly for a boy: inner lives are for girls," says Mallon. "The little girl is being trained to appreciate dailiness: her lot in life is the quotidian; her brother will do whatever transcending there is to be done" (*Book*, 210).

7. *The Diaries of Miles Franklin* (2004) are composed from an eclectic gathering of papers Franklin bequeathed to the Mitchell Library in Sydney. Taking these disparate personal jottings, diaries, notebooks, and scraps of paper—all mostly undated—the editor Paul Brunton tackled the "unwieldy mass" and "put them in chronological sequence,

nipped, tucked and created a narrative that holds the reader to the end" (Oakley, "Acid," 10). That is, the *Diaries* do not refer to any one existing diary volume, but to the mass of Franklin's personal papers in general as Brunton has edited them. Such manufacture may seem counter to commonplace assumptions about diary as a "natural" medium, though this kind of editing is certainly not unusual. Lejeune remarks that "it is likely that almost no diary has been published in the form in which it was written . . . the history of editing teems with examples of diaries that have been censored, pruned, and doctored" (*On Diary*, 226). See Bunkers, "Whose," for further discussion of critical questions raised by editing diary manuscripts.

Chapter 2. How to Be the Authentic You

1. Progoff's "intensive journal method" is derived from his series of national journal workshops carried out in North America during the late 1960s. In his best-selling adjunct to these workshops, *At a Journal Workshop* (1975), he establishes an opposition between a historical and conventional form of the genre, as narcissistic and insular, and the diary as an "essential instrument for personal growth" (24). Progoff's program is explicitly designed to promote his belief in the journal as a method of self-improvement that curbs its other potential as a narcissistic object.

2. Writers like Anne Lamott in *Bird by Bird* (1995), Natalie Goldberg in *Writing Down the Bones* (1986), or Stephen King in *On Writing* (2000) offer craft-based instruction in texts that also function as conventional memoir. Structured as narration of the author's life journey, toward what is inevitably a "vocation" or "destiny" as a writer, these memoirs explicitly connect the writer's autobiographical understanding of their experience in the world to the ability to craft authentic (whether fictional or nonfictional) stories; they offer a template for the reader who desires to experience or construct a writing life of their own.

3. This is, of course, an enduring myth of the genre and one not upheld in the various and many literary uses of the diary. See Jackson, *Diary Poetics*, or Podnieks, *Daily Modernism*, for examples explored at length.

4. "Dr. Phil" McGraw, for example, opens his best-selling self-help text, *Self Matters: Creating Your Life from the Inside Out* (2003), with a personal confession that Guignon likens to "a modern-day Paul on the Road to Damascus": the "moment of vision" when Dr. Phil realizes he has been living an inauthentic life is a powerful story. However, "Unlike the conversion experiences of such historical figures as St. Paul, St. Augustine or Martin Luther," Dr. Phil's experience inverts the Christian dyad: his "moment of vision presents him not with an understanding of his relation to God, but of his relation to himself" (Guignon, *On Being*, 2).

5. Self-reflection is a process that Progoff insists can be misused "when it is done without the guidance of dynamic principles and without a protective discipline; or when, under the guise of communication, the keeping of a journal is used as a stratagem or weapon in order to impress our point of view on someone else" (24). Progoff's journal

guides promise to correctly discipline diary and to limit such "misuse." Claiming the authority of "psychological principles," *At a Journal Workshop* offers a method in "the *how* of journal usage" that revises what Progoff calls "the basic type of personal journal used throughout history . . . an unstructured chronological journal kept either systematically by dates or written spontaneously from time to time" and without the guiding aim of self-improvement or therapy (26).

6. The Puritan spiritual diary has a clearly declared objective, and like the self-help diary, a clearly mandated form of practice. For Robert Fothergill, this condition for the diary has advantages for those who seek to adhere to tradition: "You would begin with already formed ideas of how to go about it, what sort of things to include, what tone to adopt, and so forth" (*Private*, 18). As a practice for the development and enrichment of "consciousness," however, Fothergill also finds the spiritual diary severely limited. The Puritan diary is a mode in which "the conventions tend to exclude any real interest in the outer world, except insofar as it provided a theatre for God's providences" (18).

7. In *A Voice of Her Own: Women and the Journal Writing Journey* (1996), Marlene A. Schiwy draws explicitly on a gendered tradition of diary keeping that also references other assumptions of the genre: "The diary is where women think and feel their way through key concerns and issues that determine their lives. Nowhere is the true nature of our psychic development more clearly evident. In journals we see emotion and thought, intuition and experience fused into something quite different from our usual attempts to be 'logical.' What we write and read in diaries is a language of the heart" (22). Schiwy extols journal writing as a form that can contain women's busy lives, asserting that "journal writing can be woven into the busy fabric of our daily lives, providing a moment of contact with our inner selves" (47), and advocates the diary as a place where women, who have "traditionally been the caretakers and providers of emotional support," can find their own support (114). The diarist whom Schiwy addresses is primarily a subject in need of therapeutic support: "For who among us doesn't seek healing? At some point in our lives most—probably all—of us will seek help from a therapist, in the attempt to heal the unresolved losses and sorrows in our lives" (114). This subject is female, vulnerable, and in need of healing.

8. In a much later issue of *O, The Oprah Magazine*, Winfrey reveals that she has been keeping a journal since she was fifteen. The accompanying story includes photographs of selected pages from this teenage diary and a running commentary in which Winfrey explains and contextualizes the entries (Winfrey, "Exclusive").

9. T. J. Jackson Lears, in *No Place of Grace*, uses the term in his discussion of a feature of early nineteenth-century America. A shift away from moral stoicism and a sense that life should be endured toward an "optimistic, tolerant liberal Protestant view of human nature" was celebrated by some but seen by others as the beginning of individual and spiritual decline: both "physical and moral life seemed to be suffocating in their ease and weightless in their significance" (45).

10. In *Self-Help, Inc.*, McGee links this to the rise of capitalist consumer culture, and as a shift she says may have "consequences not unlike the rise of advertising in the early

twentieth century. Just as the emergence of consumer advertising fostered social anxiety by focusing on an array of supposedly corporeal 'problems' such as halitosis or dandruff—problems that could be addressed through the purchase of various toiletries—today's retinue of self-improvement experts, motivational speakers, and self-help gurus conjure the image of endless insufficiency" (17). McGee argues that modern self-help amplifies the anxieties exploited by early marketeers. Unlike "mouthwash or dandruff shampoo," however, the commodities of self-help are not products that can be consumed and discarded once the problem is fixed: they are "a lifestyle, a series of regimes of time management or meditation, of diet and spiritual exploration, of self-scrutiny and self-affirmation" (18).

11. In 1999 Fielding's sequel *Bridget Jones: The Edge of Reason* followed up on its predecessor's success and by 2001, when the first blockbuster film adaptation was released, "the novel had sold in excess of eight million copies and had been translated into over thirty-three languages" (Whelehan, *Feminist*, 173).

12. Feminist critics responded strongly to the self-mortification they saw in *Bridget Jones's Diary*, though some also felt a subtle sense of social irony was at play. While Claire Hanson observes that the fictional diary primarily appears to promote "a kind of lipstick feminism that assumes that a woman's best weapon in life is a floaty white dress in a romantic setting," she also argues that a feminist analysis does bring politics to *Bridget Jones's Diary*, though the text itself remains passive and ultimately troubling ("Fiction," 17). In a similar vein, Stephen Maddison and Merl Storr conclude that *Bridget Jones's Diary* is a satire that fails the genre: the text, "however amusing," is profoundly conservative; it is both "neo-liberal" and "postfeminist" in that it ultimately advocates "a depoliticized understanding of an unequal world" ("Edge," 14).

13. Doris Lessing and Beryl Bainbridge were just two of the distinguished readers doing what Fielding called "getting their knickers in a twist about Bridget Jones being a disgrace to feminism" (Ezard, "Bainbridge," 7). Bainbridge famously derided the whole genre and Bridget Jones as arch progenitor, as "a froth sort of thing" (7). Similarly, lamenting "these helpless girls, drunken, worrying about their weight and so on," Lessing wondered why young women were writing "such instantly forgettable books. . . . It would be better, perhaps, if they wrote books about their lives as they really saw them" (7).

14. "Bridget Jones is no mere fictional character; she's the Spirit of the Age. Her diary presents a perfect zeitgeist of single female woes. It rings true with the unmistakable tone of something that is true to the marrow and *captures* what—alas—it is like to be female. Any woman of a certain age can recognise elements of Bridget in herself. Indeed she is far more that the patron saint of single women: she is everyman, or rather, everyperson. She is the most enchanting heroine for the millennium" (Maddison and Storr, "Edge," 3–4). In this passage, "constructed from quotes from reviews which appear on the back jackets and inside pages of *Bridget Jones's Diary* and *Bridget Jones: The Edge of Reason*" (14 n2), Maddison and Storr demonstrate the extravagance they assert the character has been awarded. Despite noting, "actually of course Bridget Jones *is* a mere

fictional character" and "her *reality* is an illusion" (4) they spend the better part of the next page explaining what in any other case might seem a startlingly simple proposition.

15. Moreover, McGee, indicating both the "vast quantity of self-literature" and the "shifting meanings of the term 'self-help'" during the period of her study (1973–2003), notes that "if one defines self-help literature as a mode of reading, rather than as a genre, then nearly any publication—fiction, poetry, autobiography, philosophy, history, or social science—could fall within the category" (*Self-Help*, 193). McGee observes that individuals may—and in surveys quite often do—consider anything from the Bible to works of literature or sociological treatises as modes for self-help, as well as those texts that claim a more direct relation to the category (193–94).

16. Furedi argues: "Therapeutic culture provides a script through which individuals develop a distinct understanding of their selves and of their relationship with others. People also read from other scripts but when it comes to making sense of who they are, therapeutics exercises a formidable impact on their lives" (*Therapy*, 23).

Chapter 3. The Ethics of Being There and Seeing

1. While diary accounts of war are a very old form, Andrea Peterson observes that published war diaries are not a historical phenomenon: "Since at least the 16th century all wars seem to have produced war diaries; but very few diaries were published anywhere near their time of writing, only a selection have been recovered and published retrospectively, and even fewer have been translated into other languages for worldwide circulation" ("War," 925). Publications like those by Goltz and McGeough (in McGeough's case, published within months of the experience) show that this condition for diary is dramatically changing. War blogging presents a further context for considering this shift (Wall, "Blogging").

2. In her study of writers' diaries, Anna Jackson makes a distinction between literary writers and professional writers, identifying the former as those who regard "writing as a life's work . . . writers [who] had a keen sense of genre and an interest in the formal constraints and possibilities of the forms in which they worked" (*Diary*, 15–16). While not literary in the way that Jackson proposes, a professional writer, such as a journalist, must also be seen as responsive and alert to genre and style. At the very least, they would be more alert to such things than those in final category Jackson selects, "diarists who were not otherwise writers" (15).

3. Zelizer observes that journalism "is most often appreciated when it turns into a nonjournalistic phenomenon. When Ernest Hemingway worked as a reporter . . . his journalistic experiences were seen as an 'apprenticeship' for his later work, and his writing was dismissed as 'just journalism.' But when he turned portions of that same material verbatim into fiction, it was heralded as literature" (*Taking*, 1).

4. "Many of the correspondents," according to Katovsky, "subjected themselves to the dangers—and terrors—of combat by often repeating these truisms: 'We wanted to

be on the front lines of history. We wanted to write the first draft of history'" (Katovsky and Carlson, *Embedded*, xviii). The appeal for readers of the embed report may be seen as based in a similar desire for "closeness" to the events described.

5. Wolf suggests that immediacy, particularly in relation to accounts of wartime experience, has become such a dominant trope that it not only risks occluding more analytic and mediated forms of life writing but also compromises the ways in which such stories are elicited and represented. "One can only imagine," concludes Wolf of a BBC series that explicitly directed contributors to provide only their most vivid memories, "what contributing veterans might have related had assumptions about what constitutes the most valuable and virtuous form of war story not deterred them" ("Mediating," 335).

6. The phrase "evidence and testimony" is from Rosenwald, who uses it to describe the likely perception of diarists regarding their manuscripts before 1800. Rosenwald notes that before this date "few diaries were published qua diaries; many, however, were quoted extensively in biographies and diarists must have considered their diaries to be, among other things, evidence and testimony" (*Emerson*, 11). Arguing that this perspective is less tenable after the emergence of published diaries, as "well-read diarists were surely considering the prospect of posthumous independent publication and thus inevitably thinking of their diaries as books" (11), we may see that the early perception of diaries as private writing that is not intended for publication continues to be a characteristic expectation of the genre, and one of its central paradoxes. What I call Goltz and McGeough's self-conscious use of the diary as evidence and testimony is a case in point here, and it is also a significant observation in regards to the Arab women's diaries considered in the following chapter.

Chapter 4. The Intimate Appeal of Getting Closer

1. Golley notes that while there exists in Arab cultures a long tradition of writing the self, women's contributions to this are relatively recent. Nonetheless, the established culture of negotiation and expression in terms of "the relationship among self, society, and history; to established social values; and to the possible mods of personal, political and rhetorical contexts" that comprises this male literary tradition is also a context for the production of new writing by Arab women (*Arab*, xxvi).

2. Al-Radi's attempts to publish her diary encounter various obstacles, which she documents at the time. Her publication, then, narrates its own transit into print, producing a particular trajectory and revealing a set of implications that I consider in detail elsewhere ("Read").

3. Quotes indicate the blog date as well as the page number of the published text, as this text exists in both digital and paper forms.

4. In his essay "The Continuous and the Discontinuous" from *On Diary*, Lejeune observes that the "diary's value lies in its being the trace of a moment" (182). The diary entry as trace overrides the need for sincerity that characterizes, for example, as Lejeune

goes on to elaborate in "Auto-Genesis," a retrospective genre like autobiography or memoir: "Reading a diary, I like to believe that I am really reading what was written in those very words on that very day and not some artifact rewritten or rearranged afterwards. This has nothing to do with sincerity. Let us assume that the diarist has made a mistake, or tried to fool himself and us on a given day; at least I am sure that it is his own bad faith on that very day that I have before my eyes. His blindness and his silences. The very words he used" (223).

5. Blogs are a descending chronological form in which the most recent entry appears as the "first" on screen. Although most blogs offer an archive, this can be clunky to navigate sequentially, and especially in "reverse" order. As a book, the blog re-acquires an ascending, forward temporality from oldest entry as first chronological date/entry to last (most recent in time).

6. The attention to personal voice and experience is an emphasis that emerges in various ways throughout *The Colonial Present*; in the annotated "Guide to Further Reading" Gregory discusses the organizing principles behind his bibliography: the majority of the works he recommends on the Israel–Palestine conflict, for example, are scholarly books that "deal with the world of high politics and lines on maps" (355). But he also wants to respond to the reader interested in bringing "the struggle closer to the lives of ordinary men and women," and he recommends cultural history titles that he thinks will fulfill this kind of purpose. However, "it's possible," says Gregory, "to get closer still," and to this end he recommends three "utterly compelling books"—a memoir, a diary, and a collection of journalism (355).

7. Susan Stanford Friedman, observing the reactions among some of the students she sets to read Riverbend's blog, many of whom are startled by the prospect of an Iraqi woman who can use a computer, discusses this as a political problem, embedded in a popular binary of Arab women as representative of "backward traditionalism" versus the West as an example of "liberating modernity" ("Futures," 1708). In *Arab Women's Lives Retold*, Golley raises this issue as a feminist one too, though she further notes that life writing is one of the ways in which such stereotypes can become better contested.

8. Riverbend not only defends her identity against direct inquiry; in late 2003 she exposes a copycat site running directly opposing content to the opinions expressed on her blog. The hoax is flattering, but it is also distressing: the fake blog is poorly written and riddled with typos and grammatical errors, and Riverbend wonders if this is "an apparent attempt to make me look more 'Iraqi,'" though she also ripostes, "maybe it's just the way this person actually writes" (29 October 2003; 120).

9. In her study of literary diaries by mid-twentieth-century writers, Jackson notes that conceptions of the diary as a particularly "female" form of life writing have limited the ways in which the genre has been theorized. Instead, Jackson argues that where "stylistic features of diary writing have been theorised as expressions of femininity or as responses to women's social conditions," they are, in fact, "common to diary writing by men and women and should be recognised as responses to the formal demands of the genre itself" (*Diary*, 4).

10. Cooke's "two camps" compose the "boringly political," which she concedes could, nonetheless, be appealing if "you are into dates and accords and UN resolutions," and the "highly lyrical," of which she says: "To many western ears, these existential accounts of the diaspora, however beautiful, however rich, are hard going—like wading through jelly. But *Sharon and My Mother-in-Law* is different" ("Emails").

11. "Customer Reviews" of *Baghdad Burning: Girl Blog from Iraq* are available on Amazon.com: "Iraq's Anne Frank?," by David Dix, posted 18 April 2005, http://www .amazon.com/review/R2615ZXDTJRZN2, and "Anne Frank in Baghdad," by "Jalus," posted 24 February 2006, http://www.amazon.com/review/R1K7UBKCLUTBTE.

12. "It doesn't have the ring of truth to it," by J. Vargo "bibliophile," posted 22 September 2006, http://www.amazon.com/review/R189R2WU3RUZIK.

13. See Gilmore and Marshall ("Girls") for a thorough discussion of how girlhoods are mobilized in this way.

14. Zapruder draws on Meyer Levin's 1952 review of what was at the time the recently published diary for her fascinating analysis of Anne Frank's diary as it has affected the reception and interpretation of children's Holocaust diaries in general. Levin, according to Zapruder, "gave his audience its first language about why the diary mattered for the girl herself, for her lost generation, and for humanity" (*Salvaged*, 2).

15. For example, Chris Hedges says: "There is no more candor in Iraq or Afghanistan than there was in Vietnam, but in the age of live satellite feeds the military has perfected the appearance of candor. What we are fed is the myth of war. For the myth of war, the myth of glory and honor sells newspapers and boosts ratings, real war reporting does not . . . All our knowledge of the war in Iraq has to be viewed as lacking the sweep and depth that will come one day, perhaps years from now, when a small Iraqi boy or girl reaches adulthood and unfolds for us the sad and tragic story of the invasion and bloody occupation of their nation" ("War").

Chapter 5. Sex, Confession, and Blogging

1. Miller and Shepherd identify several "branches" in the blog "family tree." The "use of blogs as filtering or directory services" recalls the "*log*," which is a characteristic form of "the voyage of a ship, flight of an airplane, the duty of a lighthouse keeper" and represents the function of detailed record; the "*commonplace book*," in its sense of repository for assorted personal detail, aphorism, and anecdote; the "*anthology*," in its sense of "collecting"; the "*pamphlet* or *broadside*, the *editorial*, and the *opinion column*"—genres that "highlight commentary"; and "on a separate branch of the blog family tree . . . the *journal* and the *diary*" ("Blogging").

2. "An ontological distinction may be made between the natively digital and the digitized, that is, between the objects, contents, devices and environments that are 'born' in the new medium and those that have 'migrated' to it" (Rogers, *Digital*, 9).

3. In *Memoir* (2012), G. Thomas Couser argues that memoir is best understood on a

continuum between more or less biographical or more or less autobiographical and that it is inevitably also both of these things at once (19). As a form of life writing, memoir is also proximate to other modes, such as self-portraiture or home video, as well as to the diary or journal. Couser, however, also makes a significant distinction: unlike memoir, which is always assumed to be for publication, the diary and journal are "private forms of life writing" and as such are "usually not intended for publication" (30). That a good many diaries and journals are published, and that a considerable market exists for these texts, does not inform Couser's discussion (nor does he engage with the scholarly work done on the great many diarists who have intended—whether successfully or not—to see their diaries published, something Sonia Wilson's innovative study of Marie Bashkirtseff covers in detail). Instead, he settles on the belief that *usually* publication is incidental to the writing of diary or journal narrative (this narrative is *usually* intended as private). Though critics like Rosenwald among others have offered substantial counter to such claims, it is interesting to observe how dominant this stereotype of diary writing remains that it is so little problematized in even a recent work of criticism like Couser's.

4. A 2012 study published in the *Journal of the American Society for Information Science and Technology*, for example, claims that women are more likely to write diary style blogs while male authorship is associated with less personally orientated filter blogs and offers the following definition of terms: "Diary blogs were any that commented exclusively on the author's own life, whereas filter blogs were those that commented on events external to the author's life" (Fullwood et al., "Sex," 347).

5. Certain posts suggest a level of interactivity on the blog that subsequently ceased. For example, in a post from 2003, Belle responds to a list of "Frequently Asked Questions" she says she has received over e-mail (*Diary*, "mercredi, novembre 12," 12 November 2003), and an author profile, in French, appears briefly on the blog in 2007. Neither of these artifacts are reproduced in the book version of the blog, published in 2005.

6. Belle's blog has since been superseded: under her real identity, Dr. Brooke Magnanti uses the webpage for commentary on current issues around sex, sexuality, and prostitution, for linking to her published journalism, and, recently, for promoting her popular science book, *The Sex Myth*, an education-focused exploration of contemporary culture and sexuality. The blog bears Magnanti's author photograph but has no specific title besides its infamous web address as "belledejour" (http://belledejour-uk .blogspot.com.au) and details nothing about the author's private life, and offers no personal reflection. The blog, in other words, is no longer named as and no longer functions as its author's sex diary.

7. The influence of *Bridget Jones's Diary* in the production of the sexually adventurous thirty-something's diary (and in establishing a market for its success) is routinely cited. An implicit promise that writing about the self can be liberating and transformative (as well as narcissistic and trivial) characterizes discussion about online diaries, and it is a feature in rhetoric about sexual self-disclosure. However, it is clear that neither Abby Lee nor Belle envisages herself as a successor to Helen Fielding's fictional heroine. They use their online diary to both represent and validate a particular kind of female experience, but the kind of intensive self-improvement that regiments Bridget's everyday

life is absent in their quotidian accountings. Belle in particular derides the "giggle-cuteness gosh-I'm-so-inept Love-Me! of Bridget Jones" (*Diary*, "jeudi, mars 29," 29 March 2007), and on the whole, reviewers avoid the comparison—perhaps because Belle is a professional sex worker, and thus harder to fold into the Bridget Jones "everywoman" phenomenon.

8. As Susanna Paasonen observes, "the Net is said to enable gender blending and bending, the taking up of different identities, and the exploration of the limits of "the self." . . . The medium has become invested with a general aura of possibility and subversion" ("Gender," 21). Paasonen is, however, notably cautious about the "subversive" nature of the Internet, and she remains usefully wary of assumptions that this is an inherently or naturally more liberated space for identity and the individual than the "offline" social world ("Gender").

9. The quote is from Paasonen, but she is paraphrasing John Perry Barlow, "A Declaration of the Independence of Cyberspace," available at http://homes.eff.org/~barlow/Declaration-Final.html.

10. Fullwood et al. argue that anonymity online should be understood as part of a continuum rather than in a dichotomy. Given the range of options available, from complete anonymity to selective distortion, "there are degrees of identifiability" ("Sex," 348).

11. This is not the case with all blog books. In his "Editor's Note" to the book edition of *Baghdad Burning* by Iraqi blogger Riverbend, James Ridgeway says: "The content of this book reproduces the first year's worth of Riverbend's writing as it appears in her blog, without any abridgement" (xiv). Ridgeway is at pains to note, for example, that original spellings have been retained, for instance, the spelling of burqa as "burgu3" is intended to "transliterate Arabic terms using standard computer keystrokes," and he includes where possible material from hyperlinked pages (Riverbend, *Baghdad*, xiv). A lack of similar attention to the book versions of sex blogs reveals the different value (in the case of sex blogs, a diminished one) attributed to the experience and story being narrated in these contexts.

12. Discussing the book version of Salam Pax's infamous *Baghdad Blog*, Gillian Whitlock describes the published edition as "extracted from the hot links of cyberspace, and shelved in cold copy" before wondering "why is it almost impossible to resist talking metaphorically about Pax and his webdiary as organic, living things in this way?" (*Soft*, 24).

13. Smith and Watson offer the concept of automediality as a multivalent methodology for reading digital life narrative texts, as "a theoretical framework for conceptualizing the way subjectivity is constructed across visual and verbal forms in new media" ("Virtually," 77).

Chapter 6. Graphic Lives

1. Discussing the various methods and techniques she experimented with in the process of creating her memoir, *Fun Home*, Bechdel says, "I hit on a process of writing in

a drawing program on the computer, writing in Adobe Illustrator." Once she has her "page written," Bechdel prints it out and "starts drawing, right on the cheesy typing paper" ("Creating").

2. The existence of facsimile diaries—photographic reproductions of diaries— further evidences the unique weight placed on texts like diaries or letters as forms that have an original state that both authorizes their reproduction in other forms and under- mines the published edition's claim to authenticity. However, visual reproductions of diaries are on the whole rare. Or rather, they are limited to particular kinds of diaries, and ones that clearly signal a visual register. Artists' diaries are one of the main publica- tions in this area; for example, the artist Frida Kahlo's detailed and highly illustrated journals are reproduced in *The Diary of Frida Kahlo* (2005) and the facsimile version of Edith Holden's *The Country Diary of an Edwardian Lady, 1906* (2006) reproduces her original handwritten and illustrated nature diary. The musician Kurt Cobain's *Journals* (2007) consists of photographs of the pages of his personal notebooks, a prose edition of which would necessarily elide the multiple and detailed sketches and other uses that he makes of the page. While many diary editions may include reproduced pages (or illustrations) from their subject's original diary, the key difference is that these are illustrative rather than constitutive.

3. Indeed, it is the special relationship between women's experience and visual rep- resentation that forms one of the central threads for Chute's exploration of life narrative and comics in *Graphic Women*. For Chute, the "hard-won" opportunity to visualize the "non-normative lives of women in an aesthetically engaged format" has meant that con- temporary comics artists are presenting traumatic histories that "refuse" the "lens of unspeakability or invisibility, instead registering its difficulty through inventive textual practice" (26).

4. Gloeckner has repeatedly stated that she does not believe in "art as therapy" (Spurgeon, "Phoebe"). Her comic avoids the confessional tone that critics like Leigh Gilmore observe as a feature in contemporary representations of trauma ("American") and it also precludes a kind of moral conclusiveness that certain readers might also seek in such narrative. That is, as Spurgeon puts it, Gloeckner's work "showcases an artist's desire to make a good story, not the needs of a lonely and sometimes confused teenager to understand what is happening around her"; readers are asked to admire the art more than they are required to judge or (and this seems important) to learn from the experience.

5. The back cover image for Baker's *Diary Drawings*, for example, is a photo of the stack of green watercolor pads originally displayed behind glass at her exhibition, while Someguy also references the extant journals that have formed the source material for his curated version of *The 1000 Journals Project* on his website with photographs of the piles of returned and completed journals, as a well as images of the one thousand blank journals being prepared for distribution. Eschewing the direct iconography of the "stack," Gloeckner too references the physical materiality of her original diary, including a reproduction of original typed diary pages (interleaved and spread out, as though on a bed—the location where a young Minnie spends much time typing and assembling this

part of her record) as well as a photograph of her original Hello Kitty diary, on the inside and back covers of *Diary of a Teenage Girl*.

6. Noting that Baker herself did not originally conceptualize her drawings as cartoons, Lightman observes that her work nonetheless fits a tradition of autobiographical comics in both technique and in content, and especially in its "navigation of the boundaries between life and art" ("*Diary*," 160).

7. In *Say Everything: How Blogging Began, What It's Becoming, and Why It Matters*, Scott Rosenberg observes that before September 2001, "conventional wisdom held that Web content was 'dead,'" a position that changed in the wake of citizen responses to 9/11, which also saw a new authority given to ordinary and citizen, as opposed to journalistic or media, voices: "The surrogate lamentations of the broadcast media's talking heads sounded manufactured and inadequate; people felt the urgent need to express themselves[;] . . . stepping forward to record their thoughts had unquantifiable but unmistakable value" (6).

8. Currently, the website is a more central element, though the emphasis is still on the physical production of material journals, which are uploaded and stored on a new arm of the project on the 1001 Journals site ("1001 Journals"). This allows new participants to experience the mechanisms of the original journal project, even though the original remains ostensibly uncompleted: "Unfortunately, you've got a better chance of winning the lottery, then [*sic*] of getting a hold of a journal. That's the problem when there are only 1000 of them. Now, you're [*sic*] best bet is to check out 1001 Journals where you can sign up for a journal, or launch your own traveling, location, or personal journals" (Someguy, "1000 Journals").

9. The 1001 Journals website continues the original project emphasis, but it changes the circulation process by prioritizing the digital uploading of journals to the website. Allowing individuals or groups to start their own journal projects or to join one already existing, the website has notably been developed very successfully for teen patients at the University of California San Francisco (UCSF) Benioff Children's Hospital ("1001 Journals"). There is also an iteration called the "C journals" explicitly for cancer patients and their families, and it is not linked to a particular hospital. See http://www.1001journals.com.

10. See my discussion in "Creating the Creative Subject: *The 1000 Journals Project, Creativity and Autobiographical Identity*" for a specific exploration of genre (and the significance of *journal* over diary to describe this kind of writing) in relation to the contemporary ideal of the creative subject.

11. Arguing for an attention to nontraditional and purposeful forms of autobiography that challenge to some degree the primacy of the book, such as zines, Poletti says: "Structured by well-established standards regarding acceptable variations in size, paper, production quality, font and layout, the mass-produced book is still predominantly assumed to be an invisible medium in discussions of life writing" (*Intimate Ephemera*, 53).

12. The computer diary overcomes "discontinuity in the physical medium"—the completion of notebooks—yet it also functions to produce linearity (seemingly in

contrast to the loose-leaf page system Lejeune says he prefers): "What's strange is that on the computer, for the past ten years, my diary writing behavior has been the inverse: I would never dream of opening a file for each entry" (*On Diary*, 178).

Conclusion

1.   A search of the WorldCat database produces the following results: in 2003, 1,507 nonfiction books were categorized under the search term "Iraq war," of which 18 are diary texts, 8 of these by journalists. By 2012 the number of publications had decreased, and the scope had also shifted. There were 1,058 works of nonfiction about "Iraq war," but only 2 of these texts are diaries.

2.   North American young adult television, like *The Carrie Diaries* (2013) or *The Vampire Diaries* (2009), or the film *The Diary a Wimpy Kid* (2010), as well as the British television series *My Mad Fat Diary* (2014) are just a few of the more recent and obvious examples here.

Works Cited

Adams, Kathleen. *Journal to the Self: 22 Paths to Personal Growth*. New York: Warner, 1990.

Adams, Timothy Dow. *Light Writing and Life Writing: Photography in Autobiography*. Chapel Hill: University of North Carolina Press, 2000.

al-Radi, Nuha. *Baghdad Diaries: A Woman's Chronicle of War and Exile*. New York: Vintage Books, 2003.

Amiry, Suad. *Sharon and My Mother-in-Law: Ramallah Diaries*. London: Granta, 2005.

Applewhite, Ashton. "Penguin Reading Guides. *Bridget Jones's Diary*. Helen Fielding." 2006. Penguin Group USA. http://us.penguingroup.com/static/rguides/us/bridget_joness_diary.html.

Attwood, Feona. "Intimate Adventures: Sex Blogs, Sex 'Blooks' and Women's Sexual Narration." *European Journal of Cultural Studies* 12, no. 1 (2009): 5–20.

Baker, Bobby. *Diary Drawings: Mental Illness and Me*. London: Profile Books, 2010.

———. "Performance Artist Bobby Baker." In *Art, Not Chance: Nine Artists' Diaries*, edited by Paul Allen, 31–42. London: Calouste Gulbenkian Foundation, 2001.

Baldwin, Christina. *One to One: Self-Understanding through Journal Writing*. New York: M. Evans and Company, 1977.

Ban Breathnach, Sarah. *A Man's Journey to Simple Abundance*. New Jersey: Scribner, 2001.

———. *Simple Abundance: A Daybook of Comfort and Joy*. Sydney: Hodder, 1999.

Barker, Meg. "Editorial: Special Issue on Sex Blogging." *Psychology and Sexuality* 3, no. 1 (2012): 1–4.

Bauman, Zygmunt. *This Is Not a Diary*. Cambridge: Polity Press, 2012.

Bechdel, Alison. "Creating *Fun Home: A Family Tragicomic*." Edited by MiNDTV35. YouTube, 2009. https://www.youtube.com/watch?v=cumLU3UpcGY.

———. *Fun Home: A Family Tragicomic*. Boston: Mariner Books, 2006.

Begos, Jane DuPree. "The Diaries of Adolescent Girls." *Women's Studies International Forum* 10, no. 1 (1987): 69–74.

Belle de Jour. *Diary of a London Call Girl*. http://belledejour-uk.blogspot.com/.

———. *The Further Adventures of a London Call Girl*. London: Weidenfeld and Nicholson, 2006.

————. *The Intimate Adventures of a London Call Girl*. London: Weidenfeld and Nicholson, 2005.

Bernstein, Elizabeth. *Temporarily Yours: Intimacy, Authenticity, and the Commerce of Sex*. Chicago: University of Chicago Press, 2007.

Bickler, Colin, et al. "Reporting for Change: A Handbook for Local Journalists in Crisis Areas." Institute for War and Peace Reporting, 2004. http://www.iwpr.net/special _index1.html.

Blodgett, Harriet. *Centuries of Female Days: Englishwomen's Private Diaries*. New Brunswick, NJ: Rutgers University Press, 1988.

Blood, Rebecca. "Weblogs: A History and Perspective " *Rebecca's Pocket*, 7 September 2000. http://www.rebeccablood.net/essays/weblog_history.html.

Bloom, Lynn Z. "I Write For Myself and Strangers." In *Inscribing the Daily: Critical Essays on Women's Diaries*, edited by Suzanne L. Bunkers and Cynthia A. Huff, 23–37. Amherst: University of Massachusetts Press, 1996.

Bolter, Jay, and Richard Grusin. *Remediation: Understanding New Media*. Cambridge, MA: MIT Press, 1999.

Brekus, Catherine A. "'A Place to Go to Connect to Yourself': A Historical Perspective on Journaling." In *The Religion and Culture Web Forum*, http://divinity.uchicago.edu /martycenter/publications/webforum/022004/commentary.shtml. Chicago: Martin Marty Center for the Advanced Study of Religion, University of Chicago Divinity School, 2004.

Brenton, Sam, and Reuben Cohen. *Shooting People: Adventures in Reality TV*. London: Verso, 2003.

Brooks, Peter. *Troubling Confessions: Speaking Guilt in Law and Literature*. Chicago: University of Chicago Press, 2000.

Bruns, Axel. "The Practice of Newsblogging." In *Uses of Blogs*, edited by Axel Bruns and Joanne Jacobs, 11–22. Digital Formations 38. New York: Peter Lang, 2006.

Bunkers, Suzanne L. "Whose Diary Is It, Anyway? Issues of Agency, Authority and Ownership." *a/b: Auto/Biography Studies* 17, no. 1 (2003): 11–27.

Cameron, Julia, with Mark Bryan. *The Artist's Way: A Spiritual Path to Higher Creativity*. New York: Jeremy P. Tarcher/Putnam, 1992.

Capp, Fiona. "Salinger's Toilet: The Culture of Confession." *Overland*, no. 209 (2012): 13–17.

Cardell, Kylie. "Bloodsport: Thomas Goltz and the Journalist's Diary of War." *Biography: An Interdisciplinary Quarterly* 29, no.4 (2006): 584–604.

————. "Creating the Creative Subject: *The 1000 Journals Project*, Creativity and Autobiographical Identity." *Continuum: Journal of Media & Cultural Studies* (22 April 2014). http://www.tandfonline.com/doi/abs/10.1080/10304312.2014.907872#.U3gqTliSyzk.

————. "Read My Lips: Genre, Rhetoric and the *Baghdad Diaries* of Nuha al-Radi." *a/b: Auto/Biography Studies* 27, no.2 (2012): 316–37.

Case, Alison. "Authenticity, Convention, and Bridget Jones's Diary." *Narrative* 9, no. 2 (2001): 179–81.

Cates, Isaac. "The Diary Comic." In *Graphic Subjects: Critical Essays on Autobiography and Graphic Novels*, edited by Michael Chaney, 209–26. Madison: University of Wisconsin Press, 2011.

Chaney, Michael, ed. *Graphic Subjects: Critical Essays on Autobiography and Graphic Novels*. Madison: University of Wisconsin Press, 2011.

Chute, Hilary. *Graphic Women: Life Narrative and Contemporary Comics*. New York: Columbia University Press, 2010.

Chute, Hilary, and Marianne DeKoven. "Introduction: Graphic Narrative." *Modern Fiction Studies* 52, no. 4 (2006): 767–82.

Cobain, Kurt. *Journals*. New York: Riverhead Books, 2007.

Collins, John. Review of *Sharon and My Mother-in-Law* by Suad Amiry. *H-Net Reviews in the Humanities and Social Sciences* (June 2005). http://www.h-net.msu.edu/reviews /showrev.cgi?path=135181125071047.

Cooke, Rachel. "Emails from the Edge." *Guardian*, 15 January 2005. http://observer .guardian.co.uk/review/story/0,6903,1391186,00.html.

Cottam, Rachel. "Diaries and Journals: General Survey." In *The Encyclopedia of Life Writing*, edited by Magaretta Jolly, 267–69. London: Fitzroy Dearborn, 2001.

Couser, G. Thomas. *Memoir: An Introduction*. Oxford: Oxford University Press, 2012.

Culley, Margo. *A Day at a Time: Diary Literature of American Women from 1764 to 1985*. New York: Feminist Press, 1998.

Daley, Chris. "The 'Atrocious Privilege': Bearing Witness to War and Atrocity in O'Brien, Levi, and Remarque." In *Arms and the Self: War, the Military, and Autobiographical Writing*, edited by Alex Vernon, 182–201. Kent: Kent State University Press, 2005.

Dean, Jodi. *Blog Theory: Feedback and Capture in the Circuits of Drive*. Cambridge: Polity Press, 2010.

de Man, Paul. "Autobiography as De-Facement." In *The Rhetoric of Romanticism*, 67–81. New York: Columbia University Press, 1984.

DeSalvo, Louise. *Writing as a Way of Healing: How Telling Our Stories Transforms Our Lives*. London: Women's Press, 1999.

Dowrick, Stephanie. *Living Words: Journal Writing for Self-Discovery, Insight and Creativity*. Camberwell, VIC: Viking, 2003.

Dubrofsky, Rachel E. "Therapeutics of the Self: Surveillance in the Service of the Therapeutic." *Television and New Media* 8 (2007): 263–85.

Eakin, Paul John. *How Our Lives Become Stories: Making Selves*. Ithaca, NY: Cornell University Press, 1999.

Ezard, John. "Bainbridge Tilts at 'Chick Lit' Cult." *Guardian*, 24 August 2001, 7.

Fallon, Kevin. "Richard Burton's Sexy Diaries: 13 Juiciest Bits." *Daily Beast*, 20 October 2012. http://www.thedailybeast.com/articles/2012/10/20/richard-burton-s-sexy-diaries-13-juiciest-bits.html.

Fazio, Daniel. "Paul McGeough, *in Baghdad: A Reporter's War*." *API Review of Books*, no. 44 (2006).

Felski, Rita. *Beyond Feminist Aesthetics: Feminist Literature and Social Change*. Cambridge, MA: Harvard University Press, 1989.

Ferreday, Debra. "Writing Sex Work Online: Belle De Jour and the Problem of Authenticity." *Wagadu* 8 (Fall 2010): 273–91.

Fielding, Helen. *Bridget Jones: The Edge of Reason*. London: Macmillan, 2004.

———. *Bridget Jones's Diary*. London: Picador, 2001.

Filgate, Michele. "Will Social Media Kill Writers' Diaries?" Salon.com, 4 August 2013. http://www.salon.com/2013/08/04/will_social_media_kill_the_writers_diary/.

Flood, Alison. "Bridget Jones on the Edge of Further Adventures, Says Helen Fielding." *Guardian*, 9 November 2012. http://www.guardian.co.uk/books/2012/nov/09/bridget-jones-further-adventures-helen-fielding.

Fothergill, Robert A. *Private Chronicles: A Study of English Diaries*. London: Oxford University Press, 1974.

Foucault, Michel. *The History of Sexuality*. Vol. 1, *The Will to Knowledge*. Translated by Robert Hurley. London: Penguin, 1998.

———. *Technologies of the Self: A Seminar with Michel Foucault*. Edited by Luther H. Martin, Huck Gutman, and Patrick H. Hutton. Amherst: University of Massachusetts Press, 1988.

Franklin, Cynthia, and Laura E. Lyons. "Bodies of Evidence and Intricate Machines of Untruth." *Biography: An Interdisciplinary Quarterly* 27, no. 1 (2004): v–xxii.

Franklin, Miles. *The Diaries of Miles Franklin*. Edited by Paul Brunton. Crows Nest, NSW: Allen and Unwin, 2004.

Friedman, Susan Stanford. "The Futures of Feminist Criticism: A Diary." *PMLA: Publications of the Modern Language Association of America* 121, no. 5 (2006): 1704–10.

Fullwood, Chris, Karen Melrose, Neil Morris, and Sarah Floyd. "Sex, Blogs, and Baring Your Soul: Factors Influencing Uk Blogging Strategies." *Journal of the American Society for Information Science and Technology* 64, no. 2 (2012): 345–55.

Furedi, Frank. *Therapy Culture: Cultivating Vulnerability in an Uncertain Age*. London: Routledge, 2004.

Fussell, Paul. *The Great War and Modern Memory*. Oxford: Oxford University Press, 2000.

Gammel, Irene, ed. *Confessional Politics: Women's Sexual Self-Representations in Life Writing and Popular Media*. Carbondale: Southern Illinois University Press, 1999.

———. "Mirror Looks: The Visual and Performative Diaries of L. M. Montgomery, Baroness Elsa Von Freytag-Loringhoven, and Elvira Bach." In *Interfaces: Women, Autobiography, Image, Performance*, edited by Sidonie Smith and Julia Watson, 289–313. Ann Arbor: University of Michigan Press, 2002.

Gannett, Cinthia. *Gender and the Journal: Diaries and Academic Discourse*. New York: State University of New York Press, 1992.

Gauntlett, David. *Making Is Connecting: The Social Meaning of Creativity from DIY and Knitting to YouTube and Web 2.0*. London: Polity, 2011.

Genzlinger, Neil. "The Problem with Memoirs." *New York Times*, 28 January 2011. http://www.nytimes.com/2011/01/30/books/review/Genzlinger-t.html?pagewanted=all.

Gilbert, Jason. "Samsung Patents a 'Life Diary,' Would Automatically Keep a Journal of Your Day for You." *Huffington Post*, 10 May 2012. http://www.huffingtonpost .com/2012/10/05/samsung-patents-life-diary-auto-journal_n_1943395.html.

Gilmore, Leigh. "American Neoconfessional: Memoir, Self-Help, and Redemption on Oprah's Couch." *Biography: An Interdisciplinary Quarterly* 33, no. 4 (2010): 657–79.

———. *The Limits of Autobiography: Trauma and Testimony.* Ithaca, NY: Cornell University Press, 2001.

Gilmore, Leigh, and Elizabeth Marshall. "Girls in Crisis: Rescue and Transnational Feminist Autobiographical Resistance." *Feminist Studies* 36, no. 3 (Fall 2010): 667–90.

"Girl with a One Track Mind." *Sunday Times*, 16 July 2006, 16.

Gloeckner, Phoebe. *A Child's Life and Other Stories.* Berkeley, CA: Frog Books, 2000.

———. *The Diary of a Teenage Girl: An Account in Words and Pictures.* Berkeley, CA: Frog Books, 2002.

Goldberg, Natalie. *Writing Down the Bones: Freeing the Writer Within.* Boston: Shambahala, 2010.

Golley, Nawar Al-Hassan. *Arab Women's Lives Retold: Exploring Identity through Writing.* New York: Syracuse University Press, 2007.

———. *Reading Arab Women's Autobiographies: Shahrazad Tells Her Story.* Austin: University of Texas Press, 2003.

Goltz, Thomas. *Azerbaijan Diary: A Rogue Reporter's Adventures in an Oil-Rich, War-Torn, Post-Soviet Republic.* New York: M. E. Sharpe, 1998.

———. *Chechnya Diary: A War Correspondent's Story of Surviving the War in Chechnya.* New York: Thomas Dunne Books/St Martin's, 2003.

———. "Conversation with Thomas Goltz." Institute of International Studies, UC–Berkeley, 2003. http://globetrotter.berkeley.edu/people3/Goltz/goltz-cono.html.

———. *Georgia Diary: A Chronicle of War and Political Chaos in the Post-Soviet Caucasus.* New York: M. E. Sharpe, 2006.

———. "Meet the Author." World Affairs Council of Northern California, 2003. http:// wacsf.vportal.net/?fileid=3296.

Gregory, Derek. *The Colonial Present.* Oxford: Blackwell, 2004.

Guenther, Leah. "*Bridget Jones's Diary*: Confessing Post-Feminism." In *Modern Confessional Writing: New Critical Essays*, edited by Jo Gill, 85–99. New York: Routledge, 2006.

Guignon, Charles. *On Being Authentic.* Thinking in Action. London: Routledge, 2004.

Hammill, Faye. *Sophistication: A Literary and Cultural History.* Liverpool: Liverpool University Press, 2010.

Hanson, Claire. "Fiction, Feminism and Femininity from the Eighties to the Noughties." In *Contemporary British Women Writers*, edited by Emma Parker, 16–27. Cambridge: D. S. Brewer, 2004.

Hassam, Andrew. *Writing and Reality: A Study of Modern British Diary Fiction.* Westport, CT: Greenwood Press, 1992.

Hedges, Chris. "War: Realities and Myths." AntiWar.com, 11 June 2005. http://www .antiwar.com/orig/hedges.php?articleid=6294.

Hill, Annette, and Gareth Palmer. "Big Brother." *Television and New Media* 3 (2002): 252–54.

Hogan, Rebecca. "Engendered Autobiographies: The Diary as a Feminine Form." In *Autobiography and Questions of Gender*, edited by Shirley Neuman, 95–107. London: Frank Cass, 1991.

Holden, Edith. *The Country Diary of an Edwardian Lady*. Valencia, CA: Top That! Publishing, 2006.

Holmes, Katie. *Spaces in Her Day: Australian Women's Diaries of the 1920s and 1930s*. St. Leonards: Allen and Unwin, 1995.

Huff, Cynthia A. "Textual Boundaries: Space in Nineteenth-Century Women's Manuscript Diaries." In *Inscribing the Daily: Critical Essays on Women's Diaries*, edited by Suzanne L. Bunkers and Cynthia A. Huff, 123–38. Amherst: University of Massachusetts Press, 1996.

Illouz, Eva. *Oprah Winfrey and the Glamour of Misery: An Essay on Popular Culture*. New York: Columbia University Press, 2003.

Jackson, Anna. *Diary Poetics: Form and Style in Writers' Diaries, 1915–1962*. Routledge Studies in Twentieth-Century Literature 12. New York: Routledge, 2010.

Jakubowski, Maxim. *The Mammoth Book of Sex Diaries*. New York: Carroll and Graf, 2005.

Jelinek, Estelle C. "Introduction: Women's Autobiography and the Male Tradition." In *Women's Autobiography: Essays in Criticism*, edited by Estelle C. Jelinek, 1–20. Bloomington: Indiana University Press, 1980.

Joiner, Whitney. "Not Your Mother's Comic." Salon.com, 15 March 2003. http://www.salon.com/2003/03/15/gloeckner/.

Juhasz, Suzanne. "Towards a Theory of Form in Feminist Autobiography: Kate Millet's *Flying* and *Sita*; Maxine Hong Kingston's *The Woman Warrior*." In *Women's Autobiography: Essays in Criticism*, edited by Estelle C. Jelinek, 221–37. Bloomington: Indiana University Press, 1980.

Kahlo, Frida. *The Diary of Frida Kahlo: An Intimate Self-Portrait*. New York: Abrams, 2005.

Katovsky, Bill, and Timothy Carlson, eds. *Embedded: The Media at War in Iraq*. Guilford, CT: Lyons Press, 2003.

King, Stephen. *On Writing: A Memoir of the Craft*. London: New English Library/Hodder & Stoughton, 2001.

Knightley, Phillip. *The First Casualty: The War Correspondent as Hero, Propagandist and Myth-Maker from the Crimea to Iraq*. London: Andre Deutsch, 2003.

Kreuzhage, Andrea, dir. *1000 Journals*. Andrea-K Productions, 2008.

Kuhn-Osius, K. Eckhard. "Making Loose Ends Meet: Private Journals in the Public Realm." *German Quarterly* 54 (1981): 166–76.

Lamott, Anne. *Bird by Bird: Some Instructions on Writing and Life*. New York: Random House, 1995.

Langford, Rachael, and Russell West. "Introduction: Diaries and Margins." In *Marginal Voices, Marginal Forms: Diaries in European Literature and History*, edited by Rachael Langford and Russell West, 6–21. Amsterdam: Rodopi, 1999.

Lears, T. J. Jackson. *No Place of Grace: Antimodernism and the Transformation of American Culture, 1880–1920*. Chicago: University of Chicago Press, 1994.

Lee, Abby. *Girl with a One Track Mind*. London: Ebury Press, 2006.

———. Girl With a One Track Mind. http://girlwithaonetrackmind.blogspot.com.au/.

Leech, Gary. *Beyond Bogotá: Diary of a Drug War Journalist in Colombia*. Boston: Beacon Press, 2009.

Leith, Denise. *Bearing Witness: The Lives of War Correspondents and Photojournalists*. Sydney: Random House, 2004.

Lejeune, Philippe. *On Autobiography*. Translated by Katherine Leary. Edited by Paul John Eakin. Minneapolis: University of Minnesota Press, 1989.

———. *On Diary*. Translated by Katherine Durnin. Edited by Jeremy D. Popkin and Julie Rak. Honolulu: University of Hawai'i Press, 2009.

Lightman, Sarah. "*Diary Drawings* by Bobby Baker." *Studies in Comics* 1, no. 1 (2010): 159–68.

Loane, Sally. "Interview with Paul McGeough." ABC Radio Sydney, Australia, 23 June 2003.

Lumby, Catherine, and Elspeth Probyn. *Remote Control: New Media, New Ethics*. Cambridge: Cambridge University Press, 2003.

Maddison, Stephen, and Merl Storr. "The Edge of Reason: The Myth of Bridget Jones." In *At the Interface: Continuity and Transformation in Culture and Politics*, edited by Joss Hands and Eugenia Siapera, 3–16. Amsterdam: Rodopi, 2004.

Magnanti, Brooke. *The Sex Myth: Why Everything We're Told Is Wrong*. London: Phoenix, 2013.

Mallon, Thomas. *A Book of One's Own: People and Their Diaries*. London: Picador, 1985.

Mansfield, Nick. *Subjectivity: Theories of the Self from Freud to Haraway*. St. Leonards, NSW: Allen and Unwin, 2000.

Margolis, Zoe [Abby Lee]. "The Sex Blog Confessions (with Apologies to My Dad)." *Independent on Sunday*, 13 August 2006, 34.

Marsh, Kelly A. "Contextualizing Bridget Jones." *College Literature* 31, no. 1 (2004): 52–72.

Martinkus, John. "A Slap in the Face from the Border." Review of *Manhattan to Baghdad* by Paul McGeough. *Australian Book Review*, no. 250 (April 2003): 12.

Matisse, Mistress. "Mistress Matisse's Journal." http://mistressmatisse.blogspot.com.au/.

McGee, Micki. *Self-Help, Inc.: Makeover Culture in American Life*. Oxford: Oxford University Press, 2005.

McGeough, Paul. *In Baghdad: A Reporter's War*. Crows Nest, NSW: Allen and Unwin, 2003.

———. *Manhattan to Baghdad: Despatches from the Frontline in the War on Terror*. Crows Nest, NSW: Allen and Unwin, 2003.

McGraw, Phil. *Self-Matters: Creating Your Life from the Inside Out*. New York: Simon and Schuster, 2003.

McNeill, Laurie. "Performing Genres: Peggy Abkhazi's *A Curious Cage* and Diaries of War." *Canadian Literature*, no. 179 (2003): 89–105.

———. "Teaching an Old Genre New Tricks: The Diary on the Internet." *Biography: An Interdisciplinary Quarterly* 26, no. 1 (2003): 24–47.

Mehta, Brinda. "Dissidence, Creativity, and Embargo Art in Nuha Al-Radi's Baghdad Diaries." *Meridians: feminism, race, transnationalism* 6, no. 2 (2006): 220–35.

———. *Rituals of Memory in Contemporary Arab Women's Writing*. Syracuse, NY: Syracuse University Press, 2007.

Merkin, Daphne. "Richard Burton's Diaries Reveal His Mad Love for Elizabeth Taylor." *Daily Beast*, 3 November 2012. http://www.thedailybeast.com/articles/2012/11/03/richard-burton-s-diaries-reveal-his-mad-love-for-elizabeth-taylor.html.

Mikhailova, Anna. "Revealed: Identity of Erotic Diarist behind Summer's Hottest Book." *Sunday Times*, 6 August 2006, 3.

Miller, Carolyn R., and Dawn Shepherd. "Blogging as Social Action: A Genre Analysis of the Weblog." *Into the Blogosphere: Rhetoric, Community, and Culture of Weblogs* (2004). http://blog.lib.umn.edu/blogosphere/blogging_as_social_action_a_genre_analysis_of_the_weblog.html.

Mitchell, Kaye. "Raunch versus Prude: Contemporary Sex Blogs and Erotic Memoirs by Women." *Psychology and Sexuality* 3, no. 1 (2012): 12–25.

Morris, Nomi. "Israeli Women Open Hearts and Minds to Palestine." *Globe and Mail*, 12 September 2005, D18–D19.

Myers, Linda. *The Power of Memoir: Writing to Heal*. San Francisco: Jossey-Bass, 2010.

New, Jennifer. *Drawing from Life: The Journal as Art*. New York: Princeton Architectural Press, 2005.

Nin, Anaïs. *Incest: From "A Journal of Love: The Unexpurgated Diary of Anaïs Nin, 1932–1934."* New York: Harcourt Brace, 1992.

———. *The Novel of the Future*. 1968. Reprint, Athens: Swallow Press/Ohio University Press, 1986.

Nussbaum, Felicity A. "Eighteenth-Century Women's Autobiographical Commonplaces." In *The Private Self: Theory and Practice of Women's Autobiographical Writings*, edited by Shari Benstock, 147–76. Chapel Hill: University of North Carolina Press, 1988.

———. "Toward Conceptualizing Diary." In *Studies in Autobiography*, edited by James Olney, 128–40. New York: Oxford University Press, 1988.

Oakley, Barry. "Acid in the Pen: Miles Franklin Comes to Life in Her Diaries." Review of *The Diaries of Miles Franklin*. *Weekend Australian*, 6–7 March 2004, 10–11.

O'Connor, M. "The Human Side of Occupation: Suad Amiry, Author of *Sharon and My Mother-in-Law* in Interview." *Three Monkeys Online*, 1 January 2005. http://www.threemonkeysonline.com/the-human-side-of-occupation-suad-amiry-author-of-sharon-and-my-mother-in-law-in-interview/2/.

Olney, James. *Metaphors of Self: The Meaning of Autobiography*. Princeton, NJ: Princeton University Press, 1972.

Orenstein, Peggy. "A Graphic Life." *New York Times*, 5 August 2001. http://www.ny times.com/2001/08/05/magazine/a-graphic-life.html?pagewanted=all&src=pm.

Paasonen, Susanna. "Gender, Identity, and (the Limits of) Play on the Internet." In *Women and Everyday Uses of the Internet: Agency and Identity*, edited by Mia Consalvo and Susanna Paasonen, 21–43. New York: Peter Lang, 2002.

Payne, Cynthia. "Belle Doesn't Ring True." *Guardian*, 24 March 2004. http://www .guardian.co.uk/theguardian/2004/mar/25/features11.g22.

Pennebaker, James W. *Writing to Heal: A Guided Journal for Recovering from Trauma and Emotional Upheaval.* Oakland, CA: New Harbinger Publications, 2004.

Peterson, Andrea. "War Diaries and Journals." In *The Encyclopedia of Life Writing: Autobiographical and Biographical Forms*, edited by Margaretta Jolly, 925–27. London: Fitzroy Dearborn, 2001.

Plummer, Ken. *Telling Sexual Stories: Power, Change and Social Worlds.* London: Routledge, 1995.

Podnieks, Elizabeth. *Daily Modernism: The Literary Diaries of Virginia Woolf, Antonia White, Elizabeth Smart, and Anaïs Nin.* Montreal: McGill-Queen's University Press, 2000.

———. "'Hit-Sluts' and 'Page Pimps': Online Diarists and Their Quest for Cyber-Union." *Life Writing* 1, no. 2 (2004): 123–50.

Poletti, Anna. "Intimate Economies: Postsecret and the Affect of Confession." *Biography* 34, no. 1 (2011): 25–36.

Potter, Andrew. *The Authenticity Hoax: Why the "Real" Things We Seek Don't Make Us Happy.* New York: Harper Perennial, 2010.

Progoff, Ira. *At a Journal Workshop: Writing to Access the Power of the Unconscious and Evoke Creative Ability.* 1975. Reprint, Los Angeles: Jeremy P. Tarcher, 1992.

Rainer, Tristine. *The New Diary: How to Use a Journal for Self-Guidance and Expanded Creativity.* 1978. Reprint, New York: Jeremy P. Tarcher, 2004.

Rak, Julie. *Boom! Manufacturing Memoir for the Popular Market.* Waterloo, ON: Wilfrid Laurier University Press, 2013.

———. "The Digital Queer: Weblogs and Internet Identity." *Biography: An Interdisciplinary Quarterly* 28, no. 1 (2005): 166–82.

Ray, Audacia. *Naked on the Internet: Hookups, Downloads, and Cashing In on Internet Sexploration.* Emeryville, CA: Seal Press, 2007.

Rich, Phil, and Stuart Copans. *The Healing Journey through Addiction: Your Journal for Recovery And Self-Renewal.* New York: Wiley, 2000.

Riverbend. *Baghdad Burning: Girl Blog from Iraq.* Edited by James Ridgeway. Foreword by Ahdaf Soueif. London: Marion Boyars, 2005.

Rogers, Richard. *Digital Methods.* Cambridge, MA: MIT Press, 2013.

Roorbach, Bill. *Writing Life Stories.* Cincinnati, OH: Story Press, 1998.

Rose, Nikolas. "Assembling the Modern Self." In *Rewriting the Self: Histories from the Renaissance to the Present*, edited by Roy Porter, 224–48. New York: Routledge, 1997.

———. *Inventing Our Selves: Psychology, Power, and Personhood.* Cambridge: Cambridge University Press, 1996.

Rosenberg, Scott. *Say Everything: How Blogging Began, What It's Becoming, and Why It Matters.* New York: Three Rivers Press, 2009.

Rosenwald, Lawrence. *Emerson and the Art of the Diary.* New York: Oxford University Press, 1988.

Salam Pax. *The Baghdad Blog.* Melbourne: Text, 2003.

Schaffer, Kay, and Sidonie Smith. *Human Rights and Narrated Lives: The Ethics of Recognition.* New York: Palgrave Macmillan, 2004.

Schiwy, Marlene A. *A Voice of Her Own: Women and the Journal Writing Journey.* New York: Fireside, 1996.

Seierstad, Åsne. *A Hundred and One Days: A Baghdad Journal.* New York: Basic Books, 2003.

Serafty, Viviane. *The Mirror and the Veil: An Overview of American Diaries and Online Blogs.* Amsterdam: Rodopi, 2004.

Sherman, Stuart. *Telling Time: Clocks, Diaries, and English Diurnal Form, 1660–1785.* Chicago: University of Chicago Press, 1996.

Shirer, William L. *Berlin Diary: The Journal of a Foreign Correspondent 1934–1941.* London: Penguin, 1979.

Sims, Norman, and Mark Kramer, eds. *Literary Journalism: A New Collection of the Best American Nonfiction.* New York: Ballantine Books, 1995.

Singh, Armadeep. "Anonymity, Authorship, and Blogger Ethics." *symploke* 16, no. 1 (2008): 21–35.

Singh, Jai. "Blog Power: Fresh Voices Rise from the Web. An Iraqi Woman's Postings Gives Insider's Anti-War View." Review of *Baghdad Burning* by Riverbend. *San Francisco Chronicle,* 1 May 2005, B-3.

Skurnick, Lizzie. Review of *Baghdad Diaries* by Nuha Al-Radi. *Baltimore City Paper Online,* 12 April 2003. http://www.citypaper.com/arts/review.asp?rid=5079.

Smith, Keri. *Wreck This Journal: To Create Is to Destroy.* New York: Penguin, 2007.

Smith, Roger. "Self-Reflection and the Self." In *Rewriting the Self: Histories from the Renaissance to the Present,* edited by Roy Porter, 49–58. New York: Routledge, 1997.

Smith, Sidonie. *A Poetics of Women's Autobiography: Marginality and the Fictions of Self-Representation.* Bloomington: Indiana University Press, 1987.

Smith, Sidonie, and Julia Watson. *Getting a Life: Everyday Uses of Autobiography.* Minneapolis: University of Minnesota Press, 1996.

———, eds. *Interfaces: Women, Autobiography, Image, Performance.* Ann Arbor: University of Michigan Press, 2003.

———. "Introduction: De/Colonization and the Politics of Discourse in Women's Autobiographical Practices." In *De/Colonizing the Subject: The Politics of Gender in Women's Autobiography,* edited by Sidonie Smith and Julia Watson, xiii–xxxi. Minneapolis: University of Minnesota Press, 1992.

———. *Reading Autobiography: A Guide for Interpreting Life Narratives.* Minneapolis: University of Minnesota Press, 2010.

———. "Virtually Me: A Toolbox about Online Self-Presentation." In *Identity Technologies: Constructing the Self Online,* edited by Anna Poletti and Julie Rak, 70–95. Madison: University of Wisconsin Press, 2014.

Snyder, Gregory J. *Graffiti Lives: Beyond the Tag in New York's Urban Underground.* New York: New York University Press, 2009.

Someguy. *The 1000 Journals Project.* San Francisco: Chronicle Books, 2007.

———. "The 1000 Journals Project." http://www.1000journals.com/.

———. "1001 Journals." http://www.1001journals.com.

Sontag, Susan. *Reborn: Early Diaries, 1947–1963.* Edited by David Rieff. London: Penguin, 2008.

———. *Regarding the Pain of Others.* London: Penguin, 2003.

Sorapure, Madeleine. "Screening Moments, Scrolling Lives: Diary Writing on the Web." *Biography: An Interdisciplinary Quarterly* 26, no. 1 (2003): 1–23.

Spiegelman, Art. *Maus: A Survivor's Tale.* [*The Complete Maus.*] London: Penguin, 2003.

Spurgeon, Tom. "Phoebe Gloeckner's Comics." *Comics Reporter,* 24 September 2003. http://www.comicsreporter.com/index.php/briefings/cr_reviews/2009/.

Stevens, Annie. "Should Bridget Jones Come Out of Retirement?" *Daily Life,* 20 December 2012. http://www.dailylife.com.au/life-and-love/love,-sex-and-relationships/should-bridget-jones-come-out-of-retirement-20121213-2bbma.html.

Stewart, Victoria. *Women's Autobiography: War and Trauma.* Houndmills, UK: Palgrave Macmillan, 2003.

Stohlman, Nancy, and Laurieann Aladin, eds. *Live from Palestine: International and Palestinian Direct Action Against the Israeli Occupation.* Cambridge, MA: South End Press, 2003.

Taylor, Charles. *Sources of the Self: The Making of the Modern Identity.* Cambridge, MA: Harvard University Press, 1989.

Temple, Judy Nolte. "Fragments as Diary: Theoretical Implications of the *Dreams and Visions* of 'Baby Doe' Tabor." In *Inscribing the Daily: Critical Essays on Women's Diaries,* edited by Suzanne L. Bunkers and Cynthia A. Huff, 72–85. Amherst: University of Massachusetts Press, 1996.

Tregoning, Will. "Authentic Self, Paranoid Critique and Getting a Good Night's Rest." *Continuum: Journal of Media and Culture Studies* 20, no. 2 (2006): 175–88.

Tumarkin, Maria. *Traumascapes: The Power and Fate of Places Transformed by Tragedy.* Melbourne: Melbourne University Press, 2005.

Tumber, Howard, and Frank Webster. *Journalists under Fire: Information War and Journalistic Practices.* London: SAGE, 2006.

Twiddy, David. "Library Patrons Object to Some Graphic Novels." *Washington Post,* 18 December 2006. http://www.washingtonpost.com/wp-dyn/content/article/2006/12/17/AR2006121700906.html.

University of California San Francisco (UCSF) Benioff Children's Hospital. "Journals Project Performance Shows Humanity of Hospitalized Teens." 17 March 2011. http://www.ucsfbenioffchildrens.org/news/2011/03/journals_project_performance_shows_humanity_of_hospitalized_.html.

Van Krieken, Robert. "Decline and Fall?" *Meanjin* 63, no. 4 (2004): 53–58.

Vernon, Alex, ed. *Arms and the Self: War, the Military, and Autobiographical Writing.* Kent: Kent State University Press, 2005.

Versaci, Rocco. *This Book Contains Graphic Language: Comics as Literature*. New York: Continuum, 2007.

Wall, Melissa. "Blogging Gulf War II." *Journalism Studies* 7, no. 1 (2006): 111–26.

Warner, Marina. "Chronicle of a Life Repaired." In *Diary Drawings: Mental Illness and Me*, edited by Bobby Baker, 3–16. London: Profile Books, 2010.

Warren, Frank. *PostSecret*. http://www.postsecret.com/.

Watson, Julia. "Visual Diary as Prosthetic Practice in Bobby Baker's *Diary Drawings*." *Biography* 35, no. 1 (2012): 21–44.

Weldon, Michele. *Writing to Save Your Life: How to Honor Your Story through Journaling*. Minnesota: Hazelden, 2001.

Whelehan, Imelda. *The Feminist Bestseller: From Sex and the Single Girl to Sex and the City*. Houndmills: Palgrave Macmillan, 2005.

——. "Sex and the Single Girl: Helen Fielding, Erica Jong and Helen Gurley Brown." In *Contemporary British Women Writers*, edited by Emma Parker, 28–40. Cambridge: D. S. Brewer, 2004.

Whitlock, Gillian. *Soft Weapons: Autobiography in Transit*. Chicago: University of Chicago Press, 2007.

Whitlock, Gillian, and Anna Poletti. "Self-Regarding Art." *Biography* 31, no. 1 (2008): v–xxiii.

Wilkins, Frances E. *Bodyminder Workout and Exercise Journal: A Fitness Diary*. Eugene, OR: MemoryMinder Journals, Inc., 2003.

Wilson, Sonia. *Personal Effects: Reading the "Journal" of Marie Bashkirtseff*. London: Modern Humanities Research Association, 2010.

Winfrey, Oprah. "An Exclusive Look at Oprah's Journals." *O, The Oprah Magazine*, April 2011. http://www.oprah.com/spirit/Oprahs-Private-Journals-Diary-Excerpts.

——. "What I Know for Sure." *O, The Oprah Magazine*, November 2000, 298.

Wink, Amy L. *She Left Nothing in Particular: The Autobiographical Legacy of Nineteenth-Century Women's Diaries*. Knoxville: University of Tennessee Press, 2001.

Wolf, Hope. "Mediating War: Hot Diaries, Liquid Letters and Vivid Remembrances." *Life Writing* 9, no. 3 (2012): 327–36.

Wolfe, Tom. "The Birth of 'the New Journalism': Eyewitness Report by Tom Wolfe." *New York Magazine*, 14 February 1972. http://nymag.com/news/media/47353/.

Woolf, Virginia. *The Diary of Virginia Woolf*. Vol. 1, *1915–1919*. Edited by Anne Olivier Bell. London: Hogarth, 1977.

——. *The Diary of Virginia Woolf*. Vol. 2, *1920–1924*. Edited by Anne Olivier Bell. London: Hogarth, 1980.

Young, James E. "Interpreting Literary Testimony: A Preface to Rereading Holocaust Diaries and Memoirs." *New Literary History* 18, no. 2 (1987): 403–23.

Zambreno, Kate. *Heroines*. Los Angeles: Semiotext(e), 2012.

Zapruder, Alexandra. *Salvaged Pages: Young Writer's Diaries of the Holocaust*. New Haven, CT: Yale University Press, 2004.

Zelizer, Barbie. *Taking Journalism Seriously: News and the Academy*. Thousand Oaks, CA: Sage Publications, 2004.

Index

Wisconsin Studies in Autobiography

WILLIAM L. ANDREWS
Series Editor

Robert F. Sayre
The Examined Self: Benjamin Franklin, Henry Adams, Henry James

Daniel B. Shea
Spiritual Autobiography in Early America

Lois Mark Stalvey
The Education of a WASP

Margaret Sams
Forbidden Family: A Wartime Memoir of the Philippines, 1941–1945
Edited with an introduction by Lynn Z. Bloom

Charlotte Perkins Gilman
The Living of Charlotte Perkins Gilman: An Autobiography
Introduction by Ann J. Lane

Mark Twain
Mark Twain's Own Autobiography: The Chapters from the "North American Review"
Edited by Michael J. Kiskis

Journeys in New Worlds: Early American Women's Narratives
Edited by William L. Andrews, Sargent Bush, Jr., Annette Kolodny, Amy
    Schrager Lang, and Daniel B. Shea

American Autobiography: Retrospect and Prospect
Edited by Paul John Eakin

Caroline Seabury
The Diary of Caroline Seabury, 1854–1863
Edited with an introduction by Suzanne L. Bunkers

Cornelia Peake McDonald
A Woman's Civil War: A Diary with Reminiscences of the War, from March 1862
Edited with an introduction by Minrose C. Gwin

Marian Anderson
My Lord, What a Morning
Introduction by Nellie Y. McKay

American Women's Autobiography: Fea(s)ts of Memory
Edited with an introduction by Margo Culley

Frank Marshall Davis
Livin' the Blues: Memoirs of a Black Journalist and Poet
Edited with an introduction by John Edgar Tidwell

Joanne Jacobson
Authority and Alliance in the Letters of Henry Adams

Kamau Brathwaite
The Zea Mexican Diary: 7 September 1926–7 September 1986

Genaro M. Padilla
My History, Not Yours: The Formation of Mexican American Autobiography

Frances Smith Foster
Witnessing Slavery: The Development of Ante-bellum Slave Narratives

Native American Autobiography: An Anthology
Edited by Arnold Krupat

American Lives: An Anthology of Autobiographical Writing
Edited by Robert F. Sayre

Carol Holly
Intensely Family: The Inheritance of Family Shame and the Autobiographies of Henry James

People of the Book: Thirty Scholars Reflect on Their Jewish Identity
Edited by Jeffrey Rubin-Dorsky and Shelley Fisher Fishkin

G. Thomas Couser
Recovering Bodies: Illness, Disability, and Life Writing

John Downton Hazlett
My Generation: Collective Autobiography and Identity Politics

William Herrick
Jumping the Line: The Adventures and Misadventures of an American Radical

Women, Autobiography, Theory: A Reader
Edited by Sidonie Smith and Julia Watson

José Angel Gutiérrez
The Making of a Chicano Militant: Lessons from Cristal

Marie Hall Ets
Rosa: The Life of an Italian Immigrant

Carson McCullers
Illumination and Night Glare: The Unfinished Autobiography of Carson McCullers
Edited with an introduction by Carlos L. Dews

Yi-Fu Tuan
Who Am I? An Autobiography of Emotion, Mind, and Spirit

Henry Bibb
The Life and Adventures of Henry Bibb: An American Slave
Introduction by Charles J. Heglar

Diaries of Girls and Women: A Midwestern American Sampler
Edited by Suzanne L. Bunkers

Jim Lane
The Autobiographical Documentary in America

Sandra Pouchet Paquet
Caribbean Autobiography: Cultural Identity and Self-Representation

Mark O'Brien, with Gillian Kendall
How I Became a Human Being: A Disabled Man's Quest for Independence

Elizabeth L. Banks
*Campaigns of Curiosity: Journalistic Adventures of an American Girl
  in Late Victorian London*
Introduction by Mary Suzanne Schriber and Abbey L. Zink

Miriam Fuchs
The Text Is Myself: Women's Life Writing and Catastrophe

Jean M. Humez
Harriet Tubman: The Life and the Life Stories

Voices Made Flesh: Performing Women's Autobiography
Edited by Lynn C. Miller, Jacqueline Taylor, and M. Heather Carver

Loreta Janeta Velazquez
The Woman in Battle: The Civil War Narrative of Loreta Janeta Velazquez,
    Cuban Woman and Confederate Soldier
Introduction by Jesse Alemán

Cathryn Halverson
Maverick Autobiographies: Women Writers and the American West, 1900–1936

Jeffrey Brace
The Blind African Slave: Or Memoirs of Boyrereau Brinch, Nicknamed Jeffrey Brace
as told to Benjamin F. Prentiss, Esq.
Edited with an introduction by Kari J. Winter

Colette Inez
The Secret of M. Dulong: A Memoir

Before They Could Vote: American Women's Autobiographical Writing, 1819–1919
Edited by Sidonie Smith and Julia Watson

Bertram J. Cohler
Writing Desire: Sixty Years of Gay Autobiography

Philip Holden
Autobiography and Decolonization: Modernity, Masculinity, and the Nation-State

Jing M. Wang
When "I" Was Born: Women's Autobiography in Modern China

Conjoined Twins in Black and White: The Lives of Millie-Christine McKoy
    and Daisy and Violet Hilton
Edited by Linda Frost

Four Russian Serf Narratives
Translated, edited, and with an introduction by John MacKay

Mark Twain
Mark Twain's Own Autobiography: The Chapters from the "North American Review,"
    second edition
Edited by Michael J. Kiskis

Graphic Subjects: Critical Essays on Autobiography and Graphic Novels
Edited by Michael A. Chaney

Omar Ibn Said
A Muslim American Slave: The Life of Omar Ibn Said
Translated from the Arabic, edited, and with an introduction by Ala Alryyes

Sylvia Bell White and Jody LePage
Sister: An African American Life in Search of Justice

Identity Technologies: Constructing the Self Online
Edited by Anna Poletti and Julie Rak

Alfred Habegger
Masked: The Life of Anna Leonowens, Schoolmistress at the Court of Siam

We Shall Bear Witness: Life Narratives and Human Rights
Edited by Meg Jensen and Margaretta Jolly

Kylie Cardell
Dear World: Contemporary Uses of the Diary